Those Who Can

Why Master Teachers Do What They Do

Neil Bright

ROWMAN & LITTLEFIELD EDUCATION
A division of
ROWMAN & LITTLEFIELD PUBLISHERS, INC.
Lanham • New York • Toronto • Plymouth, UK

Published by Rowman & Littlefield Education
A division of Rowman & Littlefield Publishers, Inc.
A wholly owned subsidiary of The Rowman & Littlefield Publishing Group, Inc.
4501 Forbes Boulevard, Suite 200, Lanham, Maryland 20706
www.rowman.com

10 Thornbury Road, Plymouth PL6 7PP, United Kingdom

British Library Cataloguing in Publication Information Available

Library of Congress Cataloging-in-Publication Data Available
ISBN 978-1-4758-0145-3 (pbk. : alk. paper)
ISBN 978-1-4758-0146-0 (electronic)

☺™ The paper used in this publication meets the minimum requirements of American
National Standard for Information Sciences Permanence of Paper for Printed Library
Materials, ANSI/NISO Z39.48-1992.

Printed in the United States of America

I have come to a frightening conclusion.
I am the decisive element in the classroom.

It is my personal approach
That creates the mood
That makes the weather.

As a teacher I possess tremendous power
To make a child's life miserable or joyous.

I can be a tool of torture
Or an instrument of inspiration.

I can humiliate or humor, hurt or heal.

In all situations it is my response that decides whether a crisis will be
escalated or de-escalated, and a child humanized or dehumanized.

—Haim Ginott

Contents

Preface

Surprisingly, the genesis for this book had nothing to do with my more than forty years as a teacher of students from fifth grade through postsecondary school. It had nothing to do with my one-time job as an assistant superintendent for curriculum and instruction or anything to do with twice being chief negotiator for a faculty union, a staff developer, a former college professor, or currently a student teacher supervisor. More than anything else, the impetus for this book had everything to do with transforming a seeming failure into a new and positive beginning for myself and in so doing, a new and equally positive beginning for educators and students I was unlikely ever to meet.

It began innocently enough with dreams of parlaying knowing "things" with hopes of winning unimaginable money fueling a five-year obsession to become a contestant on a trivia-based television game show. To that end, I auditioned in New York City nine times, passed multiple-choice tests on six occasions, and after each success was interviewed to determine if indeed I had the "right stuff."

Placed in the contestant pool after my last audition, I waited two years to be called to the show. When the call finally came, I was ready to demonstrate knowledge of science and Shakespeare, of literature and politics, of history and sports, of geography, biology, astronomy, and anything else I myopically believed worth knowing.

For three weeks before appearing, I alternated between envisioning plans for my "predestined" fortune and maniacally driving myself to be ready for whatever questions I would be asked. Like some child in bed on the night before Christmas, sugarplum expectations dancing in my ever-swelling materialistic head included a new car, an exotic trip, and some obscenely expensive bling.

To ensure such results, I read and reread trivia books rivaling volumes in the Library of Congress. In the middle of the night, I memorized birthstones, anniversary gifts, and astrological signs. At midday, I created mnemonic devices for the houses of British royalty, Elvis Presley songs, Hitchcock movies, and pi's value to eight places. Nothing could stop me. I would be ready for my trivia trial by fire. I would know *everything*. I would not fail.

Even on game day, after difficulty with several supposedly "beneath me" pop culture questions, I was confident, hubristically waiting for the higher-valued challenges that would surely come and that just as surely I would know.

But it was not to be. Luck-of-the-draw queries on nursery rhymes, etiquette, an old folk song's lyrics, and character names in a zombie movie sealed my paralysis-by-analysis fate. Seemingly, in an instant it was over. The clock had struck twelve, the coach had turned into a pumpkin, and the delusional and self-proclaimed "knower of all things" had morphed into Ralph Kramden on *The $99,000 Answer*.

There was no turning back. After half a decade of off-again, on-again effort, my dream was over. As a failure, I was yesterday's news. There was no unringing this bell. Or so I thought.

Yet within only hours of this initial perspective, I was in no mood for philosophical acceptance of my fate. Mirroring the far more serious stages of death-related grief, I quickly passed from "It can't be true" denial, to "It isn't fair" anger, to "If they made a mistake with a question, I'll live a better life" bargaining.

By day two, still grieving for embarrassment gained, a vacuum in personal goals created, and a life-changing opportunity lost, I settled into a feeling-sorry-for-myself "Now what?" depression. Then by day three, things changed. For, in failing to answer the most trivial of all queries, I ironically found answers to the most important questions of all.

There is a randomness to the universe defying individual mastery. And while realizing that whatever one's efforts, failure may still result from factors both unforeseen and unpredictable is hardly an original observation, the "Now what?" change for me was the simple insight that in choosing how I *perceived* disappointing events, and life in general, I was gaining the very control that had so often eluded my grasp. And if that perception was all important for me, it would be no less so for the teachers I had worked with and the students I had taught for the better part of four decades.

So, days after my fifteen minutes of game show infamy came the realization that I really could unring my humiliation bell. That epiphany began by understanding that in berating myself for wrongly answering game show questions, my extensive academic knowledge hardly defined me as a thoughtful person.

For in selectively focusing on unpleasant yet relatively insignificant events, I had failed to see the most essential answer of all. That being, by cherishing the often overlooked karmic gifts of my life—a loving family, terrific friends, hearty laughs, delicious meals, and a long career working among some incredibly talented educators—I could silence one bell *only* by loudly ringing another. And if I couldn't quickly learn to gain relief and redemption by internalizing that response, then perhaps I really wasn't so intelligent after all.

So as I had always taught my students, I began living the cliché of turning lemons into lemonade by ringing another bell in candidly writing about a career encompassing my entire adult life. To that end, this book was unapologetically written, sharing insights gained as an educational jack-of-all-trades from elementary school through college. And though my "tough love" perceptions may be difficult to accept and are likely to provoke "It's not so" defensiveness, such unvarnished honesty stems from my equally unvarnished respect for the vast majority of teachers and for the teaching profession. It is that immense respect that nourishes the steadfast belief that as a group, teachers must and certainly can do a better job educating students.

To that end, this book is dedicated to administrative and faculty colleagues too numerous to mention who have shared their wisdom with me for more than four decades. More specifically, this book is dedicated to Mike Roccoforte and Ken Sherman, whose cogent insights, boundless patience, and enduring friendships were invaluable in editing this book. But most of all, this work is dedicated to my endlessly supportive wife, Pam, and my equally wonderful son, Zac. Without their inexhaustible love and belief in me, this book could not have been written.

Introduction

Facts do not cease to be because they are ignored. —Aldous Huxley

It is "inside baseball" among school administrators that with almost perfect accuracy, one can predict in July which teachers by winter's cold will have the most parent complaints, the most student disciplinary problems, and the lowest standardized test scores. With pupil rosters not yet written and few administrative graduates from the University of Nostradamus, how can this be so? Simple. The main variable in classroom performance is not the students. It is not their parents. And it is not the principal or the board of education. It is the teachers.

Study after research study confirms that the single most important and controllable factor contributing to student success or failure is the quality of instruction (Ripley 2008). To that end, a fifteen-year University of Tennessee study "found the quality of teaching in a student's past accounted for differences in standardized test scores of as much as 50 or 60 percentile points" (Jones 1998, 22). After an analysis of achievement scores from five subject areas for some sixty thousand third through fifth graders, researchers noted that "the results show wide variation in the effectiveness among teachers . . . [and that] more can be done to improve education by improving the effectiveness of teachers than by any other single factor" (Wright, Horn, and Sanders 1997, 63; Marzano, Pickering, and Pollock 2001).

In another investigation, researchers analyzing achievement scores of over one hundred thousand students across hundreds of schools concluded that "effective teachers appear to be effective with students of all achievement levels [and] if the teacher is ineffective, students . . . will show inadequate progress academically regardless of how similar or different they are regarding their academic achievement" (Wright, Horn, and Sanders 1997, 63; Marzano, Pickering, and Pollock 2001). In still another study, evidence from nine hundred Texas school districts showed that the "effects of teaching are so strong, and the variations in teacher expertise so great that . . . the large disparities between black and white students were almost entirely accounted for by differences in the qualifications of their teachers" (Jones 1998, 22).

Moreover, the academic harm to children exposed to ineffective teachers is only compounded through exposure to several weak instructors in succession. In fact, after reviewing research on the cumulative damage of ineffective instruction, one researcher described the results as "stunning" in noting the aggregate achievement differences among children exposed to the least-effective teachers compared to their far-more-effective colleagues can represent the difference "between entry into a selective college and a lifetime at McDonald's" (Haycock 1998, 4; Marzano 2003).

Indeed, the quality differential among teachers is so enormous that another researcher estimated that the difference between a very good teacher and a very bad one is "a year's worth of learning in a single year" (Gladwell 2009, 318). In fact, since teacher effects are far more potent than school effects, a "child is actually better off in a bad school with an excellent teacher than in an excellent school with a bad teacher" (Gladwell 2009, 318). Great or even very good teachers can teach virtually anywhere. Yet without a willingness to change ineffective instructional practices, bad teachers will still be bad teachers whatever the costly or cutting-edge "bells and whistles" of their surroundings.

A NATION STILL AT RISK

In describing the once most successful educational system on earth as a "rising tide of mediocrity," a report titled *Nation at Risk* released in 1983 sounded the alarm for reform. Since then, state standards have been written, competency tests have been required, class sizes have fallen, and student spending has risen. Yet little has changed. According to the U.S. Department of Education, in 2011 only 34 percent of U.S. fourth- and eighth-grade students were reading at or above grade level, and in math the numbers were only slightly less grim (Nation's Report Card 2011, Nation's Report Card: Reading 2011).

Despite the efforts of self-proclaimed "education presidents" from Richard Nixon to Barack Obama, since 1971 meaningful improvement in math and reading scores has been nonexistent. In international comparisons, American children rank average at best and exceptional in nothing. Overall, the best that can be said about the state of education in the world's last remaining superpower is that the United States is *almost average* in international rankings of student achievement. And the longer American children attend school, the poorer they perform. Compared to pupils from similarly developed nations, achievement typically falls from average at grade four, to substandard in middle school, to worse at graduation.

In the 2009 Program for International Student Assessment measuring the performance of fifteen-year-olds in reading, mathematics, and science literacy, compared to students in other developed nations, U.S. students scored in the average range in reading and science and below average in mathematics. More specifically, out of thirty-four countries, the U.S.

ranking of fourteenth in reading, seventeenth in science, and twenty-fifth in math was roughly equivalent to nations such as Estonia and Poland spending *less than half* what is spent educating American children (Armario 2010).

"The continuing prosperity and strength of our country depends on our students achieving at levels that are at least comparable to those youngsters in our competitor nations" (Bishop 1995, 12). Yet by virtually any standard, for the better part of the past thirty years that has clearly not been so. Because of that, it is hardly debatable that still at risk, America's educational system, unlike corrupt and mismanaged financial institutions, is not too big to fail.

EXCUSING THE INEXCUSABLE

In deflecting criticism for such relatively poor results on international assessments, defenders for American public schools offer rationalizations du jour for the poor performance of American children when compared to children in similarly developed nations. Other than the threadbare and exaggerated excuse of a relatively abbreviated academic year for most U.S. schools, it is often argued that the relatively elite status of teachers in high-performing nations attracts the more able to that career. Yet even if true, who better than U.S. teachers themselves to reverse negative perceptions of their own performance? And by not doing so, whose fault is that?

Failing to accept even the possibility that any lack of respect afforded American educators is more the result than the cause of instructional deficiencies, apologists shift gears in claiming international test comparisons are bogus because other nations test high-performing students while the United States tests everyone. But the validity of that defense is questionable as well. "Due to better sampling techniques and other countries' decisions to educate more of their citizens, we're now generally comparing apples to apples" (Ripley 2010). And in comparison, our best apples don't do all that well either.

In a seemingly never-ending litany of excuses for mediocre assessment results, a more recently offered alibi is that America's diversity as a heterogeneous society acts as a drag on test scores. *Of course*, say rationalizers, with the great influx of newly arrived immigrants subject to language barriers and discrimination, U.S. test outcomes will suffer in international comparisons. However, in offering this explanation for comparatively poor results, some mitigate these outcomes by insisting America's best and brightest kids perform as well as their counterparts in other highly developed nations.

But this justification turns out to be just another unsupported attempt to excuse the inexcusable. Relatively privileged American children performing at high levels often do not compete favorably even with *average* students in well-off European and Asian countries. As economist Dr. Eric Hanushek, a Senior Fellow at the Hoover Institution of Stanford University who has studied the American educational system for the past forty years, said recently, "People will find it quite shocking . . . that even our most advantaged students are not all that competitive" (Ripley 2010).

That seems to be an understatement. As examples in Professor Hanushek's own study indicated, on a percentage basis New York State has fewer high performers among relatively privileged white students than Poland has among *all* children, and in Illinois the results are not any better. In that state, "the percentage of kids with a college-educated parent who are highly skilled at math is lower than the percentage of such kids among *all* students in Iceland, France, Estonia, and Sweden" (Ripley 2010).

Yet in explaining comparatively mediocre academic performances for American children on international assessments, the dirty little secret truth is often avoided. International students do better not because they are smarter. They do better because their schools are better. And if the single most controllable factor in student success or failure is indeed instructional quality, then in large measure their schools are better because as a group their teachers perform better. However, as much as this is a criticism of what has been, it is also a statement of what doesn't have to be. For if educational mediocrity is irrefutably more a result of ineffective pedagogy than anything else, than the potential for open-minded teachers to reverse that trend is equally undeniable.

It is not that outstanding instructors are unknown in America. Despite being unfairly stereotyped with lesser colleagues, many labor in relative anonymity "doing right for kids" each and every day. Yet such "those who can" stars are too often the exception to those who are less-than-exceptional rule. American teachers can't have it both ways. If they are willing to accept praise when students do well, they should be equally willing to accept criticism when students do poorly. And by virtually any standard, that is indeed the case.

Although unquestionably the quality of a school is largely determined by the quality of its teachers, that single and clearly focused factor is also surprisingly difficult to improve. At the least, there is often widespread faculty reluctance to coordinate K–12 efforts behind a schoolwide vision of instruction, assessment, and rigorous standards. Compounding this fragmented curriculum problem are the more publicized explanations for educational mediocrity, including veteran teachers fearing change, younger instructors lacking experience, and the motivation for improvement in both groups undermined by the complacency-inducing security of tenure.

Indeed, the 2010 documentary film *Waiting for Superman* noted as a not-uncommon example that in Illinois, out of 876 school districts, only sixty-one have *ever* tried to terminate a tenured teacher and of those sixty-one, only thirty-eight were successful in doing so. Overall, only one out of every 2,500 unionized, Land-of-Lincoln public school teachers has ever lost his or her teaching credential. Comparatively, one out of every fifty-seven doctors and ninety-seven lawyers annually lose their licenses for malpractice. What's more, in the five years between 2000 and 2005, of the 871 districts hiring outside lawyers in tenure-related cases, the average cost in legal fees was over $219,000 *before* appeals were exhausted in almost half of them (Reeder 2005). Largely a result of such budget-cannibalizing costs, in 2005 a newspaper investigation reported that out of the more than ninety-five thousand tenured teachers in Illinois, "an average of only two are fired each year for poor performance" (Hidden Costs of Tenure 2005).

However, other obstacles also undermine instructional quality. Not the least of which is that many educators view teaching as an "art" in which best practices are elusive, hard to quantify, and difficult to express. As once was said in defining pornography, one knows it when one sees it, but enumerating its essential elements escapes articulation. Hiding behind such rationalized uncertainty and widespread statistical unawareness of how badly the American public school system is broken, the least among the educational community maintain a status quo of instructional mediocrity or worse.

The United States spends more per student than any other nation except Switzerland (OECD 2011, 53), ranks fifth in the world in percent of gross domestic product (GDP) devoted to education (OECD 2011, 57), pupil to teacher ratios are at all-time lows, and since 1970 federal spending on education adjusted for inflation has risen 375 percent while the cost of a complete K–12 public school education has nearly tripled (Coulson 2011). Yet in a classic example of good money following bad, educational failure is still an option. During the last forty years, student results on domestic and international assessments have stagnated or declined.

THE MYTH OF TOO LITTLE TIME

Rationalizing such enormous spending with "it-would-have-been-far-worse"-if-not-spent alibis, mediocre assessment results are likewise rationalized at least in part as resulting from a relatively condensed school calendar. While true that U.S. children attend school less days per year than youngsters in many other nations, increasing student attendance an average of a day or two a month will hardly matter if instruction remains mediocre. "The crude policy solutions of more days in the year and longer school days do not even begin to touch the deeper truth that what has to improve is the quality of academic learning time" (Cuban 2008, 249). And besides, when mandated school attendance *hours* are examined, U.S.

children receive *as much or more* instructional time than children in many of the nations outperforming American youngsters in international comparisons such as Finland, South Korea, and Japan (Hull 2011).

Because every state has its own compulsory time requirement for schools, it is difficult to compare the United States as a whole to other nations. Yet according to a 2011 report by the National School Boards Association's Center for Public Education, what can be said with certainty is that depending on grade level, most states require between nine hundred and one thousand hours of instructional time per term and only eight require fewer than eight hundred hours. And even in most of those states, the reduced hours only apply to grades one through three, and the students in half of those states perform above the national average (Hull 2011).

More importantly, when the National School Boards' research is combined with international data compiled by the Organization for Economic Cooperation and Development (OECD), it is clear that most U.S. schools require *at least* as much instructional time as many of the world's most advanced nations including Japan, South Korea, Canada, Finland, France, Germany, Italy, and the United Kingdom.

The OECD study *Education at a Glance 2011* comparing data from thirty-four nations indicates that only five states require less than the OECD average of 759 instructional hours at the elementary level. In middle school, the OECD average of 886 hours, including such high-performing nations as South Korea, Japan, and Finland, is less than the compulsory instructional time in most U.S. states. And during high school, there is still *no* evidence that American students receive any less mandated instruction than children in nations regularly besting them on international assessments. Even at that secondary level, forty-two states require *more* instructional time than the OECD average of 902 hours (Hull 2011).

While true that time comparisons are based on required minimums and that some high-performing nations have a tradition of supplementing instruction, especially during high school, with less-formal noncompulsory schooling such as tutoring, it is undeniable that the United States does not require less educational time than other nations. It is equally undeniable that a still-longer American school year without accompanying improvements in instruction and classroom management would do little to academically level the international playing field.

For despite the quick-fix solution of increasing school time offered by politicians, it is far less important to count every minute than to make every minute count. As such, it is only when time is already well used and when students are already actively engaged in a skillfully presented and meaningful curriculum that an extended school day or year will increase student achievement (Aronson, Zimmerman, and Carlos 1998).

Of course, instructional time is an important variable that may affect instructional outcomes. However, unless additional time is used wisely, its impact will be negligible at best. Common sense and research indicate that there is little or no predictable relationship between simply requiring more time and increased student achievement (Aronson, Zimmerman, and Carlos 1998). Expecting to enhance student performance simply by increasing time in school is like expecting to lose weight simply by buying a book on dieting. While doing so may be an important first step for some, in and of itself it will not solve the problem. More time squandered on inefficient classroom management, on impotent discipline, and on irrelevant curriculums is not the answer. More effective instruction is. To that end, the perfect example of a quantity over quality school-reform failure proved that point in 2008.

In an effort to boost student achievement in Miami-Dade County, an initiative extending the school day and school year in the thirty-nine lowest-performing public schools was initiated over a three-year period beginning in 2005. Known as the School Improvement Zone (SIZ), the program lengthened the school day by one hour, four days a week, and the school year was increased by ten days. At a cost to Florida taxpayers of over $100 million largely for additional educational materials and employee compensation, the district's final evaluation report indicated that little was gained in enhancing student performance (McGrory 2009).

In comparing student achievement on state exams of the SIZ schools to a demographically similar control group of thirty-nine other schools within Miami-Dade County, the control-group schools *outperformed* the schools in the School Improvement Zone. Although Zone students did slightly better on the writing exam, according to the program evaluators the initiative "exhibited at best an inconsistent impact that was limited to the elementary grades" (McGrory 2009).

In the end, the program was terminated, the superintendent championing the School Improvement Zone improved himself with a $368,000 buyout from the school board (McGrory 2009), and interested observers witnessed a cautionary tale of what happens when well-meaning reformers seek to improve education simply by prescribing the often-cited remedy of school quantity rather than identifying the real source of educational mediocrity, a lack of instructional quality.

STRAIGHT TALK

Of all the variables that can be controlled once a child enters school, *instructor skill is the single most important factor in student success or failure* and is the primary reason why American children lag behind others in the developed world. Ultimately, whatever the importance of class size, pupil expenditures, or school-year length, people far more than policies or programs make the difference in a child's education. Thus with few if any exceptions, the quality of a school, a district, or a nation cannot surpass the quality of its teachers. Period.

Yet however difficult guidelines for adult movies may be to construct, the same cannot be said for effective instructional practices. "Despite efforts to make it so, [education] is not essentially mysterious" (Bennett 1986, v), and what the very best educators do to gain the very best student results is *not* some unknowable secret. Because classrooms are laboratories of human behavior, extensive research has irrefutably identified what instructional approaches have a high degree of probability to positively affect student learning. Accordingly, if schools are to improve, it is essential to identify those highly effective strategies and the behavioral observations and research studies supporting their use.

For as obvious as this solution is to school improvement, it is equally obvious that it is unlikely for ineffectual teachers to become excellent unless they know what excellence is. Moreover, because instruction's best practices *are* discernible, the continuance of ineffective teaching is unforgivable. Equally so, there is no acceptable reason why the average time between a conclusive research finding in education and widespread application is *ten times longer* than the comparable period in medicine (Hunter 1982).

This lag between evidence of an instructional practice's effectiveness and extensive use is even more unacceptable because refusing to apply research-based educational methods has nothing to do with a lack of money or an innate lack of teacher ability and everything to do with a lack of instructional awareness, an insistence on "teaching is an art, not a science" rigid dichotomy, and an unwillingness by many to change what clearly isn't working. Until about forty years ago, "teaching had not been systematically studied in a scientific manner" (Marzano, Pickering, and Pollock 2001, 1). That is clearly no longer so.

Only by acknowledging and accepting this reality will the discredited defeatism that schools can do little to overcome bad genes or bad parenting be replaced by a meaningfully productive "we can we do better" call for action. As recently as the 1970s, America's public schools were among the best in the world. More than forty years later, there is no acceptable reason why that can't be so yet again.

Practice One

Clarifying Vision

If you don't know where you're going, you probably won't get there. —Yogi Berra

Arguably the most important trait of master teachers is a clear sense regarding the purpose of schools. Because this conception, if internalized, largely dictates the daily pedagogical choices made in classrooms, clarifying vision is quite possibly the most important instructional practice of all. Yet, when teachers are asked to articulate their vision of schooling, they often respond with stunned silence or blankly cite boilerplate clichés that sound good but mean little.

Simply put, Practice One of the best teachers is viewing the purpose of K–12 education as not in and of itself for students to do well in school, but for them to do well in life. Once this concept is accepted, such a bottom-line mind-set changes everything. For if acknowledged without question, some commonly insipid classroom practices are seen as wastes of time, and other less pervasive but essential activities become instructional absolutes. Moreover, as important as school grades and standardized test scores are, they cannot come at the expense of a meaningful curriculum in which there is ongoing instruction in essential academic skills *and* equally essential habits of mind such as cooperation, belief in effort, goal setting, critical thinking, and a strong sense of personal responsibility.

Clearly, it is impossible to justify wasting precious class time forcing students to mindlessly learn insignificant facts, to thoughtlessly complete word searches, or to robotically read and memorize largely irrelevant material in a textbook, when such activities clearly have little or nothing to do with outside-the-classroom challenges. It's as if many schools are make-believe worlds where students are sold a snake-oil curriculum they are told is somehow good for them.

In far too many classrooms, students are coerced to learn what few, if any, adults know *or will ever need to know*. Indeed, if it were not their job to be knowledgeable about the curriculum they teach, most if not all of the teachers requiring that students learn the definition of plimsolls, the

wind speed on Saturn, or the products of South Dakota would themselves be ignorant of the forgettable material they routinely demand their
students memorize. Sadly, the *Are You Smarter Than a Fifth Grader?* definition of what it means to be well educated is too much the rule and too
little the exception.

Instructors claiming "no time" for creative writing, research, cooperative learning, oral presentations, debates, or persuasive essays among
other "authentic" activities are on very shaky ground. For if additional
teacher effort was not a factor in such real-world, labor-intensive instruction, would any educator seriously argue that assigning writing, speaking, and creative problem-solving activities was a bad idea simply because of real, exaggerated, or imagined time constraints? Of course not.

The reality is simple. As the late presidential advisor and economist
John Kenneth Galbraith once said, "Faced with choice between changing
one's mind and proving that there is no need to do so, almost everybody
gets busy on the proof" (Pritchett and Pound 1990, 17). People do what
they want to do. If they don't want to do something, they often invent a
reason for not doing it. The invented reason for not assigning real-world
activities is a lack of time, when the actual and unspoken reasons are fear
of change, fear of losing control, a lack of effort, or an undefined educational vision. However, when teachers accept that the purpose of school
is to prepare students for life after graduation, then failing to make time
for authentic "real-world" pursuits is to fail those very children teachers
are hired to serve.

REAL-WORLD SKILLS

For all students, preparation for life involves instruction in skills necessary beyond twelfth grade. If this is the case, college-bound youngsters
must be proficient in writing, speaking, and in research. Students seeking
admission into technical or trade schools must be able to listen, follow
directions, work cooperatively, and persevere on projects from inception
to completion. If the military is the goal, those abilities are no less essential. And if a student enters the workforce immediately after high school,
it would be equally difficult to succeed without proficiency in most, if not
all, of the aforementioned abilities.

Even if students choose not to further their education or seek employ-
ment shortly after leaving public school, virtually all are or will become
American citizens. As such, in joining the public debate at a school board
hearing, a town board meeting, or before a local or national election,
persuasive writing, speaking, and critical thinking are essential skills ensuring the health of our democracy. Developing an opinion, supporting it
with cogent argumentation, and fairly considering opposing views are
fundamental abilities in a free society. Could any educator seriously con-

tend they are "too busy" to offer instruction in those indispensable skills, without which our republic would be in peril? In stating over two hundred years ago that we cannot be both ignorant and free, Thomas Jefferson extolled the importance of an educated citizenry as prerequisite for the survival of our way of life. Could any educator sincerely argue that in the twenty-first century, instruction leading to that end is any less important because he or she has too much to do?

STATE MANDATES

Of course, at least as far as state-mandated curriculum and tests are concerned, some may argue that the purpose of school *is* for students to do well in school. And in the short-term they would be right. Teachers are not in private practice. They are employees of school districts and by extension, of the state. Accordingly, by signing a contract, they are agreeing to teach *whatever* curriculum is mandated. Yet, because it is often fashionable to criticize state-required instructional directives as misguided threats to local and personal autonomy, some teachers halfheartedly satisfy them at best and ignore them at worst.

However, this passive resistance is misguided. For whatever the instructional constraints imposed by state-mandated standards and assessments, if students perform poorly, those constraints will inevitably become greater still. Yet, by ignoring this reality, shortsighted instructors claim a lack of time to implement real-world instructional activities on the one hand and a lack of support for state requirements on the other. And in retreating to their instructional world of safety and security, they close their doors and enact a curriculum less focused on student futures than on their own more comfortable pasts.

CURRICULUM "FILTERS"

The easiest way, then, to look at curriculum choice is as a series of filters. The first such filter is the state-mandated curriculum, the second is reality, and the third is whether the activity, information, or assignment is irrefutably and significantly "good for kids." It is simple. *Whatever concept, fact, assignment, or activity that cannot pass through these screens should not be taught.*

The first filter is necessary because like it or not, the hiring or firing of teachers, the degree of state oversight, and the passage or defeat of school budgets are all linked to student results on tests tied to that curriculum. Additionally, state standards provide at least some guidance as to what their authors considered essential, discipline-specific knowledge teachers should impart to students. The second filter, a shorthand for the purpose of school, is essential because teachers have a moral imperative to prepare pupils for success after graduation. And the third screen focuses curricular decisions on how teachers view their professional lives. For when fear of change and additional effort lead to rationalized inaction, the "good for kids" filter should make instructional direction clear. This is so because if the purpose of school is indeed to prepare children for their futures, isn't the "good for kids" role of their teachers to ensure that result?

After all, if students are not being prepared for life after twelfth grade, what *are* they being prepared for? Doing crossword puzzles? Constructing dioramas? Memorizing the preamble to the Constitution? Lacking a sensible instructional compass guiding their daily decisions, too much of what teachers ask kids to do makes little sense. As Albert Shanker once said, "Everything we do in school is the opposite of what we do in the world" (Caulfield and Jennings 2002, 42). Yet with clarity of vision regarding the purpose of school, master teachers, in ironically asking the same "Why do we have to do this?" question as many of their students, never lose sight of what really matters.

Practice Two

Unifying Vision

To have a direct vision, that is the thing. —Pablo Picasso

While essential, screening curricular decisions through the filters of state mandates, reality, and what is "good for kids" is not enough. Though undeniably improving classroom instruction, master teachers also realize that unless that vision is shared by the entire faculty and administration, instructional benefits will be far less than they must be. For only by replacing curricular anarchy for program coherency can entire faculties speak with a voice so unified that few students can ignore its message. Thus, the job of being a great or even a good teacher does not end at the classroom door. It involves working with colleagues in fashioning a K–12 curriculum in support of instructional outcomes that are aligned with what students need to know and be able to do in the real world.

To that end, the most effective instructors support the Practice Two willingness to join together in focusing on the same core essential skills, how those skills will be taught, and how they will be assessed. In such whole-school curriculums, instructional absolutes are linked across all classes and grades. In doing so, learning is focused on what really matters rather than on the diffuse and scattershot instructional offerings found in most schools.

Yet to implement such a coherently designed program, master teachers selflessly and even *eagerly* relinquish a measure of pedagogical autonomy for the undeniable benefit of all students. For without such a collective imperative challenging the status quo, school reform will likely fail. Consequently, if there is any chance for a coordination of instructional efforts, the driving force must be a unifying vision regarding the purpose of school.

As a backdrop for more specific aspects of a schoolwide curriculum, this general statement of instructional outcomes such as the one found in this book's Appendix reminds parents, students, and most importantly teachers what the end results of their efforts must be. Most people wouldn't even leave their homes to buy a quart of milk without an unambiguous idea of where they were going. And if that is true for the most

5

simple and mundane of endeavors, shouldn't school restructuring receive at least the same consideration?

Typically, schools lack a clearly articulated, locally conceived, and
unified vision bonding all stakeholders into common and specific learning goals promoting student achievement. Realizing this, master teachers
understand that unless they fearlessly stand for a preferred future that is
that vision, their individual excellence will be diluted in a school where
teachers routinely labor at cross purposes with each other. Articulating
such a vision forces teachers to "come out of the closet with . . . doubts
about the organization and the way it operates" (Fullan 1993, 13). To that
end, a crucial first step in opening that door is conceding the curricular
disconnect among what is valued, what is desired, and what exists.

In fearlessly expressing personal purpose, elite educators invariably
become agents of organizational change by attracting kindred spirits who
might otherwise remain silent. In embracing the status quo, institutions
are inherently conservative. This inertia can only be challenged by another inertia created by trailblazing individuals willing to take a stand to
change the culture of a school. Thus, momentum leading to breakthroughs in instructional improvement begins with a school's most effective teachers realizing that collective unity of purpose paradoxically
forged by personal vision is the first step to systemic change. This collective purpose, initially promoted by isolated pockets of as-good-as-it-gets
teachers, results in productive connections among colleagues, creating
growing pressure for schools to change (Fullan 1994).

JUSTIFYING THE VISION

In schools where the only academic constant is inconsistency, the rationale for a more focused array of student products, performances, and
assessments is clear. Important, complex, and durable learning can only
be accomplished by repetitive instruction generating meaningful student
products evaluated by uniform criteria from elementary through high
school. In order to be truly learned, such "how to" procedural knowledge
must be practiced enough for students to perform important tasks with
relatively little effort or thought.

However, in the multiple-choice, fill-in-the-blank classrooms so pervasive in schools, there is little hope of such automaticity. In fact, if educators were *trying* to design an ineffective instructional approach, they
could hardly do a better job than the disjointed curriculum common in
most schools. Given this reality, the question shouldn't be why are kids
underperforming, but why wouldn't they be? Irrefutably, learning occurs
in spite of incoherent curriculums rather than because of them. To suggest otherwise is to believe what never has been and what never will be.

While randomly offered and erratically assessed learning opportunities handicap all students, those most in need suffer greatest harm. A helter-skelter curriculum where real-world instructional activities are scarce and where evaluations are based on unknown, inconsistent, and after-the-fact criteria does enormous damage to children least resilient to such instability. Moving from grade to grade and teacher to teacher, inauthentic yet easily assessable multiple-choice and fill-in-the-blank instructional offerings are overly redundant, and indispensable yet labor-intensive writing, speaking, and creative instructional opportunities are not redundant enough. As unintended victims of such disorganized and relatively unsubstantial curriculums, children become the collateral damage of faculty and administrative inaction to implement a more thoughtful, coherent, and relevant program of learning experiences.

Even when more complex and crucial learning activities are offered, rarely is consistency of process taught or of quality evaluated. One teacher demands one thing and another requires something else. One teacher criticizes one thing and another faults something else. Worse still, one teacher praises what another disparages and another assails what another commends. Exposed to such incomplete, confusing, and schizophrenic curricula, accomplished students forfeit potential, while those less able lose even the chance to succeed.

Not surprisingly, highly effective teachers realize that the journey toward a more coherent schoolwide curriculum begins with the "end in mind" (Covey 1989, 95) vision of its ultimate destination. Without such a clear target translating into the habits of mind and practice a district most values for its graduates, there will be as many different sets of criteria of what is important to teach as there are teachers. Without such end-point clarity informing instructional decisions, an aimless coverage-for-coverage's-sake instructional menu inevitably results. If *anything* can be important, then nothing is important.

In identifying essential exit abilities for students and the acceptable level for demonstrating their performance, a school's unified curricular vision provides the benefits of instructional clarity and concentration for teachers in much the same way that rubrics provide learning clarity for pupils. Even if not "high stakes," where graduation is dependent on their attainment, that these guidelines sharpen instructional focus and enhance student achievement by illuminating what scholarship is most valued is of little doubt. For other than coordinating instruction, they also "constitute an external standard that validates both the teachers who demand high-quality work and the students who choose to do more than the bare minimum" (Bishop 1995, 42). Realizing that schools will continue to fail unless such focused curricular design replaces unsystematic and incoherent curricular disorder, master teachers do whatever they can to support whole-school curriculums found in highly effective districts.

OBTACLES TO UNIFYING VISION

Paradoxically, the transformation of school outcomes from diffuse, unde-fined, and often trivial endeavors to the laser of relevant instruction is not easy. As ineffective teachers try to hang onto what has been a relatively comfortable status quo, resistance to change is often based on fears of incompetence. And in some cases, there are legitimate reasons for such anxiety, for the same light guiding instructional reform also reveals the infrastructure of pedagogical inadequacy. Thus, not surprisingly, the ed-ucators having the most to gain from this realization are often those most threatened by its disclosure.

But difficulties changing what is for what could be have always been so. As if witnessing current efforts to improve American schools, Renais-sance writer Niccolo Machiavelli observed, "There's nothing more diffi-cult to take in hand, more perilous to conduct, or more uncertain in its success than to take the lead in the introduction of a new order of things." To that end, obstructionist educators will stop at nothing to derail the implementation of virtually any reform. Their "it won't work" rational-izations protecting the status quo are limitless, and if they weren't so damaging they would be almost comical. "We tried that before" is fol-lowed by "we don't have the time," and "we don't have the money, room, personnel . . . " is followed by "we've done all right without it." And when all else fails, "Let's shelve it for the time being" is followed by an "it can't be done" finality.

With a seemingly endless catalog of reasons to resist change, perhaps the most common is "it didn't work in a neighboring district." Yet even if true, this is rarely an acceptable rationale to abandon a well-researched reform. At the least, almost anything is provable if the focus of evidence is narrowed enough. As has often been said, even a broken clock is cor-rect twice every twenty-four hours. What obstructionist educators can't see or won't admit is that no two snowflakes, no two schools, and no two of *anything* are exactly the same. Thus, with an infinite number of vari-ables leading to success or failure, an apparent "rule" may well be an exception, and a failed reform in one school hardly guarantees failure in another.

Being less fearful of change than concerned with an unsatisfactory status quo, elite educators, unlike their less open-minded colleagues, don't reflexively oppose reform. Yet realizing that hasty decisions are often wrong and that even the best-informed educators know very little about very much, elite educators withhold judgment until a thorough review of research concerning any restructuring initiative. To that end, they routinely join study teams investigating promising educational ap-proaches.

Even if master teachers initially oppose an initiative ultimately adopted, realizing they've been wrong before about the simplest of things, they reserve judgment and keep an open mind. In contrast, unaware that the smartest people are sure of very little and those far less able are far too certain of virtually everything, close-minded colleagues shun investigative involvement, and then, certain of any reform's failure, stop at nothing to sabotage results.

Yet whatever the obstructionist attempts of fearful and ineffective educators, districts must clearly indicate what ready-for-the-world twelfth-graders should be able to do and the minimally acceptable level of quality when doing it. Among countless possibilities, such performances might include writing a research paper, fashioning a persuasive essay, completing an oral presentation, creating a personal résumé, sitting for a mock job interview, or formulating a creative solution to a local, national, or world problem.

But whatever a school decides is essential evidence of a well-educated graduate, such "authentic" products achieved over and beyond the passing of state-mandated exams and more traditional district requirements align classroom activities with an instructional compass pointing toward what matters most. And without this compass, individual teachers and entire faculties can easily lose their way.

SUPPORTING THE VISION

Knowing the eventual destination of the instructional journey, while essential, is only the first step in transforming a district from mediocrity to excellence. For without the expectation that all teachers will do their share in transforming that authentic vision into reality, little will change. Talk is indeed cheap and buying into this vision will be far more costly than lip service.

It will require creating districtwide rubrics of what good is, grade-level models tangibly embodying the criteria of those rubrics, and "recipes" enumerating the process for achieving performance and product quality. That such instructional supports are essential is beyond question. For how can students or anyone else duplicate excellence if they don't know how to achieve it or even what it looks like?

Creating a more coherent curriculum is not for the faint of heart. Rethinking everything unsettles all things. Reinventing a school can expose inadequacies within the system as it reveals inadequacies within the faculty. Yet the most effective educators well understand that only by relinquishing a measure of instructional autonomy for the focused power of a schoolwide curriculum anchored on state mandates, reality, and the "good for kids" filter will essential learning for all students be more than an idealized fantasy found in mythical schools and in ivory-tower textbooks.

Even though the power of a whole-school curriculum is undeniable, less-effective teachers fearful of change and of losing control often refuse to buy in. Even given an opportunity to shape what that curriculum will look like, such malcontents sit on the sideline and remain as part of the problem rather than as part of the solution. Undermining reform through fear mongering, misinformation, and gossip, toxic educators undermine any initiative for the safety of the status quo and the self-fulfilling joy of "I told you so" failure.

On the contrary, master teachers realize that however talented they may be, their job extends beyond their classrooms. Even though they may not agree with every aspect of an instructional reform, once it is agreed to by the board, the administration, the community, and by the group of instructors fashioning the initiative, they will implement and support the change to the best of their ability. In doing so, the most effective educators step out of the comfort zone favored by lesser colleagues and become teacher-advocates for the restructuring vision. If a school is to improve, "it is imperative that the entire staff adopt an attitude of objectivity and a feeling of urgency about the need for improvement" (Coppedge 1993, 35). And as teacher leaders, elite instructors have the necessary gravitas to generate that momentum.

THE ROLE OF TEACHER-LEADER

As a profession, teaching does not encourage leadership. Even with rhetoric describing educators as "essential stakeholders" and "shared decision makers," well-entrenched factors make it difficult for instructors to accept leadership roles in school restructuring. At the least, with effective teaching being an emotionally and physically taxing job, it is difficult for instructors to view their role from a schoolwide rather than just a classroom perspective.

However, even though many teachers understand that efforts toward school improvement inevitably pay classroom dividends, there is another reason why for all but the most highly effective faculty members the term *teacher-leader* is too often an oxymoron. That reason can be summed up in the shopworn simile likening teachers to mushrooms. Thriving in darkness, when teachers stick their necks out, their heads are immediately cut off.

In too many schools, the acceptance of a so-called quasi-administrative role by a teacher in creating and promoting reform is akin to sleeping with the enemy. Fearful of change and wedded to the status quo, instructors challenging faculty involvement in school improvement programs view such efforts as a zero-sum game, where one group of educators gains what another group loses.

With a "who does she think she is" mind-set, obstructionists see teacher participation in school restructuring as transparent and selfishly motivated attempts by brownnosers and eager beavers to curry administrative favor at colleagues' expense. With a culture resistant to change so common in schools, it is any wonder why all but the most confident and effective educators often avoid any direct connection to meaningful reform initiatives?

But obstructionist teachers do more than attack their more progressive colleagues. They also routinely attack what they consider "change for change sake" administrators. That is not to say that the central office always handles school improvement well or even competently. Too often reform is based on fragmented "whatever sticks to the wall" initiatives that are ineffectively planned, insufficiently supported, and incomprehensibly justified.

With consensus, cooperation, and trust between administrators and teachers already a fragile commodity in many schools, poorly executed restructuring efforts in fueling "us against them" faculty-administrator division shatter any attempts at a critical mass vision, without which meaningful school reform is all but impossible. And even when a school renewal vision is thoughtfully conceived, it is well documented that "teachers who are asked to change features of their teaching often modify the features to fit within their pre-existing system instead of changing the system itself" (Stigler and Hiebert 1998, 10). In the end, due to underlying resistance to change and cynicism toward the change itself, what often remains of the best of intentions is "if we wait long enough, it will go away" foot-dragging and cosmetically ineffective compliance.

Whatever the collegial or administrative obstacles faced, master teachers continue to fight the good fight in realizing that in supporting a unified vision of school improvement, they are also benefitting students in their charge. As such, whatever success they've personally experienced, they understand it hardly matters how good individual actors are in a play, how dynamic particular athletes are on a football team, or how proficient specific instructors are in the classroom, without individual commitment to a group effort, systemic anarchy and mediocrity will surely follow.

The journey between now and a better educational future begins with a faculty's collective willingness to surrender the short-term safety of personal autonomy for the coherent power of a unified instructional vision. Although not without difficulty, public recognition will ultimately supplement the intrinsic reward of "doing right" for kids. For when a faculty arrives at their vision's destination; when students graduate with the knowledge, the skills, and the habits of mind to meet the challenges they will inevitably face; and when celebration replaces consternation, other schools less aware or more fearful will know where to find the blueprint from where they are to where they need to go.

Practice Three

Performing Instruction

All the world's a stage, and all the men and women merely players. — William Shakespeare

Practice Three of master teachers is recognizing instruction as a performance. Like it or not, at some levels teaching *is* a sales job. As a result, how instructors "sell" lessons is as important as what they are trying to sell. For it doesn't really matter how hard teachers work or how many degrees they hold, if instructional delivery is dry as dust, few students spoiled by their sensory overloaded world will make intellectual purchases despite a lesson's inherent value. Whatever its research-driven instructional essentials, whatever its cultural importance, whatever its purely intellectual value, and whatever conventional wisdom or ignorance says it is, teaching is in part a performance art.

Accordingly, teacher unwillingness or inability to improve instructional delivery has enormous and negative educational ramifications. For with researchers finding two-thirds of high schools students disengaged in class (Caulfield and Jennings 2002; Sedlak, Wheeler, Pullin, and Cusick 1986), and with boredom continuing to be a major complaint of students, it is difficult if not impossible for disinterested students to do high-quality work (Glasser 1990). As such, a strong research base linking student engagement and academic achievement has been well established (Brophy 2006; Hattie 2009). And equally well-established, master teachers *continually* monitor student engagement, are keenly aware of learner disinterest, and will make on-the-fly changes in focus, pacing, enthusiasm, or activities should that occur.

There is little doubt that "excellent classroom teaching has a narrative and dramatic feel . . . it has a definite theme, and a beginning, middle, and end" (Hirsch 1996, 46). Yet with effective delivery lying at the heart of quality instruction, underperforming teachers offer uninspired and uninspiring lessons with "it's my job to teach, not to entertain" rationalizations. But they are wrong. Their job is to do both.

13

"KNOWING ONE'S LINES"

Because students are less likely to learn well if not engaged, there are several strategies master teachers use to improve instructional delivery. Among the most obvious of these approaches is "knowing one's lines." There is no instructional substitute for a thorough, compelling, and immediate knowledge of one's content. Students can easily spot a fraud teacher who has not done his or her homework. Having only an "excellence gear," elite teachers never "wing it" or "mail it in." Bringing their "A game" every day and *even more so* immediately before or after a weekend or a vacation, they "are not uncertain, undecided, or confusing in the way they communicate with students" (Wubbels, Brekelmans, Van Tartwijk, and Admiral 1999, 167). Not even a little bit.

Indeed, "the master teacher will prepare for class much as the actor rehearses the lines and the character of his or her role" (Keiper and Evans 1994, 24). If the credo of real estate brokers is "location, location, location," the motto of excellent teachers is "preparation, preparation, preparation." Without such unheralded and often repetitive efforts, spectacular results are all but impossible. To that end, many effective instructors ready themselves for class by keeping a "scriptbook" sequencing of past lessons containing precise definitions and explanations of terms and concepts as well as higher-order, thought-provoking questions. This is the foundational "screenplay" likely to be taught each term.

Over time this scriptbook grows, with compelling "insider" stories making certain topics more exciting, updates to older material, and instructional notes as reminders of past problems students had in grasping material. Not surprisingly, for neophytes just starting out or for veteran educators teaching a course for the first time, use of a scriptbook improves student learning while accomplishing the same end for themselves. But the reason for this goes far beyond the old saw that "the faintest ink is better than the best memory." More specifically, the value of a scriptbook is based on far more recent understandings of how learning occurs.

Because learning is easier when new information attaches itself to existing and related knowledge, continually adding to the scriptbook from the most basic material at the onset of use to more detailed information over time, teachers develop an ever-deepening knowledge of a topic or subject. Doing so, instructors ironically become students. And as for any learner, after gaining a broad understanding of material, teachers "can mentally fit the various parts that follow into that whole, and make sense of them" (Hirsch 2001, 23). Thus, in creating a scriptbook for each subject area or course, even relatively inexperienced educators can rapidly accelerate their curricular learning curve and more quickly present material with believable authority.

Moreover, in regularly reviewing the scriptbook before a topic or unit is introduced, there is a freshness and a "singing in the shower when no one else is listening" confidence to an instructional "performance," much the same as that exhibited by the best recording artists and thespians. Rendering songs or reciting scripts dozens of times with the same power, enthusiasm, and presence as in the past, performer confidence grows, as does audience engagement. And if this is so for rock singers and Broadway actors, why should it be any less so for teachers?

For as in any performance, when inattentive to detail and unsure of one's script, there is less focus on eye contact, pacing, volume, and body language. This is as so for teachers as for any other "performers." Such uncertainty often translates into "going through the motions" presentations that are cold, robotic, and lacking in confidence. And as any self-conscious teacher knows, when content knowledge is shaky and presentations are without enthusiasm, students sensing "blood in the water" doubt, become disinterested or disruptive.

ENTHUSIASM

Undeniably, the importance of instructional passion as a characteristic of elite instructors should not be overlooked. If a teacher is enthusiastic, there is a greater probability that students will be as well. Research consistently demonstrates that "students are more likely to be interested, energetic, curious, and excited about learning when the teacher is enthusiastic" (Wedel and Jennings 2006; Patrick, Hisley, and Kempler 2000). More specifically, in a study of six Bowling Green State University's "Master Teacher" award winners, a majority of student participants cited enthusiasm *as their defining characteristic*. As one student said, excellent instructors are "more dramatic—more willing to get outside their shell" (Weaver, Wenzlaff, and Cotrell 1993, 13).

Moreover, there is little doubt that the energy level of a class is a reflection of the energy level of the instructor. As enthusiasm is contagious, so too is ennui. Students will substitute monotonal lectures for sleeping pills and will "caffeinate" off the energy from inspiring presentations. Exposed to the latter, a student responded, "I found myself highly motivated and I would do additional reading on my own . . . because I got turned on to the topic because the teacher was really excited by it" (Weaver, Wenzlaff, and Cotrell 1993, 13).

In many things, there is a fine line between mediocrity and good and between good and great. For many students, the critical difference separating a class barely tolerable from one truly memorable is often the enthusiasm of the instructor. And educators not believing that students can be "turned on" to their least favorite subject by a passionate teacher or become disinterested in their best-liked discipline by an instructor lacking energy have themselves not been paying attention.

EFFECTIVE NOTE TAKING

To further support performance quality, many excellent instructors translate their scriptbooks into bullet points listed as instructional outlines on overhead transparencies or on PowerPoint slides. These bullets indicate what is most important for students to know and provides them with a note-taking "scaffold" to fill in important details. In one study, when students were also provided with oral cues revisiting the scaffold's main points throughout the lecture, they recorded 64 percent of the lesson's details compared to only 29 percent of those details when such verbal reinforcers were not offered (Titsworth and Kiewra 2001).

Despite its overuse in some classrooms, note taking is valued as an important activity by students (Dunkel and Davy 1989), and there is strong evidence that doing so leads to higher achievement than not doing so (Kiewra 1985). And because students have more than three times the chance of remembering noted information than material not written down (Aiken, Thomas, and Shennum 1975), the ability to competently record lecture notes undoubtedly improves student performance.

In realizing that many learners record incomplete notes, master teachers also realize that requiring them to copy long passages of material from the blackboard, from overhead transparencies, or from PowerPoint presentations is not an effective solution. Even though most students will robotically and dutifully transcribe the information, in doing so they will necessarily tune out any explanatory comments made by the teacher during the transcription.

As more indeed becomes less, "forcing" students to copy lengthy material verbatim does not allow learners to process the information and is thus a counterproductive waste of time. Moreover, copying material word-for-word hardly readies students for postsecondary classrooms where mindlessness is rarely a requirement, and even if information is indeed important enough to precisely transcribe, it can be duplicated as handouts to students or posted on a website for them to access.

When lecture is used as a means to convey content information, master teachers provide younger and struggling students with organizational frameworks in the form of guided handouts or website postings mirroring the aforementioned transparency or PowerPoint lesson "scaffolds." Doing so is the middle ground between not offering students any assistance in recording lecture material and presenting them with lengthy passages to mindlessly copy. And providing students with such lecture cues signaling important ideas has been found in numerous studies to improve note taking and to raise student achievement (Kiewra 2002).

Additionally, the bulleting of key terms, concepts, or events on transparencies or as part of PowerPoint presentations acts as an instructor blueprint for a logically designed lesson sequence that is easily reviewed and if necessary fine-tuned from year to year to increase clarity, to contemporize the curriculum, and to reinvigorate past lessons inevitably growing stale. Moreover, seen from anywhere in the room, this performance script enables instructors to face the class and to stay organized, logically sequenced, and on schedule while not limiting movement being tied to a podium, personal lecture notes, or to a blackboard.

But however information is transmitted to students, the first and last parts of a lesson are key for "audience" focus and retention. As a result, there is a "tendency to remember the beginning and the end of a learning sequence more than the middle" (Sousa 1992, 21). Taking advantage of this primacy-recency effect, elite educators reserve the first and last parts of a lesson to emphasize main points of new material and to summarize and review those points respectively. The middle of a lesson is set aside for details, practice, and necessary elaboration.

CONTINUOUS MOVEMENT

Still another often overlooked performance strategy used by master teachers is continuous movement throughout the classroom *for the entire lesson.* Such nonstop motion is important because it not only stimulates student focus but it also contributes to classroom control. Students raised in a world of television, computers, and video games are visually oriented, and following a "moving target" can't help but raise their attention level.

Additionally, teacher movement is an invaluable tool to increase student engagement during class discussions. This is so because when instructors position themselves close to a student answering a question, the response is often not projected loudly enough for the entire class to hear. Also, in speaking to the teacher, the nearby student directs comments away from almost everyone in the room *except* the teacher. As such, classmates located relatively far from the dialogue will either be unable to hear what is said or will have a ready-made excuse not to even listen. Yet by continually moving as far away as possible from student speakers, a diagonal "listening corridor" is created, forcing those responding to project loudly enough for the teacher and classmates to hear (Wall 1993). Such an approach promotes student listening and attention.

As important as teacher movement is in encouraging student focus and engagement, it is equally important as a strategy fostering classroom order. As a positive side effect of enhanced attention, students invested in class discussions and activities are less likely to misbehave. Moreover, a teacher moving into the personal space of a potentially disruptive stu-

dent more directly preempts such behavior. To that end, numerous studies suggest and anecdotal experience supports the positive effect of
"proximity control—a well-known classroom management tool" (Tauber, Mester, and Buckwald 1993, 24). Simply put, discipline problems are
directly proportional to an instructor's distance from students. A teacher
planted behind a desk or mistaken for a statue in front of the room is not
only asking for students to "tune out" but is asking for control problems
as well.

CLASSROOM CLIMATE

Just as students are less likely to learn if they are not intellectually engaged, they are equally less likely to learn if the classroom is an unpleasant place to be. To that end, master teachers realize that "one of the most
significant factors affecting [student] learning . . . is the rapport they feel
with their teacher" (McGlynn 1999, 51). To that end, classroom climate
can easily be improved through teaching "performances" such as *projecting a concern and liking for all students* even when fatigued, irritated, otherwise preoccupied, and even if there is little personal affinity for a child.

If cortisol, a threat-related hormone, inhibits learning by "downshifting" the brain from higher-level thinking to more primitive survival
needs (Tomlinson and Kalbfleisch 1998), anything an instructor does to
reduce "danger" and to create a more positive classroom climate, such as
humor, praise, or taking a personal interest in students, has a beneficial
instructional impact. When teachers recognize they are partners with
their students in life's long journey, when they begin to treat them with
the dignity they deserve for simply being, then they are on the road to
becoming effective (Caulfield and Jennings 2002).

Without a classroom atmosphere of "relaxed alertness" involving low
threat and high challenge, students will invariably "be less able to engage
in complex intellectual tasks, those requiring creativity and the ability to
engage in open-ended thinking and questioning" (Caine and Caine 1994,
70; Caine and Caine 1997). From personal experience, every teacher
knows that stress can quickly downshift the brain into losing cognitive
powers. Confronted by an angry parent, an irate board member, or a
dissatisfied administrator, it's easy to feel overwhelmed and only later to
dwell on what the French call "wit of the staircase" should-have-said
regret. Why educators would believe that students who may be anxious,
troubled, or insecure are not *at least as likely* to lose the ability to think
clearly under duress is itself beyond comprehension.

There is little doubt that classroom atmosphere and the emotions it
engenders is directly related to student learning. Indeed, "a basic tenet of
brain-based instruction is that cognition is linked to emotion, which can
have either positive or negative effects on learners" (Rhodes 2003, 38).

Whereas positive emotions such as joy, excitement, or satisfaction connect new learning with feeling in the limbic system (Caulfield and Jennings 2002), negative emotions compromise learning. Realizing this, highly effective instructors are sensitive to the mood of their students and equally so are aware that good moods stimulated by teacher enthusiasm, humor, and authentically earned praise "enhance the ability [of students] to think flexibly and with more complexity" (Goleman 1995, 85; Rhodes 2003).

Conversely, student anxiety, fear of humiliation, and embarrassment sabotage learning. Over a hundred studies of more than thirty-six thousand people "found that the more prone to worries a person is, the poorer their academic performance, no matter how measured" (Goleman 1995, 84; Rhodes 2003). As has been said, it is impossible to teach someone to write with their right hand while their left is in a pot of boiling water. Whatever a teacher's academic degrees, years of experience, or even their instructional vision, without an emotionally positive and engaging environment, learning will be compromised (Caufield, Kidd, and Kocher 2000). Pink Floyd was right. Among other examples of teacher disrespect toward students, there should be "no dark sarcasm in the classroom."

When anxious, fearful, worried, or just generally upset, those emotions interfere with the ability to think long term and trigger a focus on more immediate "threats," even if imagined or exaggerated. Like one's tongue repeatedly returning to a broken tooth or lost filling, one's thoughts inevitably return to the source of "peril" and away from the lesson at hand. "Downshifted students have severe problems paying attention because their brains persevere, continuously repeating thoughts or unresolved emotional issues" (Caine 2000, 59).

Additionally, when students are classically conditioned to associate a teacher with anxiety or humiliation, such emotions are toxic to academic success. Like a Pavlovian dog salivating to a tuning fork, a student entering a classroom where emotional pain has regularly been linked to a particular instructor will continually experience unpleasant involuntary reactions detrimental to learning even if on any given day there is no immediate reason to do so.

Every teacher who has ever been upset or felt threatened knows how damaging those emotions are to clear thinking. And if that is so for adults, why should it be any less so for children? Safety and security are primary needs for all people. And since needs dictate actions, all people are motivated to satisfy those more immediate needs to the exclusion of other so-called higher-level self-actualizing prerequisites. Realizing this, the daily performance of master instructors promotes a classroom climate relatively free of negative emotion, and to the greatest extent possible, emotionally safe and even fun to experience. And to that end, laughter is but one approach toward accomplishing that goal.

It is not being suggested that a teacher who would never be confused for a stand-up comic should take lessons from Robin Williams or Woody Allen. What is being recommended is that since "humor is regularly identified by students as a characteristic of best-liked teachers" (Tauber, Mester, and Buckwald 1993, 25), more of an effort should be made to occasionally lighten the classroom's mood with humor, or at minimum, smiling more often.

At the least, laughter increases retention through the production of neurotransmitters and endorphins from 15 percent to 50 percent (Glenn 2002). Additionally, laughter oxygenates the blood, reduces stress, and "increases the ability of the student to absorb knowledge" (Tauber, Mester, and Buckwald 1993, 25). But beyond the purely physiological value of humor as it relates to learning, carefully chosen, self-deprecating comments or humorous personal anecdotes can, in exposing an educator's humanity, have the added benefit of closing the student-teacher "familiarity gap" as long as professional distance is not sacrificed for inappropriate and counterproductive instructor-pupil "friendships." Yet however skilled at fostering humor while still maintaining instructional separation with students, master teachers rarely if ever project gloom or pessimism, whatever they may be feeling inside.

On a subliminal level, a smile is perhaps the easiest way to create a more positive learning environment. Doing so will not only disarm an angry student, but for all pupils it conveys the tacit messages that "I am not a threat" and that "my only job is to help you." These messages are far more than window dressing. For conveying the impression that "I know you can do it; I won't give up on you . . . [exerts] a powerful motivating influence on students who receive the opposite message from their families and communities" (Benard 1993, 46; Weinstein, Soulé et al. 1991). Clichéd but true, many students, especially the most needy ones, don't care how much a teacher knows until they know that a teacher cares.

SAFEGUARDING INSTRUCTIONAL TIME

Still another strategy highly effective teachers have adopted from the performance arts is to be mindful of presentation gaps in moving from one part of a lesson to another. Just as "dead air" is unacceptable in a play, a concert, or a radio show, it is arguably more so during instruction. The best instructors are almost compulsively aware of how valuable class time is and are always seeking to minimize time lost to interruptions or transitions in a lesson.

Recognizing that minutes are an extremely precious and absolutely finite instructional resource, instruction starts promptly, unassigned time is eliminated, unnecessary digressions are avoided, and students are constructively engaged until they leave the classroom. Such an obsession with the productive use of time is far more than a neurotic foible or a transparent performance ploy. Its relationship with academic learning is one of the most reiterative findings in instructional research.

Other factors being equal, large increases in *productive* learning time result in correspondingly large increases in student learning. A 1980 review of thirty-five studies reported that 86 percent showed a beneficial influence of time on learning, and a meta-analysis twelve years later of more than one hundred studies showed an equally positive impact of time on learning in 88 percent of the surveys (Walberg and Fredrick 1991).

Indeed, many elite educators of middle school students and older are so mindful of conserving learning time that students in each class begin working *before* attendance is taken. Any less-driven teacher unconcerned with "saving just three minutes" a period should do the math. For in doing so, over the course of an entire 180-day term the classroom gains nine additional hours of instructional time: an extension of *more than two weeks* of typical fifty-minute classes.

After all, where is it written that instruction can't officially begin until student absences are checked? In many classrooms, pupils are greeted with a short "bell-ringing" or "do now" activity as they enter class, or quizzes are placed on a front desk for students to take upon entering the room and immediately begin *as* attendance is taken. In either case, a clear message is sent on the importance of class time, and a "learning is important" student mind-set is promoted.

The power of the environment to affect behavior is as powerful in schools as it is anywhere else. As such, the learning atmosphere orchestrated by the teacher impacts the attitude and the achievement of the children experiencing that climate. "In the best classrooms, the social atmosphere is warm and supportive . . . but at the same time businesslike and focused on the job at hand" (Hirsch 1996, 38). Conversely, the hallmark of less-effective teachers is to routinely deny this reality and then complain that "there is not enough time" for what really matters.

RELATING TO STUDENTS

In projecting a liking for all students by relating to them in a personal way can be as easy as quickly learning their names at the beginning of the term; legitimately praising their athletic, artistic, or dramatic achievements outside of the classroom; or by showing an interest in their favorite music, movies, or television shows. It can also be demonstrated by greeting them by name outside of school and making an effort to at least appear genuinely pleased to see them. "Establishing relationships with [students] communicates that you respect them as individuals and contributes to their successful learning" (Marzano and Pickering et al. 1997, 16). All people enjoy being "known." All people need to feel they are important. And students are no different.

Clearly, anything a teacher does showing a concern for pupils as individuals aside from academics positively affects instruction (McCombs and Whisler 1997). Indeed, for some students, a teacher taking interest in their lives is essential to learning. This is so because such curiosity offers unspoken evidence that students are liked and that they are valued. Since effective pedagogy presupposes strong student-teacher relationships, it is up to instructors to get "plugged into" their pupils' lives. And when doing so, "there is only one place to start and that is where they are" (Glasser 1969, 57).

Because there is a tendency to like people who say nice things to us, or who take an interest in our lives, this "positivity effect" in fostering greater student focus, effort, and compliance also promotes a less disruption-prone classroom environment. For in wanting to please someone they like and have a relationship with, it is simply more unlikely for most students to misbehave.

In a review of more than one hundred studies, "teachers reporting high-quality relationships with students had 31% fewer discipline problems, [and] rule violations, over a year's time than teachers who did not" (Beaty-O'Ferrall, Green, and Hanna 2010; Marzano, Marzano, and Pickering 2003). The cornerstones of such high-quality relationships are offering students legitimately earned praise, taking a personal interest in their lives, and especially for struggling youngsters, exhibiting empathy for problems not of their own doing. Without these essential elements of any positive association, student-teacher trust will fail to flourish, and learning will fail to flourish as well.

Long after graduation, when called on to remember what was so special about a favorite teacher, most people cite a caring personality at the top of their list. This is hardly surprising. Few would argue that a strong teacher-student relationship is all but impossible unless the learner feels recognized, respected, valued, and understood. Indeed, such relationships built on caring may well be the foundation of successful instruction. As Horace Mann said over a hundred years ago, "When students know that their teachers genuinely care, they respond by exerting greater effort to reach their potential."

Simply because effective instruction is in part a performance does not mean teachers should view efforts to help students feel understood as unacceptably manufactured efforts to demonstrate empathy. If effective instruction includes doing whatever is necessary to ensure student learning, making a conscious effort to project an understanding of and concern for student difficulties is both essential and justified.

As such, efforts promoting teacher-student communication, respect, and connectedness should neither be trivialized nor devalued. Especially for troubled learners, truly listening to concerns, validating perceptions, and attempting to compassionately see problems through their eyes may well be the "tipping points" between academic success and failure. For just as positive teacher expectations of students invariably leads to positive student results, when students hold similarly positive beliefs about their teachers, this self-fulfilling prophecy in reverse leads to similar outcomes.

Not only do student perceptions of their teachers significantly impact learning in ways congruent with those beliefs (Feldman and Prohaska 1979), those perceptions also impact the teachers themselves. Just as a class believing in their teacher likely inspires that instructor to make the most of his or her abilities, a class taught by a teacher viewed as unprepared or unconcerned likely diminishes instructional quality, as the educator so perceived struggles to overcome issues of student negativity and ineffective discipline.

"DRESSING FOR SUCCESS"

And finally, highly effective teachers dress professionally for their "role." Although less-aware or less-effective instructors might consider a teacher's wardrobe to be of little consequence, they are wrong. In rating others, people unconsciously generalize the quality of one characteristic to other unrelated details of personality. Well known by psychologists, this "halo effect" is an important determinant in how people are viewed. Thus, physically attractive people are often perceived to be more intelligent, and taller individuals are frequently judged as stronger leaders.

While unfair and often unfortunate, educators can take positive advantage of this powerful behavioral dynamic by dressing well. All things being equal, students at least initially view well-dressed teachers more professionally and positively than those who are not. First impressions do matter, people often do judge books by their covers, and "dressing for success" is at least as important in the classroom as it is anywhere else.

Practice Four

Holding Students Accountable

Nobody rises to low expectations. —Calvin Lloyd

Without question, teacher expectations exert an enormously powerful influence on learner motivation and achievement. However, in striving to be favored by students, to avoid confrontation, and perhaps in believing students are incapable of quality outcomes, too many teachers lower academic standards by rewarding less-than-satisfactory work. Expecting little from students, that is exactly what these enabling educators get. In contrast, master teachers maintain high standards by holding youngsters accountable for deficient effort and unsatisfactory results.

ACADEMIC ENABLING

Enabling students to "tune out" without comment or consequence, giving easy assessments requiring little effort, accepting "forgotten" assignments without penalty, and granting inflated credit for sloppy work all have a cumulatively harmful effect on performance (Landfried 1989). Enabling's message to students is clear: mediocrity is good enough. But in an increasingly competitive world, promoting mediocrity is clearly *not* good enough. By not holding students accountable to high academic and behavioral standards, enabling educators are not empowering students "to be all they can be" but instead to do as little as possible and be whatever they can get away with.

While teacher unawareness of academic enabling may account for some instances of this behavior, it just as often may result from motives at least partially intentional. Clearly, it is much more difficult demanding high-level work from students than accepting mediocrity. Requiring the best from pupils may well lead to confrontations with them or with their parents. This is especially so if high-quality work is expected but instruction supporting such quality is lacking.

As a result, all but the most unaware instructors realize that increasing demands and expectations on students without correspondingly making equal demands on themselves is a predictable prescription for

25

unwanted scrutiny and hassles from students, parents, and administrators. Thus, for ineffective teachers, it is simply easier to play the quid pro quo game, where passing grades are tacitly exchanged for student silence on inept pedagogy and a lack of academic rigor. According to the late educational visionary Ted Sizer, this "conspiracy of the least" where students and teachers demand little of each other transforms schools into places of "wasteful triviality" (Toch and Daniel 1996, 61).

Moreover, as the desire to be liked is as true for teachers as it is for virtually anyone else, sometimes this need also takes precedence over high academic and behavioral standards that may result in "ruffling some feathers." Demanding rigor from students contrastingly enabled by past and current instructors makes such conflict even more likely to be squarely aimed at educators having the backbone to actually require civil behavior and quality work. But whatever the reasons for enabling students "to be less than they can be," it is certain that teachers who do so academically cripple their pupils, encourage ever longer journeys on the academic path of least resistance, and clearly violate the "good for kids" filter of curricular choice.

Examples of letting students off the responsibility hook without consequence are numerous and clearly visible in all schools. Overlooking students who are chronically late or inattentive is common practice in many classrooms. Equally so, ineffective teachers endlessly repeat themselves, extend deadlines, ignore disrespect, grant meaningless extra credit opportunities, pass students not deserving to do so, and "buy into" the following student "games," reinforcing more of the same lack of student accountability and high-achievement outcomes.

"GAMES" STUDENTS PLAY

A psychological game is a repetitive series of hidden-meaning communications leading to a negative conclusion (Berne 1964). Since games are repeating behavioral patterns, when a student is playing a game, or a teacher is the unwitting victim of one, there is a déjà vu feeling of experiencing it before. And because someone almost always gets hurt or hurts themselves by the underlying agenda of a game, the term is quite misleading. That is, games are anything but fun or enjoyable because by design they are not meant to be.

Although there are many reasons why students play games, arguably the most important motive is grounded in the almost universal need to embrace the safety and security of a predictable and orderly existence. Indeed, whatever other causes for this behavior, the overwhelming desire to confirm, reinforce, and maintain one's most basic perceptions about oneself and the world is paramount. Thus, each game helps to "prove" this worldview by generating the reality, however counterproductive, that some students are comfortable with.

Simply put, the games students play are largely determined by how they positively or negatively view themselves and how that level of value compares with their perceptions regarding the relative worth of others. And because at least occasional feelings of insignificance and inferiority are an almost universal affliction, the need for students to temporarily relieve this sense of inadequacy on the one hand or to justify its presence on the other is accomplished by playing games. In the former instance, students initiate games to relatively build themselves up by putting others down, and in the latter their self-sabotaging play ensures diminished accountability, lowered expectations, and greater predictability by confirming long-held perceptions of inadequacy.

In clinging to their unpleasant but comfortable world of self-doubt, the ulterior and seemingly paradoxical theme of many student games is eschewing positive action. Seemingly counterintuitive, many insecure students would rather be "right" in generating sympathy and lowered expectations than to be "wrong" and risk losing manufactured attention by positively moving forward. Yet, in empowering students to accept responsibility for their actions, master teachers recognize the following enabling games in spirit if not in name.

Yes But

The game begins when a youngster requests help in solving a problem, academic or otherwise. The plea inevitably results in a nurturing teacher's "Why don't you . . ." response. Yet, whatever suggestion or solution is offered, "Yes but . . ." is always the reply. Though the initial request for assistance is seemingly plausible, Yes But players have a far more ulterior agenda. Their request for help is a charade. They *don't want* to solve their problem and will sabotage any effort to do so.

In rejecting any guidance, Yes Buters want to "prove" that since there is no solution to their problem they can do nothing other than to continue feeling sorry for themselves. In this way, the self-generated evidence that "I can't catch a break," or that "I'm just unlucky," is overwhelming and secure. But whatever emotional support such manipulated evidence provokes, the end result is inaction, self-pity, a lack of accountability, and the added benefit of "proving" that the teacher-patsy "hooked" into trying to help is as much of a loser as the pupil playing the game.

By continuing to offer advice to a Yes But student, enabling teachers feed into these counterproductive ends. Offering help to needy youngsters is a moral imperative for teachers. However, *endlessly* suggesting solutions to Yes Buters enables their ulterior agenda. After initially offering guidance, a teacher recognizing this game would do well to say in a flat, noncritical tone, "I have given you several useful ideas that will likely work if you try them. And since I have no other suggestions to offer, my question is what are *you* going to do about this problem?"

Simply because they are well educated doesn't mean that teachers, or for that matter any other group of adults, don't play games as well. Game playing is an equal-opportunity behavioral dynamic common to people whatever their age or college degrees. For instructors constantly complaining about their "kids" but just as constantly rejecting any collegial or administrative advice with the same "yes but" response as their students, it doesn't take a genius to figure out what game is being played, its motivation, or its eventual outcome.

Wooden Leg

Students playing this game fabricate an exaggerated or imaginary handicap, a "wooden leg," as an excuse for not doing or achieving something. In seeking absolution in alibis, students also seek lowered expectations and sympathy from unsuspecting and often enabling teachers. The ulterior message is clear. "You can't blame me today for I am handicapped," and "You can't blame me tomorrow because my handicap precludes me from being judged as an equal to those not so burdened."

In the short term, such a ploy salvages at least a shred of self-esteem. But as there are few free rides in reality, there is a price to pay in the long-term inertia of inaction, ineffectiveness, and failure. Wallowing in private moments of depression or self-pity, the Wooden Leg player is at least satisfied by a predictable world where life is counterfactually measured in "shoulda, coulda, woulda" days, where positive action is rare, excuse is the norm, and personal culpability is nonexistent.

As for the student version of Wooden Leg, teachers are no less immune to exaggerating or fabricating handicaps as a reason for not achieving something. An instructor continually rationalizing poor student results with excuses such as a "lousy schedule," or "I'm not teaching a subject I like," or "My standards are high and my class just isn't that bright" is undeniably using verbal crutches in justifying the unjustifiable. However, this last excuse is as common as it is demeaning to students *and* to colleagues of the Wooden Leg player. For if "high standards" inevitably led to student failures, does that mean that instructors not experiencing such problems have low standards?

Now I Got You (NIGY)

In justifying their own failures, some students wait for a teacher to make a minor mistake and then lash out at the unsuspecting instructor in self-righteous, inappropriate, and exaggerated anger. This "gotcha" game not only enables underperforming "players" to "get even" with authority figures, but in exposing instructor "incompetence," it also enables student rationalizations for further failure or misconduct. After all, how can anyone be expected to learn from or even listen to an unfair, inept, and ineffective teacher?

Now I Got You students often ask obscure questions not from a genuine interest in answers but as an attempt to "confirm" the teacher as a pseudointellectual fraud. Moreover, NIGY players often supplement their esoteric academic questions with others more overtly critical, such as "When did you give us that?" or "Didn't you say . . . ?" or "You expect us to . . . ?" or any other query positioning the teacher as a mindless incompetent. But however phrased, the intent and result of superficially innocent Now I Got You questions is often the same. If ignored, they can easily undermine teacher confidence and can compromise classroom discipline. Moreover, providing players of the game an excuse for failure can enable student unaccountability and underperformance to continue.

Ironically, when teachers expose the underlying motive of Now I Got You with a "gotcha" statement of their own, it will usually end the game. For all but the most hardcore of NIGY players, simply responding "Do you ask questions to seek answers or clarifications or are they attempts to make me look bad?" will be followed by impassioned student denials and not surprisingly an abrupt termination of the exposed behavior.

Inasmuch as Now I Got You is directed at authority figures, some teachers focus the game on administrators rather than on students. As in the student version of NIGY, the player waits for the "boss" to make a minor mistake to gleefully lash out in proving he or she is little more than an "empty-suited" fraud. In doing so, a typographical error in a memo or an innocent misstatement regarding test results is fair game for the "getting even" gristmill at a board hearing or a faculty meeting.

But whether a teacher is the target of NIGY or its instigator, the game's purpose extends beyond avoidance of responsibility. An added motive is that by finding fault with authority figures, Now I Got You players can relatively raise their self-esteem by lowering the self-esteem of others. For players lacking confidence, doing so can at least temporarily relieve self-perceptions of inadequacy and replace them with contrived feelings of power and schadenfreude in the suffering of undeserving targets.

THE CONSEQUENCES OF ENABLING

Whatever the seeming believability of games, excuses, or rationalizations, how does enabling students to expect sympathetic attention or pardon for boorish behaviors, a lack of preparation, or underperforming outcomes lead to achievement? If indeed the purpose of school is to prepare students for life, will accepting shoddy workmanship, chronic lateness or absence, a lack of consideration for others, or inattention to detail lead to success in *any* endeavor? Will those behaviors improve their relationships or help them gain admission to postsecondary education? Will they lead to getting or keeping a good job? Will they result in a more fulfilling life?

However, even students unwilling or unable to focus on the long-term self-inflicted damage of enabled behaviors should at least be able to understand the more immediate problems classroom disruption or inattention creates. Students need to understand that any lack of respect or attention for a teacher, even if continued without instructor comment or consequence, may be the crucial difference between passing and failing. After all, if their grades are borderline between receiving credit for a class or not, why would any teacher give a student "the benefit of the doubt" who has chronically mouthed off or has spent the term with their head inattentively planted on their desk? If for no other reason than blatant self-interest, students need to be informed to think before speaking and to at least feign interest by raising their heads above their shoulders during a lesson.

REWARDING "HARD WORK"

Counterintuitively, another way teachers enable "path-of-least-resistance" student performances is to reward "hard work" in assessing them. While compensating pupils for perceived effort prior to high school is understandable and arguably defensible, doing so for older students tacitly sends the message that unsatisfactory work is somehow more acceptable as long it resulted from "hard work."

In readying students for life after twelfth grade, how does rewarding them for "effort" without regard for legitimately rigorous performance standards do so? Where in the "real world" is one remunerated for poor results simply by asserting to have worked hard? Do claims of hard work regardless of outcome guarantee a paycheck in business, in athletics, in the arts, or anywhere else?

Students need to understand that even though without effort there is virtually no chance for success, in and of itself, exertion does not guarantee achievement. Basing a grade even partially on effort thus diverts student focus from what really matters: the *quality* of their work. And after graduation, quality is all that matters.

There are also practical and ethical reasons for not recognizing effort in assessing students. For how do teachers *really know* how much effort a student did or did not make? Since working hard is a relative term, without objectively knowing how hard classmates are working, *how do even students really know* how hard they are comparatively working? And if a student can admittedly submit high-quality work without making much of an effort, should they then be penalized for their supposed lack of exertion?

It is not being suggested that all enabling teachers are necessarily bad people. In some cases, their motive for enabling youngsters may not be a selfish attempt to be liked or an ulterior strategy to avoid student, parental, or administrative complaints. It may well be a sincerely motivated response to support pupils who are struggling. Yet in affirming the ubiquitous law of unintended consequences, that well-intentioned purpose often results in detrimental outcomes. For without extenuating circumstances, reflexively buying into a student's tears, their quivering lips, their games, or their "I can never do anything right" statements often weakens those whom misguided educators are so desperately seeking to help.

The result of low but "acceptable" expectations is clear. Seeking to do as little as possible and still pass, enabled students are more likely to set low goals for themselves, to resent authority figures insisting on quality, and to become chronic underachievers. And while virtually all teachers claim to have high standards for their students, the real question is, do they make equally rigorous demands on themselves? Clearly, master teachers have the awareness and the courage to demand both. In fact, in a study of college professors identified as master teachers, such elite educators not only demonstrated commitment to excellence through their instructional preparation, but in universally creating challenging curriculums, "not one master teacher was perceived by students to lack rigor" (Weaver, Wenzlaff, and Cotrell 1993, 14).

STUDENT DEMANDS FOR ACADEMIC ACCOUNTABILITY

Perhaps surprisingly, the most strident voices calling for higher standards and greater academic accountability are sometimes the students themselves. Rather than conforming to the stereotype of uncaring and irresponsible pupils claiming they are overworked, many insist they would do more *if only teachers demanded more.* Agreeing with Charles Schultz, they believe that "like a ten-speed bike, most of us have gears we do not use."

The nonpartisan research group Public Agenda found in a study of one thousand American teenagers that nearly 80 percent said that "they would learn more if schools made sure that they were on time to class and completed their homework" (Bradley 1997, 20). Insisting that their schools simply allow students to "muddle through," almost two-thirds said they would do much better if they tried and roughly three-fourths of those surveyed said that students should not be promoted unless they had learned the material (Bradley 1997).

Supporting the perceptions of many highly effective teachers, these findings seem to confirm that students are not being held accountable behaviorally and academically to high standards. And in likening instruction to a performance, the study also confirmed the importance of Practice Three of master educators. When students were asked what characteristics contributed "a lot" to their learning, over three-fourths responded the teacher's ability to make lessons fun and interesting and 71 percent indicated that teacher enthusiasm for their subject was important. Yet when asked what percentage of those characteristics actually fit their teachers, the numbers were 24 percent and 29 percent respectively (Bradley 1997). As master instructors well know, "hard work does not turn students away, but busywork destroys them" (Wasserstein 1995, 43).

PROMOTING STUDENT ACCOUNTABILITY

Even less-effective teachers can move in the direction of demanding higher-quality work from their students. But as for so many things in life, doing so is more a matter of "want to" than of "can do." However, to do so teachers must first clarify what quality work looks like through exemplary models, the steps necessary to create a finished product through instructional "recipes," and the characteristics of performance excellence through grading rubrics.

In eliminating any reasonable "I didn't know what to do" student excuses for submitting substandard work, such assessment guidelines grant teachers the instructional and ethical high ground to demand greater pupil accountability. And even if this were not the case, in providing greater clarity of what qualities confer excellence, students exhibit enhanced achievement and more positive attitudes toward a subject using criterion-referenced methods (Wilburn and Felps 1983).

Yet all too often, teachers make the standards for student success available only *after* the assessment of a product or presentation is complete. Such after-the-fact critiques of student work are not only disheartening but also grossly unfair. Indeed, few if any real-world assessments are done without the criteria for exemplary work made available *before* a performance is enacted.

If Olympic ice skaters or gymnasts were evaluated without a clear sense of what excellence looked like and how they were to be graded, such assessments would be viewed as absurdly unreasonable. And if teachers received unsatisfactory performance reviews without knowing the criteria on which the evaluations were based until after the assessment, does anyone doubt what their reaction would be? As one recently observed fourth-grade instructor said following such an unclear appraisal, "I had no idea what my principal was looking for—I had to be a mind reader" (Danielson 2010/2011, 35). Yet in similarly judging student work as a "gotcha game" of after-the-fact criticism, it ironically is those very teachers rightfully impugning unfair administrative evaluations who regularly require their pupils to telepathically resemble Harry Houdini.

It's not that instructors don't know the basis for their judgments. They do. But the basis for their ratings is often not shared with those likely to benefit from its disclosure until it is too late to affect their immediate performances or evaluations. Yet without doing do, students are unlikely to understand the reasons for teacher valuations of their efforts. As a result, excellent grades are seemingly given after "doing nothing," and poor ratings follow "the best essay I've ever written." Without a clear sense of teacher expectations and with an attendant inability to comply with a set of unknown or at best vague instructional standards, many students feeling at a loss to please their teachers give up and completely disengage.

Yet beyond the fairness issue of giving students a clear target to evaluate their work and to adjust their efforts accordingly, rubrics also increase the likelihood that student grades will be an accurate and uniform statement of quality compared to clearly articulated standards. While rubrics do not guarantee absolute instructor reliability of pupil work evaluations, without such standards expressing criteria for various quality levels, fair and consistent assessment of student products and performances is an impossible dream.

Although there is abundant evidence that this is indeed the case, some of the best-known research that teacher judgments are extremely unreliable measurements of student work date back some hundred years. In the 1910s, researchers copied two actual English exam papers and sent them to teachers for grading. Upon return, the marks ranged from 50 to 94 percent, and one paper graded by 142 teachers received fourteen marks below 80 percent and fourteen above 94 percent. In another instance, duplicate geometry tests were graded by 116 teachers. The returned exams were rated from 28 to 92 percent, with twenty marks below 60 percent and nine rated as at least 85 percent (Phelps 2008). And anyone suggesting such inconsistent evaluations are not equally true today has never sat in a room with teachers rating student essays or research papers without the benefit of grading rubrics.

DESIGNING RUBRICS

At the very least, competent teachers increase student accountability by providing students with instructional targets known as rubrics. These guidelines empowering students to evaluate their work against publicly revealed standards should be so clear that no student, parent, or teacher has any doubt as to how well an activity was done. Moreover, having an unambiguous idea of what excellence requires enables students to better align their energies in meeting those expectations and to assess their progress when doing so. "This is a major aspect of self-directed work and self-motivated improvement required of all human beings in real-world situations" (Darling-Hammond 1993, 24).

Mystery may be effective in Hitchcock movies, in romance, and in the works of Agatha Christie, but it *never* is effective in student assessment. Flying blind leads to only one outcome, and it is as true for students as it is for anyone else. Realizing this, master teachers design rubrics such as those found in this book's Appendix using a process similar to the following "recipe."

1. Gather samples of students' work in a particular task that illustrate a range of quality.
2. Analyze these samples. Then list the most important parts or categories of the learning activity. Called dimensions or "shells," a writing rubric, for example, may include such categories as mechanics, style, content, and organization.
3. Separate the samples of student work into piles of similar quality; for example, excellent, good, satisfactory, and below standard. Identify the essential characteristics or descriptors that distinguish samples in each pile for each of the dimensions. Start with the highest-rated products or performances. Ask yourself: By what qualities or "descriptors" will I know whether students have produced excellent work in a particular task? What traits, if demonstrated, would be impossible for a student to exhibit and still produce a less-than-exemplary product or performance? Or, what traits, if not evident, would make it impossible for a student to still demonstrate exemplary work?
4. Develop a quality or performance scale for your dimensions, such as distinguished, proficient, competent, and unsatisfactory. Again, start with the most excellent level or what an "A" looks like. Then "scale down" for as many additional levels as required.
5. Identifying four assessment levels works quite well in distinguishing between student performances. Less than this number does not adequately differentiate the great range of quality within each level, and more than this number undermines reliability among raters.
6. Gather another sample of students' work. Determine if the dimensions, descriptors, and assessment levels accurately capture the quality of products that is intuitively recognized. That is, if intuitively a particular student artifact is recognized as excellent ("distinguished"), the rubric rating should *leave no doubt* as to such quality. It's like voting whether a professional baseball player should be in the Hall of Fame. If there is much debate or uncertainty whether enshrinement is justified, there is a pretty good chance

that it is not. Equally so, if an example of student work is obviously excellent, the rubric should leave no doubt that its rating is indeed "distinguished."

7. If necessary, revise and/or realign the dimensions, descriptors, and assessment levels.
8. Try the rubric again until it accurately captures the quality levels of student work.
9. Create a student work evaluation form similar to the ones included in the Appendix that is aligned with the rubric's dimensions, descriptors, and assessment levels. Upon grading, this shorthand version of the full rubric is returned to students, clarifying areas of excellence, proficiency, competency, and below-standard performance.

INSTRUCTIONAL "RECIPES"

If students are to be held fully accountable for products and performances, common sense and fairness demand that whatever their detail, rubrics are not enough. Excellent for clarifying the essential characteristics of a learning target, they do little in clarifying how these characteristics translate into the reality of an actual artifact or presentation. Moreover, grading guidelines do nothing in providing students with an academic road map of how to reach their instructional destination. In order for students to be held fully accountable, performance models and "recipes" of exemplary work must accompany grading rubrics.

To that end, a high school "recipe" given to students writing a high-quality research paper might look like the following:

1. Pick a topic you are interested in.
2. Compile a list of likely sources.
3. As you read each source, use a legal pad to write all of the necessary citation information for each source at the top of the page, and follow this with your notes. As notes are taken, make certain to put quotation marks around any exact quotes or statistics. In the legal pad's margin beside any quoted or likely-to-be-paraphrased material, write the source's page number where the information was obtained.
4. Repeat the above procedure for each source you are planning to use.
5. When your research is complete, number your legal pad pages consecutively.
6. Read over all of your legal pad notes. As you do so, formulate a list of "research categories," such as Introduction, Conclusion, Thesis Support, Thesis Opposition, and others.

7. On an index card, color code each of your "research categories." For example, Introduction (blue) and Conclusion (red).

8. Once again, read over your legal pad notes. Using colored pens or pencils, mark your research material in the legal-pad margin with the appropriate color of the "research category" it most closely pertains to.

9. Starting with your introduction, copy onto a second legal pad all of the material colored blue as introduction material. Write *very* small but very neatly so that, if possible, all introduction notes are transcribed on a single side of a legal pad. Upon completion, this will be the "research category" sheet for the introduction. *Make certain* to indicate on the introduction "research category" sheet where (what page) the information was obtained from the original legal pad notes. This will need to be done so that it will be clear where the information came from for citation purposes.

10. Read over all of the introduction notes. Write the introduction. Once material originally on the first legal pad is used, draw a line through it. Then, repeat the above procedure with the next "research category."

11. The last thing that should be done before ending a writing session is to prepare the next "research category" sheet for the following day. In this way, the next day's writing will be well prepared for a quick start by avoiding "writer's block." Also, try writing while listening to quiet music that is emotionally moving.

12. Repeat steps 9 and 10 until all your color-coded "research categories" have been exhausted.

Rubrics, "recipes" for achieving quality work, and models exhibiting a tangible product of what "good" looks like create a win-win situation for instructors. In providing ultimate clarity of what quality looks like and the steps necessary to achieve it, highly effective teachers foster student accountability by establishing unmistakable and understandable learning standards and an efficient process for reaching them. Correspondingly, teachers are morally empowered to more readily demand greater student responsibility for creating high-quality products and performances from learners who have been clearly informed as to what excellence looks like and how best to create it.

Practice Five

Accepting Instructional Responsibility

Every damn thing is your own fault, if you're any good. —Ernest Hemingway

Lofty personal standards of the very best teachers are exemplified by their Practice Five willingness to take full responsibility for student results. This is not to say that there aren't instances when a child or even a small group of children seem unreachable. However, the most effective teachers firmly believe that such failures are extremely isolated cases. Looking first at themselves rather than at their pupils, master teachers improve student results by focusing on what they can *always* control, their own actions. Whereas the weakest teachers claim excuses for virtually everything, the strongest educators claim excuses for virtually nothing. It is thus not surprising that such "high efficacy" instructors confidently believing they have considerable mastery over their own lives also feel they have considerable mastery over the learning lives of their students.

TEACHER EFFICACY AND STUDENT ACHIEVEMENT

Instructor sense of personal mastery has clearly been correlated with enhanced student learning. That is, teachers perceiving themselves as able to make a difference achieve better student results than those perceiving themselves as unable to do so (Rhodes 2003). This may have as much to do with the greater one's sense of personal control the greater one's perseverance as it does with the likelihood that high-efficacy teachers both model and instill that same empowering mind-set in their students.

But the correlation between the potent mind-set of high-efficacy instructors and student achievement may also result from other factors. Teacher beliefs about their own effectiveness have a considerable impact on classroom management, pedagogical strategies, and on a willingness to adopt instructional innovation (Ghaith and Yaghi 1997; Gusky 1988; Woolfolk and Hoy 1990).

Teachers who are very efficacious make better use of time, criticize students' incorrect answers less, and are more effective in guiding students to correct answers through their questioning. However, teachers low in efficacy tend to spend more time in nonacademic activities and make use of less-effective techniques to guide students to correct responses (Yilmaz 2011).

Yet whatever the reasons for the correlation between teacher and student efficacy, the "if they fail, I fail" mantra of elite educators is simple yet undeniably powerful. It is a self-fulfilling prophecy. "Teachers who believe they can make a difference, *do* make a difference" (Weber and Omotani 1994, 38). Projecting an attitude of confidence and determination, "teachers with a high sense of efficacy are more likely to view low-achieving students as reachable, teachable, and worthy of attention and effort" (Alderman 1990, 28; Ashton and Webb 1986). Accordingly, the power of positive instructor beliefs and expectations to promote positive student results is more than anecdotally so. It is supported by extensive and more traditionally accepted research.

THE OAK SCHOOL EXPERIMENT

In the seminal Oak School experiment of some forty years ago, elementary school students chosen completely at random were identified to teachers as intellectual "bloomers." Also chosen randomly, the teachers were told that because of their instructional excellence these "high IQ students" were being assigned to their rooms. Further, the teachers were told that because of the academic potential of these inordinately bright learners combined with their high-quality instruction, the expectation was that student performance would improve 20 to 30 percent during the upcoming term. The teachers selected to instruct these "advanced" classes were also told that due to potential charges of discrimination, the students, their parents, and the rest of the faculty were to remain uninformed about the pupil placement plan.

Eight months later, expectation became reality when youngsters designated as intellectually promising did in fact exhibit impressive academic gains both in an absolute sense and in comparison to control students. In fact, they not only achieved the 20 to 30 percent academic gains as predicted, but their classes *led the entire district* in standardized test scores (McKenna 2002).

Moreover, these students, in actuality *representing all ability levels* from which superior performance was expected, were described as being happier, more curious, better adjusted, and more likely to experience success as adults (Rosenthal and Jacobson 1968). And their teachers fared equally well in unanimously agreeing that they had enjoyed teaching that year more than *any* year in the past (McKenna 2002).

With nothing changing other than what instructors had been falsely told, such outstanding results could only have resulted from exaggeratedly positive teacher expectations (Rosenthal and Jacobson 1968) and their more aggressively positive interactions with students resulting from those expectations. Such interactions might well have included more consistent praise, assigning more challenging work, and consciously or unconsciously expressing a more positive demeanor toward these "likely to bloom" students.

This more positive demeanor combined with any increase in instructional effort may at least partially have resulted from the belief that if these "superior" students *didn't* thrive, the onus for their underperformance would rest squarely on their teachers. After all, if "undeniably advanced" learners underperformed, who but their instructors would then be culpable for such nonfulfillment? If even unconsciously believing this to be so, this greater sense of teacher accountability correlating with enhanced student achievement provides further evidence that an increased sense of personal responsibility has the same positive effect on teachers as it does on students.

But while the relative impact of optimistic teacher expectations, correspondingly elevated student confidence, or a greater sense of instructor accountability on the Oak School results may never be known, it is irrefutable that students stereotyped as low achievers are contrastingly sent an academically disabling set of messages by at least some of their teachers. Whether actually true or not, students perceived as less able are often viewed as less worthy of sincere praise, are less likely to be called on, and when they are called on are given less time to respond (Gazin 1990). Criticized more and overtly valued less, struggling students intuitively sense a teacher's lack of interest and belief in them, and they often respond in ways validating those perceptions.

As the author of the Oak School study, Dr. Robert Rosenthal put it this way: "The only difference was in the mind, and expectations of the teacher," and having such high expectations, instructors "teach more and teach it more warmly" (Begley 2003, B1). In short, these were the very interactions those teachers *could have and should have* been displaying for all their students.

Through consistent experience, people build internal models of how they perceive themselves and the world. If all a teacher needs to do to dramatically impact learner achievement is to offer feedback challenging underperforming student models, why wouldn't they at least try to do so? Perhaps the answer is simply a lack of awareness regarding the power of expectations. Perhaps it is a gross misunderstanding of bell-curve grade distribution "inexorably" dictating a like number of "acceptable" student failures counterbalancing student successes. Or perhaps struggling students in providing a ready-made "they can't learn" instructional alibi undermine the willingness for weak instructors to even question that counterproductive mind-set.

Thus, the significance of this study and hundreds of others confirming similar results is not only that prior perceptions can affect later judgments; it is that those preconceived teacher attitudes, stereotypes, and expectations clearly influence student behaviors in conforming to them. In turn, those behaviors greatly affect student self-image and academic performance. Or as Professor Rosenthal said more succinctly, "When teachers have been led to expect better intellectual performance from their students, they tend to get it" (Begley 2003, B1).

More recently, a study of almost twelve thousand high school sophomores in 820 public, private, and Catholic high schools also found that teacher perceptions about teaching and learning directly impacted student performance. Achievement gains were "significantly higher in schools where teachers [took] collective responsibility for students' academic success or failure rather than blaming students for their own failure" (Lee and Smith 1996, 103). In particular, instructors holding themselves personally responsible for teaching all students, regardless of background, produced higher achievement in all subjects (Lee and Smith 1996). And the power of teacher expectations goes well beyond purely academic results.

THE PYGMALION EFFECT

"Students consistently treated as well-intentioned individuals, respectful of themselves and others, and desiring to act morally, are more likely to develop prosocial qualities" (Fisher 2003). Goethe was right. More than an empty cliché, treating people as if they were what they ought to be helps them to become what they are capable of being. Understanding this, teachers would do well to apply the words of Eliza Doolittle to their students. "The difference between a lady and a flower girl," the heroine of the play *Pygmalion* said, "is not how she behaves but how she is treated."

Demonstrated in hundreds of studies, this Pygmalion-effect tendency for students to perform in ways similar to prior expectations is beyond doubt. Teacher beliefs in their own effectiveness lead to positive beliefs about student potential, which then lead to enhanced student achievement. But this unconscious drive to manipulate reality to one's preconceptions can be a force for harm as well as for good. To that end, instructors believing they are powerless to affect change with an "incorrigible" student or class will validate a self-fulfilling prophecy of another sort.

In schools where the weakest educators routinely attribute student underperformance to previous teachers; to too many "bad apples"; to too little support from parents; or "bad time" excuses of pupil inattention on

Monday, Friday, before lunch, after lunch, or right before or after a vacation; the only guarantee is more of the same. Known as the Frankenstein effect, marginal expectations invariably lead to equally marginal results. This negative form of self-fulfilling prophecy can have a particularly harmful effect on students labeled as "slow" who continue to fail in part because they are expected to do so. It requires tremendous belief in oneself based on past successes to overcome a teacher's low expectations. Unfortunately, struggling students often lack the history and self-confidence to do so.

In further justifying low standards due to overcrowded classes, lack of administrative support, too little staff development, too much staff development, more cowbell, less cowbell, or any other convenient yet even *Saturday-Night-Live*-laughable circumstance deflecting responsibility, the self-esteem of scapegoating teachers is defended at the expense of the children they instruct. Yet surprisingly, such excuse-addicted educators do indeed have high standards. The only problem is those standards apply to everyone but themselves.

LOW- VERSUS HIGH-EFFICACY TEACHERS

The effective teacher practice of accepting the full burden for student results is in stark contrast to the "I'm doing all I can do" justifications of their "low efficacy" colleagues. Highly able educators realize the simple truth that *no one* is doing *all* they can do. No one. Every butcher, baker, candlestick maker, and yes, teacher can do more or at least better. Undeniably, as long as there is one teacher on the face of the earth who would have gotten better results with an "unreachable" student or class, a different strategy *could* have been used.

As experts in learning, teachers should realize that if students do not understand something it may have as much or more to do with their instruction as with anything else. After all, how many times in life is something not understood despite one's best attempts at understanding and someone else's best attempts at explanation? And how many times does a seemingly unfathomable elucidation morph into an "aha experience" upon hearing or reading a slightly different explanation?

Is it then not so that often something is not understood not because of an inability or an unwillingness to learn but because that something was not initially explained in terms one could understand? And if that has happened to all teachers, how could it not at least be equally likely to happen for students? If the fundamental goal of instructors is the transmission of explanations to ensure optimal student learning, isn't it the essential job of teachers to find the surest intellectual path leading to that destination without reflexively blaming the recipients of those explanations along the way?

However, low-efficacy teachers feeling less responsible for student achievement rationalize a lack of learning by focusing more on instructional efforts than on student results. Quick to deflect accountability, these "look how hard I've tried" teachers seek absolution by obfuscating dismal student outcomes with an unending litany of claims recounting what they did and how hard they worked in doing it.

In the real world, what matters are not the inputs of what people do but their ultimate results. And those very teachers focusing primarily on their efforts while ignoring their outcomes, in not accepting such excuses from anyone else, would be among the first to agree. None of them would care to hear how many awards a chef had won or a meal's quality of ingredients if their food was inedible. Likewise, it would be unacceptable for a mechanic to mention the parts replaced or the time spent repairing their vehicle if the car still did not run.

Why then should it be any more tolerable for a teacher to state how many papers they graded or how many activities they planned in defending unsatisfactory classroom results? The answer is that it isn't any more acceptable. As the comic strip character Pogo was fond of saying, "We have met the enemy and he is us." And the most highly effective teachers, in focusing entirely on an "Am I getting it done?" mind-set, know that.

Practice Six

Monitoring Thoughts

Our life is what our thoughts make it. —Marcus Aurelius Antoninus

Whatever their intelligence quotients or diplomas on the wall, teachers are no less immune to destructive thought patterns than anyone else. All people behave in ways consistent with their assumptions about life. And when those assumptions are inaccurate, their perceptions of events often lead to detrimental outcomes. For teachers, such illogical thoughts often translate into academic and disciplinary problems with students. Yet "educators who bring their counterproductive self-talk to a level of awareness, and who rethink and reverbalize these inner dialogues, stand a good chance of improving their performance" (Neck and Barnard 1996, 25).

There is little doubt that beliefs and attitudes are not only reflected in a teacher's emotional world and personal actions, but there is evidence that they also "drive important decisions and classroom practice" (Stuart and Thurlow 2000, 113; Renzaglia, Hutchins, and Lee 1997). Teachers do what they do because of their perspectives on instruction, on children, on their roles as educators, and on themselves. To that end, an instructor's emotional health has a direct and significant impact on student learning. Unquestionably, the healthier a teacher is the greater his or her likelihood of connecting with students. And the stronger that connection, the more learning will likely occur. Because this is undeniably so, educators must understand that recognizing ineffective teaching practices is only part of the remedy for poor instruction. It is equally important for teachers to identify the mind-sets prompting the use of these deleterious practices in the first place.

LINKING THOUGHTS AND BEHAVIORS

As successful people do in any profession, highly effective teachers monitor their self-talk in order to establish and maintain healthy thought patterns. In contrast, coping poorly with life's inevitable problems, many less-successful people drift from counterproductive thought, to unhappy

emotion, to negative behavior, without recognizing their interconnected-
ness and without realizing the possibility of personal choice and control
among any of them. Clearly, we are the cumulative total of our perceptions. And since it is not possible to change what isn't acknowledged, the
first and arguably most important step in becoming a master teacher is to
understand how disempowering and self-destructive thinking leads to
problems in classrooms, in school, and in life.

At the least, it is important to recognize that in daily affairs, events
rarely cause negative emotions such as anger, insecurity, or anxiety.
What if those reactions resulted from our interpretations of those events?
What if those interpretations were merely inaccurate assumptions based
on distorted views of the relationship between ourselves and the world
that we were taught to believe as small children? And if feelings were
really reactions to thoughts and perceptions, and if by changing our
thoughts we could also change how we feel, what would such control do
for the quality of our lives?

Undeniably, people disturb themselves through faulty thinking. An
incident takes place, the event is interpreted, and a person thinks, feels,
acts, and creates his or her own reality in accord with that interpretation.
For example, a teacher's conference with a parent ends in a shouting
match fueled by unjustified accusations and threats to take the issue to
the administration. Feeling guilty about losing control during the meeting, angry for being scapegoated by an "unappreciative" parent, and
anxious about a possible meeting with the superintendent, the teacher
becomes severely depressed. However, conventional wisdom notwithstanding, the confrontation with an irate parent did not cause the depression. It resulted from the confrontation being viewed through an array of
irrational beliefs.

With all due credit to Albert Ellis and his Rational Emotive Behavior
Therapy, the commonly held unreasonable beliefs that led to the teacher's despondency may have included:

1. "I Must Be Liked by Everyone."
2. "People Must Always Treat Me Fairly."
3. "I Must Always Perform Perfectly."
4. "It Is Catastrophic When Things Are Not the Way I Want Them to
   Be."

It is less important which illogical belief led to the teacher's melancho-
lia than understanding that whichever one was primarily its cause, it
played an essential role in stimulating the despair. The activating experience leading to the emotional consequence of depression was clearly the
confrontation with the parent. But for that feeling to have been elicited,
the event was colored by one or more of the aforementioned erroneous
beliefs. Clearly, by challenging and eliminating those beliefs, a teacher's

emotional results would likely be eliminated or at least diminished as well.

While not easy to do, questioning one's internal propaganda leading to habitually negative reactions is both a curse and a blessing. Such challenges are a curse because once initiated, the emotional consequences of an unpleasant event often continue because questioning a thought's legitimacy does not immediately guarantee emotionally negating it. Yet questioning long-held perceptions is also a blessing because only one thing, if changed, can make a lasting difference in the quality of jobs done and lives lived. And that is what people irrationally tell themselves.

But dysfunctional thinking is not limited to a few very specific illogical beliefs. Several more general thinking distortions reinforce such beliefs and amplify their damage. Both in school and out they include:

Awfulizing

Just as prom night blemishes are continually focused on by student lotharios, the improbable consequences of a minor problem are obsessively revisited and exaggerated as a near certain disaster by some of their teachers. Thus, an isolated discipline problem irrationally portends losing control of an entire class, a student forgetting his pencil is cause for his public humiliation, and lower-than-usual standardized test scores unreasonably lead to an "all but certain" denial of tenure. In stating, "The crisis of yesterday is the joke of tomorrow," H. G. Wells surely understood that such catastrophes rarely, if ever, occur. And what the master of science fiction knew some hundred years ago is apparently still not grasped by classroom masters of personal melodrama today.

All-or-Nothing Thinking

Some teachers see specific events as absolutely good or bad or right or wrong without allowing for shades of gray. As a result, a high failure rate for a single class in a single marking period is viewed as a total failure, a disrespectful comment by an otherwise well-behaved student in September will influence an attitude grade throughout the term, and a parent wanting to remove their child from one's class will serve as personal proof of ineffective instruction despite far wider evidence to the contrary.

Overgeneralization

At times, specific failures are extended into unrelated and negative personal characteristics. Doing so, a teacher incorrectly computing a report card average views himself as incompetent; in making a thoughtless comment at a faculty meeting, a female instructor labels herself as chronically stupid; or in belittling a disruptive student, an otherwise ethical educator defines himself as a bad person.

Personalization

Teachers will sometimes negatively apply external events to themselves even when there is no objective basis for making that connection. Thus, when an administrator reminds faculty to be punctual for class, self-conscious instructors may believe the comment was personally directed even without evidence that was indeed the case. Or a principal's constructive appeal for teachers to remain open to new instructional methods may be heard as personal attacks on instructional skill and on an unwillingness to improve. Even reading this book, some instructors may indignantly view its entire text in much the same negatively self-directed manner. Yet reflexively personalizing reminders, appeals, or words in a book is far more likely the result of latent guilt or a persecution mind-set than of poorly camouflaged and individually targeted criticisms of unethical behavior or pedagogical incompetence.

Delusions of Grandeur

Amid large numbers of students, administrators, and colleagues, teaching is ironically an isolating job. Making small talk in faculty rooms, the cafeteria, or even assigned to adjacent rooms, teachers often work in close proximity to one another for many years and never really know their level of skill relative to other instructors. Certainly, through word of mouth or overheard student conversations, reputations both good and bad on both extremes of the quality spectrum are often widespread and may be legitimately earned. However, teachers of more middling ability or those not yet labeled as excellent or incompetent labor in relative isolation from their peers as unknown quantities.

Largely unaware of fellow faculty members, mediocre or worse teachers often exaggerate personal efforts and effectiveness in comparison to co-workers. With no real understanding of the daily struggles, exertions, skills, or successes of their colleagues, such delusional instructors embellish their own burdens, industry, and abilities and in doing so inoculate themselves against any possibility of improvement. For already "working so much harder than anyone else" and being so "near to perfection," there is no reason to fix what is perceptually unbroken. Yet in maintaining the status quo, such "nearly perfect" teachers virtually guarantee their students will continue receiving an education little more than perfectly second rate.

To make matters worse, an exaggerated sense of self leads teachers infected with delusions of grandeur to an inflexible unwillingness to relinquish autonomy in support of a schoolwide curriculum or well-documented restructuring efforts. "Going rogue" becomes a badge of honor in protecting one's "academic freedom" in the assignment of instructional tasks and in assessments without "out-of-touch and change-addicted" administrative interference.

Rather than joining with "lesser" colleagues in offering a unified program of what students are expected to do, and the level of quality they are expected to do it at, learners are offered a fragmented "every teacher for themselves" education, where able students get short-changed and those struggling continue to do so. And even when school improvement teams, after months or even years of research, analysis, deliberation, and consensus-building, offer a reform initiative, the grandiose response from Clark Kent more than Superman instructors is that it won't work and it's foolish to even try.

Selective Perception

In seeking the safety and security of a predictable world, most people also seek to avoid change. Whereas people often insist they embrace new experiences, novel ways of doing things, and change in general, what they really mean is they want change for everyone but themselves. Staying comfortably defended in the past, the thinking distortion often reinforcing such inaction is selective perception.

Also known as the fallacy of positive instances, selective perception is the tendency to not accept any information contradicting one's point of view. In "cherry-picking" evidence and ignoring or rationalizing whatever contradicts that perception, a larger but false reality is constructed and any initial judgment of people, events, or ourselves is maintained. Moreover, in seeing only what one wants to see, growth is inhibited as originally held points of view become believable, defensible, and virtually unchangeable.

But selective perception is more than simply "stacking the cards" by choosing evidence supporting a deeply held perception. It also involves a "confirmation bias" of actively seeking, exaggerating, and accentuating any experiences or facts corroborating well-defended convictions (Wason 1960). This cognitive distortion combined with "motivated reasoning" of more forcefully challenging information not fitting one's perceptions than questioning any information supporting one's assumptions (Kunda 1990) almost guarantees the continuation of a belief system, whatever its absurdity or harm.

Few people haven't heard of the supposed connection between the assassinations of Abraham Lincoln and John F. Kennedy. Without chronicling the numerous similarities between those two events, their coincidental parallelisms are often portrayed as evidence in linking them in an unexplainable or even mystical way. Yet often unrealized is that almost anything can be proved by selectively perceiving certain evidence to the exclusion of obvious contradictions.

True, there *are* many similarities between the murders of these two presidents. However, there are infinitely more differences than likenesses in the crimes. Yet by selectively perceiving evidence of two events separated by one hundred years and innumerable contrasts, the case is made "proving" an interesting set of coincidences is far more than that.

Similarly, in focusing on only certain trees, some teachers often fail to see the forest as a whole. In a day of almost infinite stimuli, a teacher feeling victimized will "prove" that assertion by focusing on a principal's comments to raise test scores and will not even hear positive comments on progress already made. Or a teacher feeling unappreciated will dwell on a student not saying thank you after extra help and will ignore another student's "aha smile" of recognition and satisfaction after successfully writing a research paper for the very first time. Ironically for educators, such "thoughtless habit[s] of believing that one's unexamined, superficial, or parochial opinions and feelings *are* the truth" is as much as anything else the sign of a poor education (Wiggins 1989, 57).

In looking at only certain pieces of evidence supporting a perception and ignoring the wider and often conflicting reality, some teachers grossly devalue or rationalize positive comments or events. Others, in seeing the proverbial glass as half empty, greatly exaggerate the impact of negative occurrences as victimization "proof" of their "never catch a break" worldview. To be sure, even relatively unaware instructors have seen these very behaviors in their own students chronically playing "persecution cards" and in reflexively viewing certain teachers negatively based on comments from former pupils rather than on any personal and immediate evidence supporting such evaluation.

It is not surprising that selectively perceiving reality is so common an impediment to clear thinking. What *is* surprising is that *teachers* often lack awareness of its existence or that they are personally doing so. For surely as educated people, they have written innumerable letters, emails, memos, and research papers. And just as surely, they must have experienced missing innumerable writing errors even after several proofreadings.

How could that even be possible if they were not selectively perceiving their own text to see whatever they wanted to see? And if this has routinely occurred in reviewing a finite number of words they themselves had written, isn't it just as likely to have routinely happened in reviewing events, people, or instructional programs composed of an infinite number of variables of which they were infinitely unaware?

For nearly two thousand years after Aristotle first insisted that the heavier an object, the faster it would fall, the most educated people in the world believed this as so. Even in 1589 after Galileo was said to have dropped two balls of differing weights from the Tower of Pisa, professors

standing at the structure's bottom selectively perceived what they expected to see in denying the objects landed at the same time. And today,
over four hundred years later, some of the most learned people in the
world *still* disavow reality in continuing to see what they want and expect to see, and as others did in the past, not even knowing they are
doing so.

THE POWER OF CHOICE

Just as teachers need to be mindful of cognitive thinking distortions, they
need to be equally mindful of emotional ones. That is, just as people can
become addicted to heroin or cocaine, they can become similarly addicted to the internal chemicals of anger, jealousy, persecution, or guilt.
But the next "fix" is not dependent on any dealer. It is dependent on
those so enslaved satisfying their self-perpetuated addictions by continually perceiving or even creating experiences generating the internal
"drugs" producing those emotions. Chemical withdrawal may be no less
difficult for drugs produced by one's bodily "pharmacy" than it is for
those purchased on the street. Such physical needs combined with an
emotional need to maintain a predictable world results in rigid and negative thought patterns perpetually creating and envisioning the reality one
thinks is true and that is often believed to be deserved.

As for all people, teachers are born with infinite possibilities of how to
think, how to react to events, and how to feel in response to those events.
Yet over time in seeking a consistent world, they often come to believe
that there is only one way to think, feel, and to respond. What was once a
birthright of limitless behavioral choice becomes an incremental and intellectual straitjacket impeding the ability to view new situations with an
open mind.

As a result, it is not uncommon for teachers to stridently insist that
they *had* to act, feel, instruct, or discipline in a certain way. But if this
were so, then *all* teachers would act similarly in response to a particular
stimulus. However, since this is clearly not so, one's unique perceptions
actually dictate one's unique responses, emotional and otherwise. The
perceived world is not "out there" immutably independent of one's dis-
tinctive consciousness in interpreting that reality. As perceptions are indeed in the eye of the beholder, master teachers fearlessly accepting "I
was wrong" insights well understand that at least initially, "seeing" is
not always believing.

If the same wave hits two children playing at the seashore and one
starts crying and the other begins laughing, how could this be if there
wasn't a choice in response? A football team winning ten games after
winning only one game the previous season results in fan celebrations
and talk of future Super Bowls. Yet the same stimulus, a ten-and-six

record for a perennial powerhouse team, results in depression and finger-pointing criticism from fans. How could this be if there wasn't a choice in how to respond? A sixty-degree day in January results in Floridians donning thick sweaters. Yet the same stimulus, the temperature, results in Vermonters seeing evidence of global warming and marveling about a wintertime heat wave. How could this be unless how one sees the world prompts one's responses to it?

After teacher observations, an administrator suggests alternative instructional approaches. One educator openly accepts recommendations as constructive criticism, while another defiantly refuses, claiming a destructive attack on pedagogical excellence. Again, an identical stimulus offered to two teachers of equal seniority and similar ability led to *completely* different responses. How could this be if in an absolute sense there wasn't a choice in reply?

Yet even if believing how something is viewed depends primarily on past history and present context, in accepting control over one's thoughts, doesn't one also control how a situation is viewed *whatever its context*? And if there still is doubt about the power and possibility of perceptual choice, how then can a situation be perceived *by the same person* one way today and far differently tomorrow? After all, who hasn't experienced a change in mind-set upon personal reflection, advice from a friend, or even a good night's sleep?

Indeed, we *are* our own worst enemy. Yet our power to inflict self-imposed pain can also be our salvation. For as John Milton said, the same mind that "can make a hell of heaven" can also make "a heaven of hell." In our daily lives, paradise can be perceptually gained in much the same way as it can be lost. To that end, if we accept that we are primarily responsible for our misery through our self-defeating perceptions, we can also accept that we are just as responsible for our joy by learning to change how we view the world and each other.

No one can say something producing hurt, rage, insecurity, or doubt in someone unless the person experiencing those emotions had similarly criticized themselves. Thus, in stimulating those emotions, verbal "assaults" remind us that more work needs to be done in changing what we don't like about ourselves or to be more accepting of whom we are. In that, the person blamed for our unpleasant emotions is more teacher than attacker. And this "inner leadership" understanding is certainly no less important for educators than it is for anyone else.

Practice Seven

Monitoring Actions

Before you can be an effective teacher, you have to be an effective person. —
Unknown

Dysfunctional and largely out-of-awareness thought patterns are not
alone in undermining quality instruction. Unexamined actions protecting
self-esteem by shielding teachers from unpleasant realities also hinder
optimal pedagogy. These behaviors allow ineffective educators to de-
ceive themselves and at least temporarily protect positive self-images.
Yet if successful in blocking troubling thoughts and emotions, the following "robbing Peter to pay Paul" actions maintain blind spots in behavior
and lessen the urgency to overcome problems causing the need for self-
deception in the first place.

Identification as a master teacher has as much to do with engaging in
certain habits of mind and actions as it does with not engaging in others.
This is not to say that there aren't extremely rare instances of unintention-
al thoughtlessness or even of less-than-ideal preparation from elite educators. The best the teaching profession has to offer are no less human
than highly effective people in any occupation. However, in daily exhibiting a personal standard of excellence, the likelihood of elite educators
repeatedly exhibiting the following behaviors is only slightly greater than
being struck by lightning twice on the same day.

REACTION FORMATION

A person disturbed by their feelings or actions will often replace them for
their exaggerated opposites. In so camouflaging troubling realities by
behaving in a manner counter to one's inclinations, anxiety is reduced
and self-esteem is temporarily maintained. For example, rather than seriously considering a change in career, a teacher no longer liking his job
may continually express exaggerated joy in instruction. Or fearing a loss
of face, a teacher depressed over poor test results or discipline problems
will exhibit a confident demeanor in defiantly refusing to accept help. In
either case, what is threatening to self-esteem is masked by an excessive

demonstration of its opposite. But there is a cost to this charade. And by attending classes taught by frustrated, unhappy, or ineffective instructors, innocent students end up footing the bill.

PROJECTION

Objectionable motives, desires, or shortcomings a person is unwilling to recognize in themselves are sometimes attributed to others. In doing so, an educator justifies inappropriate actions, diverts attention away from personal failings, and attacks innocent targets without guilt. As what we like least about ourselves is often projected onto others, the best defense is indeed a good offense. Accordingly, a teacher feeling guilty about inadequate preparation will unfairly claim his students were unprepared. Perpetually angry educators claiming that "administrators don't listen" are often the very instructors refusing to hear what others are saying. Or a teacher continually bullying colleagues will insist the principal persecutes her staff.

RATIONALIZATION

People often excuse embarrassing or questionable behavior by justifying it to make it appear acceptable. Seemingly plausible, such excuses defend one's self-esteem by intellectualizing reasons for acting in a way that are in truth indefensible. A teacher defiantly insisting a "mental health day" was taken because *everyone* else does it"; claiming that grades were not submitted on time because "I was giving students extra help"; or waiting until the last minute to review a budget because "I work best under pressure" is attributing behavior to motives having little or nothing to do with those behaviors.

Moreover, rationalization is an all-purpose defense against honestly confronting the reasons for poor student results. In an endless litany of excuses, the class is too large, the students are unmotivated, the administration is unsupportive, parents don't care, or students in a neighboring district also failed lead the list of explanations for what is often inadequate instruction.

It doesn't matter that the class average for a test was 45 percent. It doesn't matter that half the students routinely fail one's courses. And it doesn't matter that students having a long track record of ultrahigh performance and respectful behavior for every other teacher barely pass and are discipline problems in another teacher's classroom. There is always a fill-in-the-blank justification for the unjustifiable.

Master teachers realize that it is their professional responsibility to avoid blaming parents, television, societal permissiveness, other educators, the Internet, or anything else for student shortcomings. Although these "usual suspects" *may* indeed negatively impact education, perpetual hand-wringing doesn't change anything. The only question that matters is not whether educators can change the world but whether they change the only world that matters. And each day, that is the world faced by children walking through the schoolhouse doors.

COLLECTING PSYCHOLOGICAL "TRADING STAMPS"

Similar to the long ago practice of collecting "trading stamps" when making purchases and then redeeming them for merchandise, these are the bad feelings people collect that are later used to justify some negative behavior such as arguments or physical confrontations. Instructors experiencing problems with disruptive or inattentive students often internalize unpleasant feelings that cumulatively color their reactions to future and unrelated student exchanges. Additionally, when staff development is offered, a certain percentage of a faculty will be sure to collect persecution stamps in claiming the presentation was in actuality an administrative criticism of instructor effort and effectiveness.

When emotional stamp books are filled with real, imagined, and exaggerated affronts, ineffective educators self-righteously cash them in by expressing criticism or anger toward anyone unlucky enough to be in the way. Redemption time phrases such as "I've taken all I can take" or "that's the last straw" make clear what is about to happen. And for an unsuspecting student or colleague "guilty" of being in the wrong place at the wrong time, the teacher's response will neither be appropriate, understood, nor deserved.

In closely monitoring their own behavior, master teachers rarely collect stamps, and even if they do, they vent their negative emotions in constructive ways through exercising or finishing up chores rather than displacing their anger or frustration onto innocent students or colleagues. Yet even when an unpleasant classroom event does occur, elite educators, in refusing to collect negative feelings, begin each lesson anew devoid of emotional stamps internalized from the preceding day.

CONTRIBUTING TO PROBLEMS, NOT SOLUTIONS

As a signature behavior of master teachers is a tireless devotion to improving the working and learning environment of the school, an equally representative behavior of less-effective colleagues too often contributes to its detriment. Complaining of low morale, going-through-the motions instructors engage in gossip, innuendo, and character assassination in adding far more to a negative climate than those they self-righteously attack. Ever the "victims," even so-called good schools at times harbor a toxic subculture of educators reflexively eager to undermine administrative initiatives or to "poison the well" by spreading rumors and misinformation to anyone willing to listen.

"Too busy" to provide extra help to students or to join school improvement committees, ineffective teachers have no trouble finding time to while away hours in the faculty room reading the paper, whining about their contract, or criticizing colleagues supporting reform. And even when invited to participate in contributing to school improvement solutions, those complaining the loudest will voice "I have too much to do" rationalized inaction and attack a newly minted proposal as too expensive, too impractical, too time-consuming, or too ineffective.

OFFERING INADEQUATE STUDENT FEEDBACK

Lacking professionalism and good instructional practice, ineffective teachers routinely offer students inadequate feedback on their work. Claiming they are too busy, responses to student efforts often consist of letter or number grades and little else. Accompanied by hastily scribbled and nearly illegible comments of "Good work" at best or "I'm disappointed in this" at worst, little is communicated with enough specificity to motivate either effort or success. Yet in some classrooms, such ambiguous comments, even if promptly offered, may be all that can be expected. The best coaches quickly and effectively inform their players what they must do to improve. Master teachers are no different.

Exaggerating personal efforts and complaining that their hard work often goes unnoticed, ineffective instructors discount the efforts of students by not returning their work for weeks or even longer. It matters little that specific and prompt feedback enhances learner performance and motivation (Larson 1984). It matters little that without prompt feedback, it is difficult for students to evaluate how they are doing. And for ineffective teachers, it matters little that student achievement routinely takes a back seat to personal convenience.

Failure to return student work within a reasonable amount of time tacitly sends the message to pupils that their efforts are unimportant and that their learning does not matter. And from the perspective of ineffective and unprofessional educators, this assessment is much closer to the truth than they would ever care to admit.

Yet for student writing, many teachers don't provide students with *any* feedback. This is so because other than short-answer questions on tests, in too many classrooms students rarely do any writing at all. In claiming they are too busy to assign such work, or that "writing is the job of English teachers," students receive too few opportunities to improve this essential skill. As a result, American public schools routinely graduate many students virtually incapable of writing coherent paragraphs or even grammatically correct sentences.

That many students receiving high school diplomas approach functional illiteracy is arguably one of the biggest failures of American education. This is so because along with reading there is no more important academic skill than writing. As a complex task, writing requires planning, reviewing, editing, and the perseverance to improve a product over time—all skills important for life success whatever the endeavor.

Moreover, because many good readers are poor writers yet it is virtually impossible to find good writers who read poorly, some argue that writing rivals reading in intellectual and academic importance. But whether writing is as important as reading remains an open question, there is little doubt that few learning opportunities are better at enhancing higher-order thinking (Marzano 1993). And in denying students the opportunity to improve this skill, teachers are also denying them an opportunity to improve an ability unquestionably important for success in life.

POINTING FINGERS

There are few behaviors indicating a greater lack of professionalism than scapegoating virtually everyone for virtually everything. If whatever can go wrong will go wrong, rest assured that highly ineffective teachers will point fingers at parents, administrators, students, and their colleagues rather than looking far closer to home for the source of their failures. Incredibly, nowhere is a lack of responsibility heard more often than faulting others for poor morale.

Think about it. In a job where teachers commonly implore students to accept responsibility, "do as I say not as I do" educators *cannot even accept responsibility for their own mood.* Blind to such nonsense and unaware that excepting perhaps an exile to Devil's Island, no one can make you emotionally feel anything without your consent, it is little wonder why inadequate instructors are mediocre at best. For if by their own admission they are powerless to master even their own disposition, how can they be expected to skillfully master the learning of their students?

JUSTIFYING INADEQUACY

A related behavior to "pointing fingers" at others for "poor morale," ineffective teachers often rationalize their pedagogical inadequacy. Seen objectively, justifications for poor instruction would be almost comical if they didn't have such a seriously negative impact on student learning. Whereas go-to-the-head-of-the-class teachers take responsibility for virtually everything, their weakest and most unprofessional colleagues choose excuses in defending the indefensible.

Poor student discipline? No problem. There is too little administrative support. A high rate of student failures? No problem. Kids spend too much time on the Internet. Unsatisfactory teaching evaluations? No problem. Cronyism is rampant, my class assignment is not to my liking, and the principal is out to get me. But there *is* a problem, and it is staring at the authors of such nonsense in the mirror each morning.

IGNORING DETAILS

While master teachers generate excellence with an almost compulsive need to "dot every *i* and cross every *t*," their far more mediocre colleagues routinely do neither. Insisting they were too "busy" or sheepishly claiming that they "forgot," they routinely rationalize their inattention to detail. Found on virtually every staff, these "busy" and "forgetful" teachers show their lack of respect for others in failing to respond to voicemails and emails, in ignoring administrative memos, in routinely "forgetting about" or arriving late for meetings, or in handing back student exams and projects with all the speed of a lethargic snail.

Protected by tenure, it is hardly surprising that such passively aggressive actions are also signature behaviors of the most ineffective instructors. Equally not surprising, these are the same "educators" demanding inflexible obedience from their students and who fail to notice that their very best colleagues have no trouble attending to those very details they find so impossible to heed.

Prone to melodrama, hyperbole, and "all about me" focus, underperforming educators spend as much time complaining as in planning lessons. Is it any wonder why these "victimized" instructors have low morale? After all, isn't it so that their classes are larger, their students more difficult, and their schedules more unfair than for their more favored coworkers? And despite all these catastrophes, isn't it self-righteously so that they work harder, overcome more obstacles, and are better teachers than their colleagues?

By sitting in the faculty room doing crossword puzzles, exchanging gossip, or endlessly retelling war stories, unprofessional teachers are not above exaggerating how busy they are. It is this exaggeration that is the all-purpose excuse for their chronic inattention to detail. After all, with "so much to do," isn't it understandable why meetings are missed, lateness is common, and grades are unsubmitted? Of course, when none of these deficiencies is a problem for other faculty members, it is because their "schedules are easier" or that "they don't do as much helping kids."

This "I am busier or working harder than you" holier-than-thou mind-set as an all-purpose rationalization for ignoring details is also divisively extended to other schools or departments *within the same district*. As children argue over whether vanilla is better than chocolate or sports fans endlessly argue whether their team is superior to another, equally immature educators debate whether the elementary faculty works harder than teachers in the high school or whether "disrespected" middle school teachers "have it tougher" than anyone else. But even if there is a shred of truth in any such nonsense, and if laboring under such "Draconian" conditions is indeed well less than ideal, who then are the fools for choosing a more stressful, less respected, and more difficult job for the same salary?

While underperforming educators wallow in self-aggrandizing puffery and compensate for failures playing "mine is worse than yours" games, master educators, in almost obsessively planning for class, really are too busy for such egocentric, counterproductive, self-indulgent, and petty nonsense.

SEEING COLLEAGUE RECOGNITION AS A ZERO-SUM GAME

With more than a little truth, the public is far too quick to criticize even quality teachers and not quick enough to recognize their countless acts of going well beyond the call of duty in helping kids. Yet while undeniably so, it is also undeniable that egocentric educators acting as children longing for ever more gifts on Christmas morning are no less guilty of such self-absorbed behavior themselves.

When a teacher is publicly recognized for excellence, it is difficult for some colleagues to express authentic joy for one of their own. Invariably, an "all about me" response rears its ugly head. That is, rather than viewing teacher recognition as well-deserved and perhaps the beginning of more widespread acknowledgements to come, envious instructors see only the twisted logic of a zero-sum game in which what another teacher gains is equal to what they have lost.

Seemingly toiling in anonymity, bitter about their own lack of recognition, and believing that validation is a finite resource, what such "scarcity mind-set" (Covey 1989) educators have been denied others may not enjoy. Denied their "rightful" but unacknowledged share of praise and bitter over another's applause, contributions of those celebrated are often responded to with devaluation. Barely audible "what about me?" comments, such as "Sure, she created an after-school help program; with no kids of her own and her husband leaving, she's got time to burn" or "Sure, his students had great test scores; he's got small classes, the best kids in the school, and all he does is teach to the test" are heard well enough.

Unknown to master teachers, such unprofessional, resentful, and toxic reactions impact far more than petty office politics. When widespread, such egocentric behaviors undermining teacher collegiality and cooperation negatively affect the working and learning environment of the entire school. For in stifling the cross-pollination of instructional innovation among faculty members, such self-centeredness directly impacts students.

In keeping with their overriding theme of putting kids first, master teachers spare no efforts in helping students, and indirectly that imperative often involves helping colleagues. However, while master educators eagerly share their work with co-workers, their more egocentric zero-sum associates fearing others will gain recognition from ideas not of their own creation guard their "prized" assessments and project descriptions as if they were Fort Knox gold. Thus, in obsessively hoarding fruits of their intellectual labors, "me first" educators may well be denying colleagues "undeserved" credit, but in failing to share the instructional benefits their ideas might have otherwise achieved, such pettiness invariably puts students last.

In sharing and even cataloging lesson plans, rubrics, project ideas, and assessments, master teachers do more than offer support for students and co-workers today. In making such instructional resources available, they are also offering help to teachers and children in the future. Preparing for the worse yet hoping for the best, master teachers realize that should they leave the classroom due to sickness or retirement, replacement instructors armed with their teaching materials will have much-needed help in maintaining high standards.

However, not seeing the long-term value of archiving instructional materials, self-centered instructors often resist doing so. Whether such resistance is due to fears their "prized" materials may expose their mediocrity or is more simply an "I'm not sharing" immaturity is unknown. Yet there is little doubt that should *their* child ever have a replacement teacher who flounders, they would be among the first to complain that student learning has been compromised due to a lack of curricular guidance from the administration or from the prior instructor.

CONFORMING TO GROUP PRESSURE

Whereas even the most inadequate teachers assert to going the extra mile for students, in rationalizing opposition to virtually any instructional reform they expose the hypocrisy of that claim. Even when they privately agree that an initiative would be "good for kids," if the winds of dissent are blowing in another direction their fearful silence registers as tacit agreement.

Indeed, the ability of group pressure to foster conformity is so powerful that even when a teacher approaches an administrator with a problem and a mutually acceptable solution is reached, after-the-fact collegial opposition often results in revisionist history *even from the instructor initially asking for help*. It is not that a better solution is later offered after input from other teachers. It is that the initial problem is minimized, claimed never to have existed, that the solution violated the teacher's contract, or that the "administrator's solution" was a reprehensible attempt to extract additional effort from an innocently unsuspecting faculty member.

Embracing this last response to a teacher's willingness to put kids first, less-inclined instructors too often believe their well-meaning colleagues need protection from slippery-slope administrative exploitation. To that end, faculty consent to volunteer for extra duty, begin an after-school program without pay, or even to regularly stay late to give kids extra help may provoke group pressure to cease and desist. Fearful of looking bad in comparison and insisting that such "beyond the call of duty" efforts *must* have resulted from administrative coercion, "us versus them" instructors pressure their "going the extra mile" colleagues to travel less far.

In the end, group pressure often carries the day, and administrator-faculty cooperation in arriving at reasonable and agreed-upon solutions to what are often *teacher-initiated* concerns results in a situation where nothing is solved, faculty-administrator trust is compromised, and "teachers who can and will" are "convinced" to become "teachers who could and won't."

Psychologists recognize the need for approval as so great and feelings of insecurity as so widespread that groups pressure conformity to even obviously incorrect judgments. But Alice in Wonderland and the Easter Bunny don't exist, whatever the level of conviction expressed or whatever the verdict of a seemingly unanimous majority expressing otherwise. Yet for many, being liked and accepted by "going along with the crowd" is apparently more important than being right. If as Robert Kennedy said, 20 percent of people will oppose anything, almost twice that number will do nothing to oppose seemingly unanimous group perceptions whatever their harm or absurdity.

Known as groupthink, the tacit agreement of group members to blindly conform in not questioning or even acknowledging a troubling truth inevitably results in defective decision making. Such is the fruit of self-censorship. And this is as true for historical mishaps and disasters as the Watergate scandal, the Vietnam War, or the space shuttle *Challenger* tragedy as it is for flawed decisions affecting the education of children by a group of teachers, board members, or administrators.

No matter how incongruent with objective reality, only the most confident of people will take a principled stand, resist group judgments, publicly state the "emperor has no clothes," and as devil's advocate refuse to ride obstructionist bandwagons stuck in neutral. Yet in formal meetings and impromptu gatherings sometimes all it takes is one brave person to stem the tide. All it takes is one bold person inspiring others to resist group pressure to stand pat in the face of educational failure. All it takes is one courageous person who was wondering why somebody wasn't saying something to realize *that they could be that somebody*. And in schools, those valiant few willing to be a majority of one, those willing to paraphrase Abraham Maslow in asking "If not me, who?" and "If not now, when?" are almost always the most highly effective teachers.

"RESCUING" INCOMPETENTS

Quick to adopt an "us versus them" mind-set, short-sighted teachers reflexively support ineffective colleagues when "attacked" by administrators, making Torquemada look like Mr. Rogers. Hearing only the "victim's" perspective; lacking knowledge of events leading to his or her "persecution"; and voicing the fallacy that the art of teaching is difficult, if not impossible, to objectively evaluate; well-meaning but uninformed instructors too often support the most incompetent of their number.

It's not that overly aggressive administrators can't be unfair in their approach or wrong in their evaluations. Of course they can. Yet, what superficially looks like an error in judgment may be exactly the right decision, or the best "lesser of two evils" move under the circumstances. Many so-called bad administrative decisions in personnel or program might look far more justifiable if teachers knew more about the situation or had a greater schoolwide perspective. However, often armed with little or no objective information, some instructors rush to judgment, claiming teacher harassment or worse, whenever a fellow faculty member is "written up," is refused tenure, is supposedly denied academic freedom, or is threatened with termination. They will often do so *even if they are well aware* of the "victim's" inadequacies.

Yet in attempting to rescue underperforming colleagues, teachers are little different than enabling parents rationalizing misbehaviors of their child as untrue, exaggerated, or caused by the teacher, the principal, or other children. And as every educator knows, in shifting the focus of misbehavior from its source to an innocent target, the behavior is all but guaranteed to continue.

Accordingly, "rescuing" dead-wood educators is a pact with the devil. Although it may save them in the short run, by cumulatively undermining the instructional quality of the entire school, it will eventually harm their protectors and more importantly, the children they instruct.

JUMPING TO CONCLUSIONS

Realizing how easy it is to be totally wrong about the simplest of things, master teachers rarely make impulsive judgments, and even when they do, they are open to new data that may completely change their initial conclusions. Indeed, how can there be great certainty about very much when a person often bases an analysis on limited information, filtered through one's unconscious biases of which one is infinitely unaware?

How can there be certainty why a student behaved inappropriately or why an administrator arrived at a decision when one has been completely wrong about the outcome of a sporting event, or even the date of the next faculty meeting? How can a colleague's motivation for embracing school reform be reflexively disparaged when at times one has been unaware of words said or even how a cut or a bruise was suffered? Or how can one be sure that a new program, policy, textbook series, or child will fail years hence when one has been totally wrong about the placement of car keys one day or student placements the next? After all, didn't equally certain teachers describe the inventor of the light bulb as "too stupid to learn anything" and the author of $E = mc^2$ as so lazy and insubordinate that he would "never amount to anything?"

Realizing this, master teachers practice critical thinking in continually asking, "What assumptions have I made?" or "Have I fairly considered other points of view?" or "Have I too quickly passed judgment without sufficient evidence to do so?" All too happy to inhabit an Einsteinian world where realities are relative, constants are rare, and absolute truth is often fool's gold, elite educators are quick to ponder and slow to certainty.

While highly effective teachers recognize and admit to errors in judgment, their less-effective colleagues practice critical thinking by thinking critically about everyone but themselves. Despite all evidence to the contrary, in smugly maintaining their initial evaluations and in not realizing that they don't even know what they don't know, they stifle their own growth and indirectly do at least as much to limit the students they claim to further.

In monitoring thoughts and actions, it is not surprising that such traits as personal responsibility, self-motivation, critical thinking, impulse control, and social competence, all essential for successful students, are no less important for successful teachers. Because these dispositions cumulatively referred to as "emotional intelligence" have even been ultimately learned by children growing up under the worst of circumstances (O'Neil 1996), is there any doubt that in understanding their value, instructors can and should internalize them at least as well?

Practice Eight

Maintaining Discipline

Discipline is the bridge between goals and accomplishments. —Jim Rohn

In "getting it done," the best teachers are able to almost magically supervise and discipline even the most disruptive students. Often categorized under the heading of "classroom management," the importance of this ability is beyond doubt. Indeed, education majors report they are very concerned with "discipline" (Parkay and Stanford 2004), maintaining control is perceived as the foremost problem of new teachers (Veenman 1984), and more than anything else, in chaotic classrooms learning is undeniably compromised. To that end, research indicates that teacher actions involving classroom management have "twice as much impact on student achievement as assessment policies" (Beaty-O'Ferrall, Green, and Hanna 2010; Marzano 2003; Marzano and Marzano 2003).

If "misbehavior is to a classroom what pain is to a body . . . a useful status report that something isn't working" (Sylwester 2000, 23), highly effective teachers have a seemingly innate ability to diagnose and remedy the problem before the infection of misconduct spreads. Yet their ability to do so has nothing to do with sorcery, sixth sense, or a degree in medicine. Folk wisdom to the contrary, maintaining a smoothly running classroom relatively free of disruptive behavior has nothing to do with not smiling before Christmas, turning the lights on and off, or isolating troublemakers from the rest of the class. It has to do with emulating the habits of practice and mind of master teachers.

"WITHITNESS"

While the strongest instructors assert control through curricular choice, instructional delivery, high standards, clearly articulated rules and procedures, and by demonstrating personal interest in their students, the best teachers also preemptively prevent potential problems from escalating into actual ones. This "eyes in the back of the head" keen awareness of, and immediate response to potentially disruptive behavior referred to as "withitness" is what "most consistently separates the excellent classroom

managers from the average or below-average classroom managers"
(Marzano, Marzano, and Pickering 2003, 5).

In order to defuse a situation that could undermine classroom control,
the best teachers continually monitor pupils for possible disruptions.
Never long behind a lectern or desk, such "with it" instructors continually walk around the classroom exercising proximity control. Doing so,
such teachers regularly scan the entire room, making eye contact with as
many students as possible, and are acutely aware of any behavior that
might become disruptive.

Realizing that student frustration is a precursor to student misbehavior, "with it" teachers recognize early markers of such stress and preemptively deescalate potential problems before they become actual ones.
Nonverbal behaviors including fidgeting, sighing, pencil tapping, paper
tearing, or a student putting his or her head down on the desk are often
the opening acts of a drama leading to a more disruptive and unpleasant
dénouement.

If a student exhibits such forms of passive aggression, and if eye contact alone doesn't end the behavior, the best teachers use proximity control by approaching the youngster in a calm and nonjudgmental manner.
Failing that, some effective teachers let offending students know, nonver-
bally if possible, that their actions are unacceptable (Marzano, Marzano,
and Pickering 2003). Actually, nonverbal disapproval in the form of a
relatively private face-saving "cut it out" facial expression is one of the
simplest and most commonly exhibited disciplinary procedures, but it
will only work if a teacher has earned the respect of his or her students.

Additionally, hypervigilant educators preempt potential problems by
mentally reviewing before class what might go wrong with certain pupils
and by creating a "battle plan" of how those problems will be addressed
if in fact they do arise. As with even minor car accidents, once a problem
is well underway, it already is too late to stop it without at least some
damage. But in this case, the harm is not to a bumper or fender but to
classroom climate and student self-esteem.

REMAINING CALM

However, whatever other strategies comprise such a plan, it never includes a teacher internalizing problems with a student on a personal
level. Once an educator loses emotional objectivity, views a discipline
issue as a personal affront, and becomes angry or hurt, they are on the
way to amplifying an unpleasant situation into something far worse. At
the least, when giving into exasperation or anger a teacher loses the respect of students just as surely as they lose the ability to thoughtfully
function. "Demanding respect is not as effective as earning it, and how
[a] teacher comports himself or herself has much to do with how he or

she is viewed and respected by students" (Beaty-O'Ferrall, Green, and Hanna 2010).

Disciplinary interactions with students oddly resemble a tennis match. The harder the teacher hits the "emotional ball," the harder the offending pupil is likely to return the serve. The most effective teachers in calmly and thoughtfully responding to misbehavior reduce the pace of the "disciplinary volley" and rarely allow the exchange to counterproductively escalate. Failing that, educators risk losing students' respect and invariably the "match" as well. For if the teacher continues to argue, uses sarcasm or threatens, and students recognize that things are not under control, they are apt to create more problems that incite further misbehavior (Collette and Chiappetta 1989; Walker, Colvin, and Ramsey 1995).

AVOIDING INTIMIDATION

While intimidation can diminish undesirable student behaviors in the short term, because of negative longer-term side effects, doing so often results in a "win-the-battle-and-lose-the-war" Pyrrhic victory. At the least, overly harsh reactions to student misconduct may encourage those very behaviors the teacher wants to extinguish. Just as bad food is better than no food at all, for students feeling powerless to gain positive attention, negative attention is better than no attention at all. Overly punitive teachers satisfy that hunger.

Moreover, in seeking a predictable world, normalcy demands that students treated harshly or abused at home will often seek more of the same at school in order to "confirm" their status as perennial victims. Thus, responding in an overly severe manner to the transgressions of such students, teachers are unwittingly giving those youngsters the detrimental constancy they counterproductively want and need.

Still another negative side effect to overly stern consequences for student misdeeds is that people and places associated with those unpleasant outcomes will through classical conditioning also become unpleasant. Thus, a student regularly scolded or embarrassed will continually reexperience the anxiety, the dread, and the feelings of inadequacy associated with those moments every day walking into school, entering classrooms, and when seeing the teacher administering such discipline. It is impossible to overstate the harmful impact on that child's ability to learn that any of these emotions will continue to have. As has so often been said, students may forget what a teacher says, but they will never forget how a teacher made them feel. Those feelings, both good and bad, directly affect academic performance.

Lastly, if overly harsh consequences for student transgressions become common practice, their power to lessen those behaviors, unless their severity continually escalates, diminishes over time. Like Muzak in an elevator or the constant hum of a fan, the sound of either soon becomes unheard. So, too, with discipline. Continually sending an overly aggressive disciplinary "message" to students has an extremely short shelf life. Unless the punishment ante is regularly and detrimentally increased, youngsters become desensitized, and teachers in countless faculty rooms will continue to wonder why students "don't listen."

Realizing the counterproductive results associated with aversive or overly punitive conditioning, master teachers project calm, confidence, and to the greatest extent possible, nonjudgmental demeanors. Misbehaving students are given a choice to comply with the teacher's request or to accept the consequences. The options for behavior are clearly and unemotionally explained, and penalties for misdeeds, unless there are highly unusual mitigating circumstances, are always implemented. More generally, fairness demands that classroom rules, procedures, expectations, and consequences for violations are announced on the first day of class, applied immediately if necessary, and are periodically reinforced throughout the term. It is essential that students know that teachers know that they know what is expected of them.

In an elite educator's classroom, there is no yelling, no intimidating threats, no endless "furthermores," and no "fuel on the fire" melodramatic confrontations. Students soon learn that anger has no place in the classroom and that agreed-upon outcomes, however unpleasant, are the logical results of *their* choices. There must be no doubt that in choosing behaviors, students are also choosing outcomes. Complying with respectfully stated teacher requests leads to positive results, and defiance results in less-than-positive ends. When there is certainty about consistently applied consequences, most students most of the time quickly learn to self-correct their counterproductive impulses and choose wisely.

In addition to projecting an air of calm in the classroom when disciplining students, master teachers avoid "parental" body language likely to stimulate student resistance. Examples of such negatively dominant and emotionally charged actions include:

1. scowling
2. index-finger pointing
3. foot tapping
4. head wagging
5. hands on hips
6. arms folded
7. rolling eyes
8. sighing

Great awareness of such provocative nonverbal communication is supplemented with an equally great awareness of word choice and verbal delivery. Again, staying calm is the key. If possible, when disciplining youngsters the pronoun *you* is avoided, as it can lead to defensive and/or rebellious results. Equally so, the following "parental" slogans are also likely to stimulate combative rather than reasoned responses from students:

1. "If I were you."
2. "How many times have I told you?"
3. "You do as I say."
4. "I'm going to put a stop to this once and for all."
5. "How dare you."
6. "Because I said so."
7. "Shut up!"
8. "That does it."
9. "If I've told you once I've told you a hundred times."

Flatly delivered control prompts of highly effective teachers include:

1. "These are your choices for behavior, and these are the outcomes of those choices."
2. "For me to teach this class, I need everyone in the class to be quiet."
3. "Were those actions helpful to anyone in this class?"
4. "I find it difficult to teach when students are getting out of their seats."
5. "I will be happy to discuss this issue once we are speaking calmly to each other."
6. "I realize that many students find this class demanding. However, by not handing in assignments, this course will be almost impossible to pass."

REFRAMING

Ironically, as the best educators shorten the physical distance to students through proximity control, they emotionally increase the distance from problem students through the process of "reframing." Rather than seeing problems with students as personal attacks, elite educators address disciplinary issues in an unemotional, businesslike, and matter-of-fact manner without becoming emotionally distraught and without personalizing the actions of difficult youngsters.

Such instructors well realize that while they may want to "win" a struggle with students, the disruptive pupil to save face often feels that they *must* win with teachers. Understanding this, the best instructors rarely forget that it may take one person acting foolishly to talk back but it takes two foolish people to escalate a thoughtless comment into a last-word competition. And since teacher behavior directly impacts the behavior of students, staying calm and in control leads to a classroom atmosphere reflecting those qualities.

Admittedly easier said than done, thoughtful teachers "reframe" disciplinary incidents by seeking explanations for student behavior that change the entire meaning and feeling tone of those events. Thus, rather than seeing a pupil outburst as a personal attack challenging their authority that "must" be responded to in kind, the most effective teachers habitually reframe and depersonalize the behavior as perhaps a desperate compensation for low self-esteem due to academic frustration or inadequacy. By changing the way things are looked at, the things looked at also change (Dyer 2009).

MONITORING IRRATIONAL BELIEFS

In addition to changing the "frame" of how student conduct is perceived, making-the-grade educators stay in control by understanding that unpleasant events with pupils do not directly cause a negative and counterproductive teacher response such as anger or sarcasm. That is, when an incident with a student occurs, many teachers on automatic pilot are "programmed" to think, feel, and act in accord with their interpretation of the event. However, in many instances, the perception of the incident is based on irrational and unchallenged beliefs. Once those beliefs are understood and changed, the negative emotional consequences linked to them change as well.

For example, a student asked to stop talking answers in a defensively rebellious "I'm being persecuted" way. Hearing a challenge to authority and not wanting to look weak, the instructor escalates a relatively minor misbehavior by reflexively belittling the student. Not wanting to publicly lose face, the student further escalates the situation by angrily claiming that other students were allowed to talk because "they are teacher's pets." Hearing an attack on his competence and fairness, the exchange intensifies yet again with a sarcastic teacher response and predictably a student disciplinary referral to the principal's office.

By examining the irrational beliefs precipitating the confrontation, it is easy to understand the reasons for the teacher's exaggerated and spontaneous response. Although a talented educator, as a perfectionist he believes he must always perform flawlessly, and when inevitably that doesn't happen, he doubts his own competence and in so doing turns a relatively small issue into a catastrophe.

As noted earlier, in expecting perfection the teacher was "guilty" of "all or nothing" thinking, and "making a mountain out of a molehill" is a textbook example of "awfulizing." In the first instance, one perceives events in black-and-white terms. That is, if results are imperfect they're looked upon as total failure. In the second instance, a relatively small problem, failure, or frustration is illogically exaggerated into an end-of-the-world disaster.

These thinking distortions combined with the ego-fueled irrational belief that in order to maintain authority over the class he *had* to respond to the student's impertinence in the strongest possible way led to the teacher's exaggerated and counterproductive actions. However, the reality is that his reply was the product of unthinking and unreasonable beliefs that he had no choice but to act as he did and that a strong teacher maintains authority by silencing disruptive students through coercion.

Obviously, the teacher had a myriad of ways to respond to the student, including to calmly inform the youngster that "the discussion" would be continued after class. Further, in realizing that with a history of success, his exaggerated responses were more compensatory reactions to unrealistic feelings of inferiority and an excessive need to demonstrate power than student conduct so egregious that brow-beating a pupil was the only possible response. Finally, the perception that strong teachers maintain authority through intimidation was the illogical belief that led to a heated classroom exchange and a damaged relationship with the youngster.

This shift in how things are perceived changes everything. For by changing thinking, one inescapably also changes how one feels and behaves. Thus, by separating pupil conduct from the pupil by reframing and by realizing that it is not events that cause emotional reactions but one's interpretation of events, destructive power struggles are avoided, the teacher models the essential skill of self-control, and the classroom's learning environment is safeguarded.

But effective classroom discipline involves more than a teacher remaining calm by reframing students' negative behaviors and questioning unfounded beliefs. It involves more than a teacher exhibiting a high level of self-awareness, self-confidence, and the ability to maintain self-control despite student provocations that could easily lead to confrontation and crisis. The signature of the most effective instructors is the regular use of strategies making discipline problems in the short-term less frequent *and* long-term growth and success in children more probable.

USING POSITIVE DESCRIPTORS

Beginning early in the term, one such growth strategy is the use of positive descriptors for students. By defining who and what a child is, attributions such as "You are smart" or "You are a good person" *when they are legitimately earned* act as self-fulfilling prophecies in making certain behaviors likely and others far less so. For in justifying those positive descriptors, students are intrinsically motivated to do the right thing not through fear but because they have come to believe *that is who they are.*

In seeking a safe and predictable world, children most often generate the reality they think is true and that they deserve. Pupils continually told, tacitly or otherwise, that they are lazy, stupid, or irresponsible will likely create experiences "proving" those descriptors. Conversely, students truthfully told they are intelligent, hardworking, and conscientious will find it difficult to act in a way contrary to characteristics defining their core personality. As plants grow toward light, children grow toward labels.

PRAISING STUDENTS

When positive attributions are supported by *authentically earned* praise, it is a potent combination furthering strong discipline and a productive learning environment. Yet as a dog whistle is blown but is unheard, positive student behaviors often happen but go unnoticed. However, in understanding it is far more important what a person sees than what is looked at, master teachers have an acutely sensitive eye for observing and responding to good behavior in their pupils. By linking such praise to salutary labels, a more constructive sense of self is reinforced, making misbehavior less likely and academic achievement more possible.

Instructor praise has been empirically linked with student on-task behavior (Apter, Arnold, and Stinson 2010), with increasing academic performance, and with decreasing behavioral problems (Gable, Hester, Rock, and Hughes 2009; Scott, Alter, and Hirn 2011). However, it is often reported as an underused pedagogical strategy despite statistical evidence strongly supporting its use (Shores et al. 1993; Sutherland, Wehby, and Yoder 2002).

When deserved, elite educators rarely miss an opportunity to tell students how pleased they are with their work or that a less-able class is doing as well as a more-able group. They rarely miss a chance to tell a class that "you made my day" or that another teacher complimented one of their students. Using words such as *intelligent, smart, clever,* and *mature* to describe youngsters, high-performing instructors *never* humiliate or use sarcasm with students. Students are praised in public and when necessary, criticism is administered in private. Destructive comments have no place in the classroom. And with class time such a finite commodity, teachers would do well to spend it honoring the "good for kids" instructional filter by legitimately praising and encouraging students rather than by destroying them.

Between a stimulus and an inappropriate or counterproductive student response is a moment of time. And when that moment is filled with embedded descriptors and remembered praise incompatible with such negative reactions, their likelihood is diminished. Beyond inoculating students from negatively impulsive actions, praise and positive attributions are gifts that keep on giving. For in "catching pupils being good" by honestly recognizing their positive behaviors, teachers are not only stating current fact but in satisfying "universal needs for love, acceptance, belonging, competence, self-esteem, a sense of purposefulness, and identity" (Abrams and Segal 1998; Sabatino 1987), they are also maximizing their potential.

As if the reasons for maintaining classroom discipline were not obvious enough, the prerequisites for that discipline of structure, consistency, and strong teacher-student relationships should be no less obvious factors in establishing a positive classroom climate. Especially for struggling students coming from chaotic homes without clear expectations, rules, or routines, a well-ordered and supportive classroom can provide a safe haven of a more predictable world without which their journey toward self-actualization would unlikely reach that destination.

THE MOST POWERFUL DISCIPLINE STRATEGY OF ALL

In the end, the most effective classroom management strategy is to preempt student problems through a meaningful curriculum engagingly delivered. Though not a guaranteed panacea, the overwhelming majority of students, if intrinsically motivated to pay attention because they enjoy class and feel it benefits them, are far less likely to be frustrated, aggressive, or disruptive.

Yet the reverse is also true. If instruction is boring and is seen as having little value, misbehavior may well occur unless the teacher practices coercive discipline through a pedagogically unsound intimidating presence. As such, by a wide margin the typical cause of chronic behavioral problems for teachers has more to do with poor curricular choice and ineffective instructional delivery than it does with "incorrigible" children. In recognizing this truth, chronically ineffective teachers are inescapably confronted by another: blame for chaotic classrooms rests far less with students than with themselves.

Practice Nine

Questioning Skillfully

I use the Socratic method here. I ask a question —you answer it. I ask another question —you answer it. Now you may think you have sufficiently answered the question, but you are suffering a delusion. You will never completely answer it. —Professor Kingsfield (John Houseman), *The Paper Chase* (1973)

Teacher questions serve many purposes. At the least, what is arguably the most universal instructional strategy is used to check student understanding, to create an engaging classroom dynamic, to differentiate instruction, to review previously learned material, and to create an acceptable but necessary level of tension increasing academic focus. But whatever the pedagogical value of these reasons, its greatest benefit is that when used skillfully it can enhance student learning (Wilson and Clegg 1986).

THE BENEFITS OF HIGHER-LEVEL QUESTIONING

Master teachers well understand that questions posed to students are foremost among stimuli triggering thinking and in setting level of cognition. That the stratum of student thought is directly related to an instructor's questioning skills is beyond doubt. That is, questioning levels mirror student thinking expected in the classroom (Beyer 2000; Crowe and Stanford 2010). Thus, the questioning culture of a particular class is clear evidence of its predominant intellectual temperature. And that temperature correlates to student achievement.

Because the characteristics of pupil responses are strongly related to the level of teacher questions, higher-level questions stimulate higher-level responses, and lower-level questions predictably stimulate correspondingly less-complex replies. Thus, not surprisingly, pupils taught by higher-level questioning score significantly better on application and evaluation test items than do youngsters primarily exposed to lower-level questions.

However, in many classrooms teachers spend a disproportionate amount of time asking simple memory-type questions requiring student regurgitation of textbook information or lecture notes. Even though thoughtfulness is essential for success in life, rote memorization is often far more essential for success in school. It has been estimated that only about 5 percent of verbally asked student questions require a thoughtful response (Williams, Alley, and Henson 1999), and on written tests the percent of in-depth questions is not much higher. In point of fact, because the K–12 education of many teachers themselves was largely focused on rewarding the comprehension of existing knowledge, their reluctance to encourage divergent "outside the box" thinking with students is at least somewhat understandable.

Yet if questions account for 80 percent of classroom talk (Borich 1992), and if the purpose of school is to prepare students for life, it is hard to rationalize this disconnect between the questions students experience in typical classrooms and the thinking skills students will need once they graduate. For whatever students end up doing after twelfth grade, one thing is certain: they will all have to think.

Comparatively, master teachers routinely inspire in-depth thinking through discussion questions requiring students to consider their views in broader contexts, to clarify and evaluate their positions, to solve problems, and to make predictions. Indeed, there is evidence that more effective instructors ask more questions and evoke more high-quality student participation than their less-effective colleagues (Henderson, Winitzky, and Kauchak 1996). But the creation of a dynamic and interactive classroom environment moving students from passive to active learners is not the product of happenstance. It is the product of planning.

COMPOSING HIGHER-LEVEL QUESTIONS

For teachers using a low-level questioning approach, it might seem difficult to elicit student responses beyond merely factual recall. However, by categorizing questions into Bloom's *Taxonomy of Educational Objectives*, such a seemingly daunting task proves quite manageable. Thus, questions promoting a variety of thinking skills are relatively easy to compose by focusing on the verb stem that describes the question for the student.

Most simply, the first three levels of Bloom's analysis stimulate lower-order thinking and are considered to be "reproductive" or essentially imitative, while the last three levels promoting higher-level thought are considered to be "productive" or primarily creative in nature. It is these "productive" questions that the overall body of research has linked to enhanced student achievement (Tienken, Goldberg, and DiRocco 2009).

Yet it is no surprise that numerous research studies have found that the clear majority of teacher questions fall into the "reproductive" category (Tienken, Goldberg, and DiRocco 2009). So in a world increasingly requiring imaginative and critical thinking, students are overwhelmingly asked questions fostering little more than mimicry and recall. Thus, not coincidentally, as teachers do not take full advantage of questioning's potential, neither do their students.

Second nature to master educators, extemporaneously asking questions stimulating higher-level student thinking are ironically often composed with little or no conscious thought. For their less-aware colleagues or even for more advanced instructors who want to raise the level of classroom interaction, it is but a small matter to compose higher-level questions and transcribe them to overhead transparencies or PowerPoint slides when planning lessons. In doing so, elite teachers do not leave the development of students' thinking to chance, and neither should their less-able colleagues.

If lawyers or journalists wouldn't think of going into trial or an interview without carefully planning their questions, why then should it be any different for teachers? In any event, once the following questioning levels are committed to instructor memory through constant repetition, raising the level of student discourse as part of a "full mental jacket" curriculum requires no advanced pedagogical training, no complex technology, and no budget-busting expenditures. Promoting higher-level student thinking requires little more than a teacher's willingness to do so.

TAXONOMY LEVEL #1: KNOWLEDGE

In asking this level of question, the teacher expects students to remember an idea, a term, or fact in somewhat the same form as it was learned. For example, KNOWLEDGE questions might ask learners to express the formula for the area of a triangle, to spell the word *taxonomy*, list the parts of speech, or recite a poem.

KNOWLEDGE questions often start with these "stem" words:

Describe	List	Quote
Define	Identify	Name
Label	Cite	Locate
Repeat	Tell	Who
What	When	Where

TAXONOMY LEVEL #2: COMPREHENSION

For COMPREHENSION questions, the teacher is expecting students to show understanding of recalled information. Such queries also involve interpreting ideas, concepts, terms, or events in their own words. For example, a student may be asked to reword the Pledge of Allegiance, clarify the definition of *gross domestic product*, or explain the purpose of a verb in a sentence.

As recall and the ability to correctly explain things in one's own words is the foundation for more advanced learning, KNOWLEDGE and COMPREHENSION questions *should not be underestimated* simply because they are categorized as the first two levels of Bloom's analysis. Indeed, by setting the stage for more thought-provoking questions, lower-level queries can ultimately facilitate the learning of high-level objectives.

COMPREHENSION questions often start with these "stem" words:

Paraphrase	Interpret	Change
Explain	Restate	How
Discuss	Retell	Why

Interestingly, when the verb stem *why* is used to initially ask a question, a relatively low-level comprehension response is elicited, and yet when a teacher uses the same verb stem in asking a student to explain or justify their *reply*, higher-order thinking and discussion are likely to follow.

TAXONOMY LEVEL #3: APPLICATION

A teacher asking APPLICATION questions is expecting students to use what he or she knows to solve problems. That is, this questioning level requires learners to apply ideas to new situations by using charts, rules, principles, or procedures. Application is often the practical evidence of student comprehension. For example, students might be asked to use the periodic table to solve a chemistry problem, to use the Dow Jones Average to "invest" money in the stock market, or to write a research paper using an instructional "recipe" listing the steps to follow in accomplishing the task.

APPLICATION questions often start with these "stem" words:

Apply	Utilize	Operate
Employ	Use	Put to Use

TAXONOMY LEVEL #4: ANALYSIS

In asking ANALYSIS questions, highly effective teachers are expecting students to deconstruct things into their component parts or to uncover the unique characteristics of a "thing." From the Greek "breaking apart," *analysis* requires reducing a complex topic into smaller parts in order to gain a clearer, more manageable understanding. For example, an instructor might ask learners to take apart a computer, to scrutinize *The Last Supper* to uncover as many principles of art as possible, or to identify the essential elements of a persuasive essay in an op-ed commentary.

ANALYSIS questions often start with these "stem" words:

Classify	Compare	Analyze
Dissect	Contrast	Examine
Distinguish	Simplify	Discover
Differentiate	Divide	Deduce

TAXONOMY LEVEL #5: SYNTHESIS

For the SYNTHESIS level of questioning, the teacher asks students to think creatively, to construct original products, or to formulate novel solutions by combining ideas in an inventive way. For example, learners might be asked to develop an original way to teach the concept of adjectives, create a new ending for a book, or formulate an imaginative approach to reducing crime. However, because the very essence of synthesis questions inspires creative thinking, such queries are *inherently resistant* to single right-answer, multiple-choice, completion, and true-false assessments so common in American classrooms (Wiggins 1992).

SYNTHESIS questions often start with these "stem" words:

Create	Plan	Propose
Compose	Build	Predict
Design	Formulate	Conceive

Synthesis questions are arguably the most powerful bridge for encouraging students to creatively extend their thinking. This is so because synthesis implies the creation of something new, which necessitates the asking of "what if" hypothetical questions. Typically, such queries take the following forms:

1. What if this had not happened?
2. What if this were true?

3. What if everyone . . . ?
4. What might be an unforeseen result of this situation?
5. What would happen if . . . ?
6. Is it possible for someone to . . . ?
7. Why is it unlikely that . . . ?
8. What's good/bad about . . . ?

Another form of synthesis questions takes advantage of the natural urge in students to complete what is unfinished. Such questions often take the following forms:

1. How would you write a new beginning for the story?
2. What would be a different way to end the book?
3. What goes in the blank space?
4. What is the missing piece or step? (Cardellichio and Field 1997, 36)

TAXONOMY LEVEL #6: EVALUATION

EVALUATION questions require students to make judgments about people, ideas, events, or points of view and to state, explain, and defend reasons for their opinions. Open-ended questions require students to justify their points of view. For example, learners might be asked to decide which candidate would make the best president, to rank the most important inventions of all time, or to critique a movie, a book, or an advertisement.

EVALUATION questions often start with these "stem" words:

Evaluate	Rate	Weigh
Judge	Prioritize	Defend
Decide	Rank	Critique
Grade	Appraise	Rule On

In addition to a thorough knowledge of questioning levels, highly effective teachers are also mindful of the following questioning considerations:

1. For higher-level questions, the teacher should not have a preconceived right answer in mind. The intent of such thought-provoking questions is that they are open-ended, with many answers acceptable and "right." Consistent with real-life problems, such questions often have an infinite number of possible solutions and, accordingly, are "authentic" in the truest sense of the word. Because such thoughtful questions are inherently compelling, students will be

engaged, discipline problems will likely diminish, and somewhere Professor Kingsfield will be smiling.

Yet ironically, the closer instruction gets to the reality that students will face after graduation, the further it is removed from the multiple-choice, true-false, and fill-in-the blank questioning reality so common in many classrooms. The singular purpose of questioning should not be to find out what a student doesn't know. As Einstein said, its purpose should also be to "discover what the pupil knows or is capable of knowing."

2. A key to fair assessments is that there is a good match between the levels of questioning used for both instruction and testing. That is, it would be grossly unreasonable to ask students knowledge-level recall questions during everyday instruction, then present them with written tests demanding synthesis and evaluation responses. Elite educators *always* teach what they test.

3. Effective teachers mix higher-level and lower-level questions in both their instruction and assessments. Such a blend of thought-provoking reasoning questions and rapid-fire recall queries cuts across all levels of Bloom's taxonomy.

4. Master instructors often orchestrate "cross fire" discussions by referring questions and answers from one student to another in a piggyback fashion. Promoting focus, after a student responds to a question others are asked, "What do you think?" or "How would you have answered that?" or "Why do you agree or disagree?"

5. Many instructors not only ask too many low-level questions but also they tend to ask questions, whatever their degree of complexity, far too rapidly. While shorter pauses between speakers can be justified for simple recall–rote memorization questions, the same cannot be said for higher-level queries. Typically, after asking *any* question, teachers allow on average *less than one second* for student responses (Honea 1982). If the answer does not almost immediately begin, they often call on other students or answer the question themselves.

By relying too heavily on rapid-fire questioning, pupils have little time to formulate thoughtful answers. Thus, their responses are often short, incomplete, and superficial. Moreover, when students are immediately called on after an unanswered question, other students feeling intellectually "off the hook" often disengage from the ensuing answer. Well aware of this, highly effective teachers encourage student alertness and involvement by using "wait time" after posing a question. This strategy, also known as the *pausing principle*, "provides an environment in which substantial changes in teacher and student behavior occur" (Tobin 1987, 89) and "is an important instructional variable when higher cognitive level learning is the objective" (Tobin 1987, 87).

Research reveals that on average teachers wait a mere 0.9 seconds for students to respond to questions (Rowe 1974). Research also indicates that when "wait time" is longer than three seconds, the length and depth of student responses increases and the number of students failing to answer is reduced (Tobin 1987; Rowe 1986). These benefits are especially important for lower-achieving learners who often are reluctant to respond to teacher questions. And even if a student fails to answer after a sufficient amount of "wait time," highly effective teachers rephrase the question, provide additional information, or ask a different but related question.

An immensely powerful discussion strategy used in conjunction with "wait time" is "Think, Pair, Share." It is so simple to implement and elicits such positive classroom energy it is unfathomable why it is not used more often. Cognizant of higher-level verb stems, the teacher asks a thoughtful question, *insisting* that students not call out and not raise their hands. This is followed by a minute or two for student reflection. After this pause, students are told to share their thoughts with a nearby classmate. After two or three minutes of pair interaction, the teacher randomly calls on student pairs for a wider class discussion.

A variation of "Think, Pair, Share" is to provide time for each pair to share their thoughts with a neighboring twosome before sharing their ideas with the entire class. As with its simpler version, "Think, Pair, Square" stimulates higher-level thinking and discussion in even the most reluctant-to-speak students.

6. Low achievers are asked fewer higher-level questions than high achievers (Cotton 1988). Indeed, they are asked fewer questions at *any* cognitive level (Gazin 1990). And even when they are asked to respond, if they pause, look hesitant, or seem bewildered, they are frequently "let off the hook" by teachers, who direct their questions elsewhere. In fact, the manner in which a teacher responds to an incorrect answer or a lack of a response sends a strong message to students (Hunter 1969).

Obviously, students are more likely to remain interested, involved, well behaved, and motivated if they feel positive toward classroom interactions. This is especially so for underperforming learners who may feel insecure after failing to respond correctly to a question. As "success breeds success," it is thus important to ask such students questions at their level of ability. However, this does not mean that struggling students should be asked insultingly easy or "dumbed down" questions. The key is asking these less-able students questions maintaining a relatively high level of scholarship without compromising their willingness to engage through disrespect or failure.

When a struggling youngster does answer incorrectly, it is important to emphasize what, if any, part of the response was correct or that seemed to be moving in the right direction. Providing hints or a restatement of the question may also be helpful. Equally so, asking lower-achieving students opinion questions is a good way to engage them without fear of responding incorrectly to right or wrong recall questions and also to demonstrate that their ideas are valued.

7. Not surprisingly, able learners are called on more than struggling classmates because a correct answer self-servingly validates a teacher's instructional skill, ensures lesson momentum, and avoids uncomfortable moments or student embarrassment ensuing from "I don't know" or "leave me alone" responses. But whatever the reasons for such discrimination, it is essential that all students remain engaged by being given equal chances to respond. This is so because those most likely to "tune out" from class because they are "safe" from questions are often those most likely to be academically at risk.

   In order to ensure maximum learning, students must be "kept on their toes" through seemingly random questioning patterns. And if a teacher realizes that their pattern has become discriminatory toward students of greater ability, there is no reason not to prepare a list, mentally or otherwise, of recently "ignored" students needing to be reengaged through classroom questioning.

8. Strictly speaking, Bloom's taxonomy should not be viewed as a rigid and linear value statement for the importance of each questioning level. Overall, higher-level questions *do* stimulate higher-level thinking. However, that does not mean that in any absolute sense evaluation is always superior to synthesis or that application is always less meaningful than analysis. And while master teachers do make more of an effort to ask students higher-level questions, they also make certain to offer students a varied menu of questioning levels as often as possible.

Practice Ten

Modeling What Matters

No written word nor spoken plea can teach young hearts what they should be, nor all the books upon the shelves but what the teachers are themselves. — Rudyard Kipling

Practice Ten of highly effective instructors is expressed in the commonly accepted but often forgotten saying that "when the teacher sneezes, the whole class catches a cold" (Whitaker 2004, 56). Because children often mirror the characteristics of their instructors, it is essential for teachers to model behaviors translating into success in school and in life. While importantly reinforcing constructive behaviors from "good" homes, it is even more imperative for educators to lead by example in displaying a positive behavioral pattern for children less fortunate.

Getting education right involves more than reading, writing, and arithmetic. To the greatest extent possible, it also involves sending productive and emotionally healthy young people into the world. And since values are best taught through behavioral modeling, teachers need to create a positive moral climate supporting that end (Williams 1993).

Despite the undeniable fact that parents should provide instruction in good character, the sad reality is that what should be and what is are often two very different things. In the absence of positive role models and character instruction in many homes, if teachers are to uphold the Practice One vision of preparing students for success in life, it is essential to fill that vacuum by "modeling what matters."

With character education increasingly a part of the formal academic programs in many schools, unless teachers support those efforts within the "hidden curriculum" of their own behaviors, the power of such programs will surely diminish. For without creating a positive moral and behavioral climate through their daily actions, teacher admonitions to behave properly will ring hollow and fall on deaf ears as garden-variety examples of "do as I say, not as I do" doublespeak. To that end, "modeling what matters" should, at a minimum, include teacher punctuality, self-control, responsibility, respect, critical thinking, goal setting, and effort.

MODELING SELF-CONTROL

When an instructor continually arrives late for class, is easily provoked, blames others for failures, humiliates students, and assigns "busywork," such actions speak louder than any words about what is important. In fact, such actions often encourage those very student behaviors the teacher is seeking to avoid. This is especially true for instructors who in failing to model self-control chronically yell at students. As any effective teacher or parent knows, by regularly raising one's voice, youngsters soon grow "deaf" as they become desensitized to such drama. Moreover, because students quickly identify educators whose "buttons are easily pushed," provocative youngsters eager to "start a show" use such teachers for entertainment purposes.

But self-control involves more than not "flying off the handle." It also involves a willingness to endure short-term "pain" for longer-term gain. While this is not easily modeled by instructors, teachers would do well to at least inform students of the importance of self-discipline in delaying gratification.

In the so-called marshmallow study at Stanford University in 1972, over six hundred preschool children were brought one-by-one into a room and had a marshmallow, a pretzel stick, or a cookie placed in front of them. They were told that if they waited for an adult to return from an errand they could have two treats, but if they ate one in front of them before the adult returned, that is all they would receive. About one-third ate the treat on the spot, some waited a few minutes longer, and only about one-third of the youngsters were able to wait fifteen minutes for the adult to return (O'Neil 1996).

When the children were contacted some fourteen years later, researchers found that the test was an extremely accurate predictor of how they ultimately did in school. The youngsters denying themselves the single marshmallow, cookie, or pretzel for the promise of two "were more emotionally stable, better liked by their teachers and their peers, and were still able to delay gratification in pursuit of their goals" (O'Neil 1996, 7). However, the more impulsive children were more irritable, more sensitive to stress, more likely to pick fights, and were not as well liked. And most telling, *on average their SAT scores were 210 points lower* than youngsters exhibiting self-control more than a decade earlier (O'Neil 1996).

MODELING RESPONSIBILITY

Perhaps more than any other trait, the most effective teachers also model responsibility for their students. For as much as any other characteristic, modeling accountability for one's actions can't help but positively impact student achievement in school and in life. And as certainly, the reverse is also true. Just as a parent reflexively blaming the school for their child's failures enables that youngster to continually struggle, a teacher reflexively blaming students for failures, discipline issues, or their own "you made me angry" outbursts models the same crippling "it's not my fault" message to those least able to question its immediate validity or long-term harm.

The reason for this disempowering result is simple. By pointing the finger of culpability elsewhere, one loses the drive and the leverage to affect positive change. For if "everything" is someone else's fault, and since one has limited control over the "everything" of other people's actions, then one is equally limited to improve a situation. As a result, such excuses invariably lead to impotence, lethargy, and drift. However, in talking the talk *and* walking the walk of responsibility, a teacher inoculates students against a "going nowhere" existence by internalizing the belief that success in virtually anything begins by looking inwardly at yourself. In so doing, such educators help students seize control of their lives.

MODELING RESPECT

In addition to being on time, being in control, and being responsible, the most effective teachers are always mindful of respecting their students. Admittedly, in an emotionally and physically taxing job such as teaching, this is not always easy to do. If as Vince Lombardi once said, fatigue makes cowards out of all of us, it also pries teachers from their moral center in impatience, shortness of temper, a lack of sympathy and, at times, sarcasm. As a result, pupils are ubiquitous and convenient targets to vent frustration. Without acceptable ways to respond to such disrespect, student embarrassment, humiliation, or even anger may result.

Most people can recall a time when an authority figure treated them unfairly or inappropriately. A sarcastic or cutting remark, if humiliating enough, lives forever as if etched in granite. Students may pretend to forget such moment-in-time thoughtlessness, but as the emotional scars remain, they never will (Whitaker 2004). Life is a series of tipping points where seemingly insignificant and random childhood experiences can set in motion choices activating a chain of events leading to otherwise improbable outcomes. Because students are impressionable targets for such teacher-initiated crossroad experiences, when they are sufficiently negative their harm to a child may be everlasting.

When teachers don't respect students, when they express "I don't have faith in you" in words or actions, when they don't believe they are inherently worthwhile, and when they don't believe that exposed to quality instruction they can become productive and moral adults, then that message will be sent *and felt* loud and clear whether it's intended or not. If even once a term an educator fails to think before belittling a student, emotional damage may ensue that may never be completely undone. Mindful of this, whatever the situation, the lateness of the day, or however weary they become, master teachers, in realizing they have been sent the best kids the community has to offer, treat them as if parents were in the room and respect all youngsters the way they expect their own children to be respected. Ralph Waldo Emerson once said, "The secret of education lies in respecting the pupil." And he was right.

Over time, the physical and emotional toll of teaching can lead to rare but no less negative behaviors from even high-performing educators. In the heat of the moment, even the strongest teachers can weaken and unthinkingly demean, insult, or embarrass a student. However, what separates the most effective teachers from their lesser colleagues is that should they lose self-control in acting aggressively or unfairly to students, they have no problem initiating "emotional repairs" by quickly and sincerely apologizing for such behaviors. Expressing heartfelt regret for impatience, ineffective instruction, or impulsively lashing out at students can positively reset a damaged classroom atmosphere and tacitly model responsibility for acting inappropriately.

MODELING CRITICAL THINKING

Modeling respect involves more than sensitivity to the feelings of others. It also involves recognizing the inherent worth of all people without making reflexive evaluations based on how they look, where they're from, or what they believe. To see things from multiple realities, to withhold judgments, to weigh evidence, and to be open-minded is the foundation for tolerance based on critical thinking. This essential disposition commonly needs to be a regular part of every classroom's hidden curriculum. And in classrooms taught by master teachers, it very often is.

Aside from using wait time, use of higher-level verb stems when questioning students, and playing devil's advocate, there are numerous ways elite instructors model critical thinking. At the least, they often remain silent and briefly ponder their responses to student questions, they often think aloud in formulating answers to questions, they outwardly examine important decisions from a cost-benefit perspective, and they rarely rush to judgment in considering information or issues from differing points of view.

When reflecting on questions, critical-thinking teachers speak the language of "I think" or "It is likely" or "The evidence suggests," rather than the language of absolute certainty that is absolutely often wrong. There is a world of difference in stating something is "possibly" or even "probably" so than to make ex cathedra pronouncements implying an all-knowing monopoly of truth. In thinking classrooms, teachers tell students what they are doing and why, they extol a lack of instant-on conviction concerning complex issues as a positive trait, and they regularly explain and cite examples of cognitive distortions such as awfulizing, selective perception, overgeneralization, personalization, and all-or-nothing thinking.

MODELING GOAL SETTING

Just as curricular vision directs behaviors for teachers, goals do the same for students. More specifically, goals are directive (Locke and Latham 2002). If a goal is set to spell at least eight out of ten new spelling words correctly, the learner has an elevated awareness for this intention and is more likely to work toward its realization. An added benefit is that goal-setting students are more likely to notice their own behaviors supporting or undermining the goal that without a target might otherwise have "flown under the radar" (Locke and Latham 2002).

Additionally, anyone committing to a creative goal knows it leads to a hyperawareness, whereby seemingly random environmental stimuli often support that endeavor. A well-publicized example of this phenomenon was said to have occurred in 2004 for Facebook creator Mark Zuckerberg. During the initial stages of designing what became a worldwide sensation, when a friend asked him if a particular female student was "available," Zuckerberg, portrayed in *The Social Network* as barely paying attention to the question, instantly realized that adding "relationship status" to Facebook would springboard his Internet brainchild to unimagined popularity. Yet without his goal of creating a social networking site as a magnet for randomly generated supportive ideas, his friend's "boy meets girl" question would have meant little.

But one doesn't need to be a genius, a *Time* magazine "Person of the Year," or one of the world's youngest billionaires to realize the power of goals in stimulating creativity. Thus, a music student struggling to write a love song and hearing a story of unrequited love will suddenly have little trouble composing lyrics or a channel-surfing student with writer's block who is writing a research paper on the civil rights movement will gain needed context by coincidentally watching a documentary on Abraham Lincoln.

Ideas bolstering creative endeavors are "out there" for the taking, and goals as lightning rods attract such ideas by increasing student sensitivity to receiving them. Like a net trolling for fish, goals allow irrelevant ideas to pass through while snaring more important prey. Thus in defining genius, Thomas Edison was only partially right. For as much as perspiration undoubtedly led to his inventive breakthroughs, goal setting likely "attracted" or "caught" the inspirations without which such insights would likely not have occurred.

However, student goal setting does more than inspire creativity in overcoming writers' block for song lyrics and research papers. Positively and specifically visioning life after secondary school can also serve as a creative goal for students in reaching that destination. As with more everyday aims, once that life objective is visualized, it attracts seemingly random environmental stimuli illuminating paths toward its realization. With a keen eye merging student abilities and interests, master teachers can help students formulate "Have you thought of a career in . . . ?" life goals and in doing so, take the first steps on that journey.

As goal-directed pursuits often lead to peak emotional experiences, at times referred to as a state of "flow," cognitive and physical efforts are stimulated, as is persistence (Locke and Latham 2002). Undeniably, such intense focus is important in developing self-efficacy and often translates into academic achievement. As such, high-achieving students set goals more frequently and more consistently than lower-performing classmates (Zimmerman and Martinez-Pons 1986). When goals are meaningful, challenging but attainable, and self-made rather than imposed, students are motivated to try harder, risk failure, and set higher standards for themselves (Wang, Haertel, and Walberg 1993, 1994). And if new skills are required to attain a self-generated goal, students are more likely to identify and devote energy into learning the new strategies (Locke and Latham 2002).

As for other beneficial behaviors modeled by teachers, if students continue to set goals after graduation it will positively impact adult life. In an admittedly small 2010 study conducted by Dr. Gail Matthews at the Dominican University of California, the benefits of adult goal setting were strongly suggested if not confirmed (Lee 2010). By *simply thinking* about goals participants hoped to realize within a four-week period, almost half reported successfully achieving them. When another group was asked to write their goals, the rate of success rose to 61 percent. A third group accompanying their written goals with an action plan to accomplish them and who also shared their aspirations with a friend reported an achievement rate of 64 percent. And when a last group was asked to contact that friend with a weekly progress report, the goal accomplishment success rate increased to 76 percent (Lee 2010).

Asked why there was such an achievement disparity between the groups, Professor Matthews replied, "It has to do with making an implicit commitment to yourself when you write down your goal . . . it helps to focus your attention on what you want or need to do" (Lee 2010). And the value of goal setting for adults is no less so for students.

In recognizing the self-regulated gains of goal setting, master teachers encourage its practice through personally modeling its value, and more directly, in helping students formulate their own academic and behavioral objectives. Indeed, for some children, the school may be the only source of goal development. Certainly such encouragement could be offered through personal and seemingly impromptu stories of how goal-motivated actions ultimately led to desirable outcomes. Training for a marathon, earning a college degree, saving for a vacation, or even grading students' research papers by a certain date all exemplify how teacher achievements can be realized by setting meaningful yet challenging goals.

Verbalizing goal attainment can be a powerful model for students to emulate, as is breaking a larger goal into smaller, more manageable steps. Such "chunking" the goal encourages student confidence and is an effective antidote to "all at once" procrastination anxiety and "I'll never be able to do this" negative thinking. Knowing full well how counterproductive self-talk can rob a student of motivation, perseverance, and ultimately success, master teachers, having been down their own roads of self-doubt, can help students weather their inevitable "I'm not good enough" apprehensions by challenging negative thoughts. An obvious way to do so would be to encourage students to recall other "I don't have what it takes" fears that proved false. To that end, if such thoughts were so unfounded in the past, why should they be any less unfounded today?

These personal illustrations can easily be reinforced with classroom examples of finishing a learning unit within a given time period or establishing class targets for grades, behavior, or homework completion. But however goal setting is modeled, master teachers demonstrate its value beyond the classroom and themselves by offering its power to individual students. And as with other "modeling what matters" behaviors, encouraging goal setting among students requires little more than a teacher's willingness to do so.

Although students are more motivated to accomplish self-made goals than those imposed on them by others (Snyder, Feldman, Shorey, and Rand 2002), it is especially important to guide younger students in their formulation, and together with parents reinforce their realization. It is also necessary for goals to be sufficiently challenging to inspire satisfaction from attainment and sufficiently meaningful as not to foster a "who cares" indifference. Additionally, because students need to track their progress, goals need to be specific and measurable. As such, "do your best" or "try harder" or "be a better person" mottos are likely to disappear into the dustbin of vague and unrealized New Year's Eve resolutions so common to the world of adults.

In the end, encouraging students to set goals, assisting in their formulation, and monitoring progress toward their attainment are essential practices of master teachers. As a motivational tool enhancing academic and behavioral achievement and objectives, there are few strategies more important to improving student performance. Goals provide the daily and long-term "what should I do now?" activating self-talk without which apathy and drift are more likely. However, there is a more important reason for teachers to promote this practice. In gaining a greater sense of control, students who set goals and create plans to achieve them also gain a greater sense of confidence, potency, and responsibility for their lives. And in furthering the master teacher vision of preparing students for the world beyond the classroom, isn't that education's most important goal of all?

But as important as goals are, without a dogged willingness to stay the course and overcome inevitable setbacks, they are little more than empty words and unfulfilled promises. Wanting and expecting immediate gratification, when rewards don't come easily many students give up well short of accomplishing even modest ambitions. Just as exertion pursuing ill-defined aims dissipates energy on projects leading nowhere, goals without industry result in little more than couch-potato dreams. Knowing that rarely is anything of value accomplished without the stamina and determination to endure what is often a long and difficult road toward realization, legendary UCLA basketball coach John Wooden once said, "Nothing will work unless you do." And because without this mind-set, achievement in school and in life is all but impossible, master teachers model a persistent and unwavering effort.

MODELING EFFORT

Obviously, by instructing from "bell to bell," by grading papers and returning them before the next solar eclipse, and by instructing with as much or even more enthusiasm on Fridays and immediately before a vacation as on any other day, the teacher-initiated message of hard work is clearly expressed. Unquestionably, when there is greater teacher effort in classroom activities there is a greater likelihood that students will follow that example. When an instructor is unprepared, forgets to give proper directions, does not grade or return assignments promptly, and is excessively absent, many students will follow that example as well.

Obviously, no amount of lesson planning, no clarity of curricular vision, and no understanding of instruction as performance means anything if a teacher is home taking a "mental health day." Described as epidemic in some districts, excessive and unfounded teacher absences send all the wrong messages to impressionable students. In recognizing that in a far more tangible and immediate way chronic teacher absenteeism undermines student achievement, master educators rarely miss class.

In contrast, too many of their colleagues never internalized the platitude that "just showing up is more than half the battle." In "dire need" of stress reduction, they justify their slacking with "quality of instructional time is more important than quantity" rationalizations. But this is clearly not so. The overall performance of a school is negatively affected by increased teacher absenteeism (Manlove and Elliot 1979). And even if "quality *is* more important than quantity," where is it written that teachers shouldn't or can't provide both?

Through no fault of their own, as a group substitute teachers are typically less effective than regular classroom instructors (Olsen 1971). At the least, temporary instructors are afforded less student respect, are unaware of specific student learning needs, are the face of instructional discontinuity, and are often required to do little more than oversee student "busy work." Thus, not surprisingly, research indicates that when comparing the same teacher in different years, students do worse in years when their teacher compiles a greater number of absences (Rockoff 2010).

Additionally, when comparing student results on standardized tests, teacher absences before those exams impaired scores. And because there is often less preparation for short-term absences than for more extended teacher leaves, several single-day absences spread throughout a term are academically far more detrimental than an isolated absence of far longer duration (Rockoff 2010).

Effort demonstrated through good attendance, well-prepared lessons, and prompt grading of assignments is more than "simply" a trait for instructors to model for students. Whenever possible, it can and should be a part of the instructional program. Accordingly, "effort belief," the conviction that with few exceptions, success can only be gained through consistent and unyielding hard work, is so important that in giving students 100 percent of themselves nearly 100 percent of the time, it is also Practice Eleven of master teachers.

Practice Eleven

Promoting Effort Belief

The big secret in life is that there is no big secret. Whatever your goal, you can get there if you're willing to work. —Oprah Winfrey

People in general and students in particular typically ascribe achievement to ability, luck, or effort (Marzano, Pickering, and Pollock 2001). And because the reasons one assigns to success or failure largely dictate outcomes, master teachers understand the relative effect these three factors have on student actions and expectations.

OF SUCCESS AND FAILURE

Whereas successful students often point to hard work as the tipping point between success and failure, underachieving youngsters credit native ability or luck as key factors in determining results. Between these two groups of students, this is a telling and unfortunate difference in perceptions. For in believing that innate ability or happenstance largely determines outcomes, factors beyond one's control, students internalize a sense of helplessness and inhibit achievement by undermining their own capacities to affect positive change. While students believing that intelligence can change through hard work will actually increase efforts after failure and "are more likely to accept challenges and persist on tasks" (Bransford and Vye 1989, 181; Dweck 1986), students believing that intelligence is fixed will actually expend *less* effort after defeat (Alderman 1990).

Superficially, belief in inherent ability might seem positive. After all, if students believe they have ability, virtually any task is doable. However, regardless of how much ability one thinks one has, inevitably there will be tasks for which necessary skills are lacking. In such cases, insecure students internalizing an innate view of intelligence will often handicap themselves through procrastination, inattention, the manufacture of a personality conflict with the teacher, or simply by not trying very hard. By inwardly "proving" that failure was caused by reasons other than an inborn lack of ability, self-esteem is protected, an underperforming status

quo continues, and the fiction of blameless defeat is maintained. As Columbia University psychologist Carol Dweck so aptly said, such fixed
intelligence students "care so much about looking smart that they act
dumb" (Gladwell 2009, 367–368).

Lacking confidence and fearing failure, it is psychologically safer for
such students to mismanage study time, deny the need for extra help, or
claim "I didn't even try" rather than face what they believe are unchangeable personal limitations. Even when a student believes he or she has the
natural ability to successfully complete a task, such a belief might undermine the work ethic because if one already has such a natural ability,
trying hard may be seen as less necessary.

The disempowering belief among struggling students that innate ability is the primary determinant for success is more widespread than many
people realize and may partially contribute to the poor showing of
American students in international comparisons. In a study of parental
beliefs regarding school success, Japanese mothers identified effort and
hard work as key factors, whereas American parents associated inherent
ability as the essential element in academic performance (Barker 1996).
Yet by culturally "brainwashing" their children into believing their futures are genetically preordained, American parents are unwittingly also
convincing them to devalue the importance of effort in determining outcomes. And in doing so, parents also undermine their child's control over
their own learning.

But American parents are not the only authority figures to disempow-
er children with the "you are what you are" mind-set, encouraging if not
guaranteeing achievement paralysis. When asked to explain differences
in student achievement, American teachers also cited "student ability."
Predictably, when asked the same question, Japanese educators answered "hard work" (Stevenson 1990). Moreover, when 93 percent of
Japanese teachers explain student differences in math performance as
due to studying hard, compared to only 26 percent of American instructors (Toch, Bennefield, and Bernstein 1996), it is clear U.S. educators often
see academic success as a function of *who* a student is whereas their
Japanese counterparts see achievement differences as resulting from *what*
a student does (Danielson 2002).

Apparently, the brainwashing has been successful. American students
often insist that success in a particular subject was the result of being
"good" at it. Predictably, when they do poorly, it was because they were
not "good" at it, or because they were unlucky, or because the teacher
didn't like them (Danielson 2002). By giving themselves such permissions
to fail, American youngsters guarantee more of the same. In contrast,
students in Asia or in Europe often "attribute their successes to hard
work and a lack of success to insufficient effort on their part" (Danielson
2002, 13).

Belief in luck also inhibits achievement. Such a belief places control of a task's outcome beyond the command of the student. Doing so also undermines the work ethic and disempowers the youngster. For why should one try if luck runs out or if one is perceived to be unlucky in the first place? Thus, if one believes oneself powerless to recast the "immutable" realities of luck or innate ability, such impotence quickly morphs into an inertia of fatalism, excuse, inaction, and failure. After all, why try bettering oneself if one is believed to have marginal talent and equally little luck?

THE KEY FACTOR IN SUCCESS

The only variable leading to success or failure one can fully control *is* effort. Along with perseverance, it is regarded by educational researchers as a key attribute "necessary for developing self-controlled, self-regulated learners" (Wang, Haertel, and Walberg 1993, 1994, 75). In saying that "I'm a great believer in luck, and I find the harder I work, the more I have of it," Thomas Jefferson got it right. Accordingly, children need to learn that "all in" effort can largely compensate for a perceived lack of innate ability or good fortune and that with few exceptions success can only be gained through unyielding exertion. And understanding this relationship between one's effort and outcomes can translate into a willingness to engage in difficult tasks over an extended period.

Indeed, a growing body of research reveals that inborn aptitude may be greatly overstated as a primary determinant of outstanding achievement. Although students may believe they are limited by an absence of native ability, superior achievement in any field results at least as much from effort as it does from winning the genetic lottery. According to K. Anders Ericsson, a psychology professor at Florida State University, "There is surprisingly little hard evidence that anyone could attain any kind of exceptional performance without spending a lot of time perfecting it" (Levitt and Dubner 2011, 61; Ericsson, Krampe, and Tesch-Romer 1993). Thus, educationally speaking, the good news is that "expert performers—whether in soccer or piano playing, surgery or computer programming—are nearly always made, not born" (Levitt and Dubner 2011, 61; Ericsson, Krampe, and Tesch-Romer 1993).

Not surprisingly, the research also "strongly suggests that students who believe in their own capacities—to learn, to cause good outcomes by their actions, to exert control over their lives . . . do better in school" (Caine 2000, 60; Schmitz and Skinner 1993). Inevitably encountering academic obstacles, such self-regulated learners believing that effort will ultimately pay off, take charge, take responsibility, and find a way to succeed.

This understanding that "true grit" is essential to manipulating reality toward positive ends not only promotes achievement in students from so-called affluent communities, it is equally effective for children seemingly less advantaged. "Children in inner-city Detroit schools achieved more when they were directly taught that intellectual development is something they all can achieve through effort, as compared to something only some people are born with" (Benard 1993, 46; Howard 1990).

Sadly, whatever their economic strata, the message linking perseverance with success has neither been taught nor reinforced in many homes and schools. In realizing that many students "have missed the connection between effort and outcome" (Rimm 1997, 18) and that "student effort is modifiable through the actions of teachers" (Covington 1992, 16), the most effective instructors, by consistently modeling and promoting "effort belief," enable students to internalize the mind-set that effort pays off, even if they initially don't accept that connection.

In fact, because how individuals explain their academic outcomes is a learned trait (Seligman 1975), students who have been taught about the relationship between effort and success increased their level of achievement more than students who were taught techniques for time management and comprehension of new material (Marzano, Pickering, and Pollock 2001).

EXTERNAL AND INTERNAL MIND-SETS

As a prerequisite for establishing the connection between effort and success, it is helpful for teachers to understand that students adopt one of two dominant and general philosophical mind-sets for explaining success or failure. Externally oriented learners believe they have little control over what happens to them. At the mercy of the environment, they hold that luck, circumstance, task difficulty, or fate shapes their lives and that personal effort makes little difference. Obviously, crediting factors beyond one's control with determining life's circumstances is a recipe for failure in the classroom or virtually anywhere else.

In contrast, internally oriented students believe they are largely responsible for their own happiness or misery. Believing their life circumstances are largely within their control, they agree with Sartre that "a man is what he wills himself to be." Internalizing this worldview, students attribute outcomes to factors within themselves, such as ability or effort. Although both of these variables may account for outcomes, because it can be controlled, only belief in effort is an appropriately beneficial philosophy leading to achievement.

And even if students conditioned by parents and society resist this empowering "no one else is to blame" message, master teachers can foster internally oriented mind-sets by asking students a simple question: "If you are unsure whether you want to be an internal or external person, why not choose the belief that is far more likely to get you where you want to go?"

EFFORT BELIEF INSTRUCTION

In words, deeds, and instruction, master teachers relentlessly communicate to students that effort is the key to success. But this message should also be communicated to students through the policies and the practices of the schools they attend. Doing so may be as simple as recognizing student "personal best" achievements that otherwise might have been ignored as less-than-absolute excellence. Additionally, allowing students falling short of "top-of-the-class" standards to enroll in advanced courses makes an undeniable statement that since effort matters, every class is yet another opportunity for students to make a powerful "I can do this" statement.

Obviously prior to enrolling in such an advanced course, students, whatever their academic histories, should be informed as to its rigor and that success will require a considerable commitment of time and effort. Assuming that students have the prerequisite skills for success, an "open admissions" policy for such classes tacitly expresses confidence in the efforts of learners to succeed today despite falling short of an absolute grade threshold yesterday. Such a policy also says that the school is in the business of opening doors for kids rather than slamming them shut without giving them a chance to rise or fall based on their most immediate efforts.

More specifically, "effort belief" instruction may be offered by assigning projects about "ordinary" people doing extraordinary things through "fall seven times, stand up eight" perseverance. Teachers might also encourage student research of decidedly unordinary athletes, entertainers, scientists, or political leaders who ultimately succeeded primarily because they refused to give up. To that end, when asked how he was able to make discoveries so long eluding others, no less a stick-to-itiveness authority than Sir Isaac Newton replied, "By always thinking about them." Thus despite what some *American Idol* wannabes believe, success doesn't "just happen." According to some experts, the key to great achievement in any field is practicing a specific task for at least twenty hours a week for ten years: the so-called ten-thousand-hour rule (Gladwell 2008).

Perhaps the best way to teach the connection between hard work and success is for students to share personal stories about overcoming difficulties, even those involving the most mundane of endeavors. Virtually all students have experienced achievement in something that was initially perplexing but over time became doable at a high level of competency.

Whether students were shooting baskets, riding skateboards, or playing video games, the common denominator leading to success was persistent effort. That relationship between exertion and mastery so commonly experienced outside of school is no less true in the classroom.

Still another way to introduce "effort belief" on the first day of school is to ask students: How many students would succeed if passing grades led to a thousand-dollar reward? The laughter and sheepish grins following this query reinforces the "effort belief" message that if virtually everybody would indeed pass to earn the money, then the question is not whether one can or can't pass, but whether one will or one won't.

Throughout the term, there is no lack of effort belief examples to focus on either through formal instruction or during occasional "teachable moments." At the least, the strategy of students setting their own goals with teacher oversight emphasizes the importance of internal control over results. But whatever strategies an instructor uses to reinforce effort belief, it must be *explicitly* taught. Simply exhorting students to "work hard" or "make more of an effort" is not enough. Only by understanding the dynamics of effort belief are students empowered to better control their own motivation. And in realizing the importance of directly forging student links between effort and achievement, master teachers have few problems in making their own efforts to do so.

For by instilling in students that they can do great things with great effort, elite instructors are teaching kids the essential life lesson that they *can* transform their dreams into realities. It matters little what talent cards a child is dealt if they are played poorly or not at all. And not playing the cards one is dealt confirms the adage that fewer things in life are more common than talented people who are unsuccessful.

Well aware of the power of effort belief, highly effective teachers model and create learning experiences helping students to accept that their futures are largely determined by what they do rather than who they are. One's innate ability is not merely a finite resource but a potential that can be enhanced or squandered depending on effort. Failing to make effort belief an instructional priority virtually dooms many youngsters not receiving this message at home to be far less than they can be.

However, even with extraordinary effort a "be-all-you-can-be life" is not guaranteed. Undeniably, effort is necessary, but it may be not enough. Yet without perseverance and the belief that one *can* achieve positive results, children have virtually no chance of maximizing their potential whatever path they choose. Because perception is *not* reality, it is only *someone's* reality, what students accept as true is all important. Or, as Henry Ford once said, "Whether you think you can or think you can't . . . you are right."

Practice Twelve

Understanding Motivation

It is not enough to be busy. The question is, what are we busy about? —
Henry David Thoreau

Even if a teacher uses the previous eleven practices of effective instruction, what often separates the "merely" good educators from excellence is
"packaging" those practices with a Practice Twelve understanding of
learner motivation. The fact is that most students *are* motivated to learn.
However, as all teachers know, while they may be motivated to recite
sports statistics, song lyrics, or video-game strategies, they may not be
interested in learning what instructors are trying to teach them.

Although in an absolute sense, even the best teachers can't directly
motivate their students to learn, they can use strategies such as "effort
belief" instruction promoting that end. But empowering students to seize
control of their own learning by linking hard work and achievement is
not enough. Teachers need to also focus on learning's motivating factors
and on the creation of a positive classroom climate without which motivational strategies will prove ineffective. And because pupils enter classrooms with diverse interests, learning styles, and abilities, knowledge of
motivation's basic principles is not only important, it is essential.

SUPPORTIVE LEARNING ENVIRONMENT

The indispensable precondition for student motivation is a supportive
learning environment. In poorly managed classrooms where the only
routine is chaos, where discipline is lacking, where bullying is ignored,
and where students feel anxious, uninspired, or invisible, few children
will be motivated to learn whatever the quality of curriculum. When
under threat, it appears "the brain shuts down to a fight or flight mode
that precludes higher-level learning" (Caulfield and Jennings 2000, 8;
Caine and Caine 1994). Because of this, a negative classroom climate will
trump anything else a teacher can do to motivate students.

Yet in classrooms where learners feel safe, respected, and encouraged
to take intellectual risks without fear of ridicule, an instructional program

constructed with attention to learning's essential motivating factors will likely be embraced. Some sixty years ago, Abraham Maslow posited that unless the universal need for safety and security is satisfied, there is little motivation to pursue higher level but less immediate needs. And in maintaining a supportive learning environment, master teachers today know what "the genius from Brooklyn" knew in 1954.

MOTIVATION'S ESSENTIAL FACTORS

In order to persuade anyone to learn, or for that matter to do virtually anything else, the task must be *both* doable and important. If *either* factor is absent, little effort will be expended at best and no effort will be made at worst, *no matter how much of the other variable is present* (Feather 1982). The reason for this is simple. If tasks are doable but perceived as unimportant, few people will spend much energy on such "trivial" pursuits. If assignments are important but not seen as doable, most people will give up rather than struggle with seemingly "impossible" undertakings.

Further, the motivational calculus is strongly linked to offering students tasks that challenge enough to stimulate success satisfaction and are seemingly achievable enough to prompt efforts to even attempt. If tasks are too easily doable, they are often devalued as unimportant, and if they are extremely difficult, even if successfully completed, success may be attributed to luck. When learning is too easy, thinking is suppressed as the brain enters a state of relaxation, and when learning is too challenging, the brain downshifts into a self-protective mode. In either case, neither promotes satisfaction driving further effort. Only success at moderately challenging tasks gives rise to feelings of pride, competence, determination, and personal control (Danner and Lonky 1981).

Said differently, "motivation is determined jointly by the expectation that the effort will lead to the goal and that the goal is worth attaining" (Wilson and Corpus 2001, 57; Csikzentmihalyi and Nakamura 1989). Mindful of this and by adding the third factor of fun, the most effective teachers are able to intrinsically motivate all but the most apathetic of students.

TASK DOABILITY

At the least, instructional strategies increasing doability for performance tasks such as essays, research projects, and oral presentations should include rubrics detailing evaluation criteria, exemplars of what performance excellence looks like, and sequential "recipes" for how to create quality work. However, for material such as concepts, terms, and vocabulary, it is also *essential* to create a consistent and cumulative review schedule so that students will be able to self-regulate their study and recall.

Well understood by master teachers, this often-overlooked instructional approach of distributed practice is the "one indispensable key to effective learning" (Dempster 1993, 437). This is so because the regular review of newly learned information or tasks is the "best approach to achieving retention in long-term memory" (Hirsch 1996, 37).

DISTRIBUTED PRACTICE

There is little doubt that the common instructional approach of once-is-enough "massed practice" unit tests and final exams results in learning that is neither meaningful nor enduring. Typically, students cram before a major assessment, mindlessly parrot back information, and then quickly forget what they never actually learned in the first place. The fact is *nobody*, even serious students, really learns that way.

In order for durable learning to occur, students must "overlearn" material by recalling it throughout the term on a *regular, predictable,* and *cumulative basis.* Initially spaced close together, reviews of previously "learned" information should gradually be sequenced at ever-lengthening intervals. Anecdotally so and intuitively obvious, many studies indicate that frequent assessment and feedback effectively promote learning (Wang, Haertal, and Walberg 1993/1994). Aware of this, master teachers realize that without a reiterative assessment schedule, students will be hard-pressed to internalize and begin applying what they have been taught. Because repetition reinforces brain connections, "practice doesn't make perfect; it makes permanent" (Wolfe 1998, 63; Hunter 1982).

But the value of distributed practice goes far beyond fostering knowledge retention. A repeating practice schedule not only enhances recall of facts, concepts, procedures, and vocabulary; it also fosters a relatively automatic processing of pattern recognition. When experts encounter familiar problems, they rely on automatized learning to quickly recognize its signature pattern and solution. And when comparatively little attention is needed to identify such well-known patterns, they are able to invest more effort, should it be necessary, in dealing with other aspects of the problem (Bransford and Vye 1989).

In contrast, students often lacking pattern fluency in recognizing words, writing competently, or in solving math problems invest a disproportionate amount of attention initially figuring out what to do. When experiencing difficulties, this often leads to frustration, attentional fatigue, and failure. In greatly enhancing student pattern recognition, an ongoing distributed practice schedule can, academically speaking, do for students what such an ability does for experts, and that is to enable them to identify and solve repeating problems with relatively little difficulty and "I've seen this before" confidence.

The power of a secure knowledge base in improving retention and pattern recognition is so great that "when children acquire unusual levels of knowledge . . . they often perform as well as, or better than, adults on tasks that depend on that knowledge" (Resnick and Klopfer 1989, 5). An example of such precocity is clearly illustrated in a study measuring the short-term recall of young children compared to college students.

When the research task was to memorize randomly generated number strings, not surprisingly, the college students excelled. However, when youngsters, who were avid chess players, were asked to remember briefly seen game positions on a chess board, they easily outperformed students twice their age (Bransford and Vye 1989). If after repeated practice young children can learn such automatic pattern recognition in chess, why shouldn't this be equally so after distributed practices composing research papers, solving math problems, or in internalizing strategies to promote reading comprehension?

CONNECTING NEW KNOWLEDGE TO OLD

Because a "fundamental principle of cognition is that learning requires knowledge" (Resnick and Klopfer 1989, 5), as students truly commit information to long-term memory, related material is easier to learn as it mentally attaches to what is already known. "Since the mind can handle only a small number of new things at one time . . . a new thing has to become integrated with prior knowledge before the mind can give it meaning [and] store it in memory" (Hirsch 1996, 37). And this relationship between one's relatable prior knowledge as a framework for understanding and assimilating new learning is more than anecdotally so. The correlation of learning ability with the level of general knowledge is a statistically significant +.811 (Hirsch 2001, 22; Lubinski and Humphreys 1997).

In determining what is doable and important enough to expend effort on learning, the brain scrutinizes new information for recognizability. When a place is found to fit the new information within the context of an existing knowledge base, it is added to what is already known. It is by matching incoming sensations with related information stored from previous experiences that the brain attempts to make sense of the input it constantly receives (Gazzaniga 1998).

More simply, people use what is already known to construct meaning from new information. From personal experience, we all know this to be so. Driving a new car, using a new computer, or teaching in a new school, our brains scan past experiences for similarities. The greater the similarity between the novel and the known, the easier learning will be.

As such, highly effective teachers often begin classes with a review connecting the new topic with students' prior knowledge. What Madeline Hunter called an "anticipatory set," this introductory bridge linking what students already know to what they are about to learn provides the "Velcro" new information readily attaches itself to.

A simple example from Social Studies might be a teacher announcing, "Remember our discussion on the differences between our two major political parties? Well today, we'll be looking at the candidates for the upcoming presidential election to see how closely their statements conform to the party beliefs we talked about last week." Master teachers recognize that without the intellectual Velcro of previously learned knowledge for new learning to adhere to, what is being taught will stick as poorly as food to a Teflon-coated pan.

Still another method creating Velcro hooks for new material to attach to is assigning pertinent readings to students *before* a topic or unit of instruction is taught. Provided with the "big picture" to come, students are more able to fit subsequent material into that newly created knowledge base. And to "encourage" students to take such global overview readings more seriously, a brief quiz should follow its assignment.

Yet because even the most able students have difficulty knowing what to focus on for a reading quiz assessment, a good rule of thumb is to weight each question at roughly half of its arithmetically correct value. Thus, on a ten-question quiz the worth of each question should be five rather than ten points. The purpose of this grading "curve" is not to give students something for nothing but rather to increase the likelihood that the assignment will be thoughtfully read without unfairly penalizing them for not knowing what the teacher felt was important about a topic they initially knew little or nothing about.

To further reinforce learning, master teachers regularly and cumulatively quiz their students on material both new and old. They add a few older questions to unit exams, especially those often missed in the past or those of particular importance because of their regular appearance on state tests. So too, they may encourage students to make problem-solving corrections on assessments by partially "reimbursing" them for points lost when initially taking exams. Moreover, practice-savvy instructors also distribute "cognitive maps" listing according to when taught, important terms, concepts, and essential questions students will be held responsible for at the end of each learning unit. Collectively, these materials along with review-focused homework assignments provide students with excellent study guides, taking the "mystery" out of end-of-term exams should they be required.

When these distributed strategies are regularly used, new information becomes integrated with previously learned material, and higher-level thinking likely results. This is so because the more one knows about a topic and the longer that knowledge is deeply considered, the greater the chance for application, analysis, synthesis, and evaluation. This relationship between a secure knowledge base, time, and insight is undeniable.

Research indicates that distributed practice does more than simply increase the amount of information learned. "It frequently shifts the learner's attention away from the verbatim details of the material being studied to its deeper conceptual structure" (Dempster 1993, 436). Anyone ever arriving at a profound insight after much "patient thought" knows this to be so.

> Charles Darwin gathered biological facts for twenty years without seeing any binding relationship. Then one day when he was walking through an English country lane, the idea of evolution suddenly came to him. That's what thinking is—the flashing emergence of an idea after the facts have been mulled over for a long time. (W. E. McNeil as quoted in Dale 1984)

However, if a forgettable and fragile knowledge base is a "mile wide and an inch deep," meaningful interpretation becomes all but impossible. Instructionally, we know this to be so. If two students of equal ability read an article about the Civil War, the works of Shakespeare, or anything else, and one has a deep and secure preexisting informational foundation and the other has at best a superficial familiarity with the subject, there is little doubt that the former student will make greater sense of the material. What has been learned in the past acts as both a magnet to attract the new information and a lens to analyze its accuracy in light of what is already known.

Perhaps more than anyone else, teachers should thus recognize how important an automatic and secure knowledge base is to thoughtful cognition, pattern recognition, and effective problem solving. Every seasoned educator has personally experienced the difference between trying to survive as a rookie instructor and the relative ease of being a veteran teacher. As a novice educator with so much content and procedure as yet unlearned, one's intellect is focused on making sense of a still-new situation. As such, there is little time, Velcro, and psychic energy for profound insights, which ultimately occur only after the basics of the job have been habitually mastered. As master teachers know, if this was once true for themselves it is now equally so for students.

While several tests given shortly after instruction leads to rapid acquisition of new material, unless assessments are continued at ever-lengthening intervals new knowledge will quickly evaporate. Thinking back to their own days as students and the parroting back of information on final exams without the yearlong benefit of distributed practice reviews, every teacher knows how rapidly such "learning" was lost. Thus, testing their own students even several times shortly after instruction and rarely if ever thereafter is irrefutably a sham exercise in futility. And as this is true for the "knowing what" of declarative knowledge in learning concepts, terms, and vocabulary, it is equally so for the "knowing how" of procedural knowledge in learning far more complex performance tasks.

Whether the assignment is to write a research paper, make an oral presentation, compose a persuasive essay, conduct an original scientific investigation, pen a short story, or for younger students, fashion a simple paragraph, distributed practice is an essential instructional strategy for learning to do so. Assigning such real-world tasks without a distributed learning loop is certainly better than not doing so at all. But undeniably, it is not much better.

There are also ethical and practical reasons for creating distributed practice schedules. After all, if something is important enough to teach, isn't it also important enough for students to remember and to actually *use* in their lives? If something is important enough to have been taught, isn't it also important enough for that learning to be durable enough for students to easily access in order to make better sense of new and related information? Moreover, as for all the best habits of master teachers, distributed practice is a cost-free strategy to greatly increase student learning. And with schools continually under pressure to do more with less, what could be a better way to academically accomplish that result?

The research is clear. The real question is not whether material has been covered but whether it has been internalized, is durable, and is of sufficient depth to provide context interpreting novel situations and to secure a foundation for new knowledge to attach to. And because such outcomes of genuine learning require frequent reinforcement, an ongoing and cumulative distributed practice design scheduled over increasing intervals of time is a part of every master teacher's instructional arsenal.

Irrefutably, when expectancy of success fostered by a reiterative assessment schedule is combined with meaningful assignments, student learning inspiring increased motivation is likely to result. The reason for this is simple. The more students know about a topic, the greater the likelihood they will be interested in it (Marzano, Pickering, and Pollock 2001; Alexander et al. 1994). As for most people, it is difficult for students to have an interest in anything they know little or nothing about. Knowledge may indeed be power, but "knowing" also powers the desire for more of the same. And that is as true for sports statistics, celebrity gossip, or computer game strategies as it is for reading, writing, and arithmetic.

TASK IMPORTANCE

The second essential element promoting student motivation is importance. Accordingly, the most effective teachers are able to convince even "Why do we have to do this?" pupils that what they are being asked to learn is worth knowing. "Because all human beings organize their thinking and perceptions around what they regard to be important . . . when we disregard student purposes and values, we are tossing out the essential glue that acts as the key to the depth of understanding we wish students to acquire" (Caine and Caine 1997, 112).

In asking youngsters to learn endless and largely irrelevant "factoids" having little innate importance other than to pass teacher-constructed tests, many students, even "good" ones, believe that much of what they are being asked to learn is not worth the effort to learn it. And they are right.

> Suppose you get a job in a factory making both black shoes and brown shoes. You are well managed and do quality work. But soon you become aware that all the brown shoes you make are sold for scrap; only the black shoes are going into retail stores. How long would you continue to work hard on the brown shoes? As you slack off, however, you are told that this is not acceptable and that you will lose pay or be fired if you don't buckle down and do just as good a job on the brown as on the black. You are told that what happens to the brown shoes is none of your business. Your job is to work hard. Wouldn't it be almost impossible to do as you are told? (Glasser 1992, 691)

Because students, and for that matter everyone else, will spend little cognitive energy on seemingly unimportant matters, perceived importance is essential to learning virtually anything. Since the brain's primary role is its continued survival, anything that it "determines is important is much more likely to be attended to, stored, and later retrieved than that which the brain decides is meaningless or of little consequence" (Westwater and Wolfe 2000, 49).

"The brain/mind resists meaningless information imposed on it: isolated pieces of information unrelated to what makes sense to a particular learner" (Caine and Caine 1997, 105). As a result, when increasing motivation the answer is not to "convince" students to work harder through coercion. "The answer is to increase the quality of what we ask them to learn" (Glasser 1992, 691).

How common is the experience to "forget" an often-used phone number or a frequently used recipe when the written details of either have been misplaced? The reason for this inability to remember something that seemingly should be easy to recall is simple. In either case, with written information as an aid, it was unconsciously deemed unnecessary and thus unimportant to memorize, that is, to learn, an old friend's number or Aunt Minnie's recipe for pumpkin pie.

In a very real sense, we are evolutionarily programmed to pay attention to and remember only what is deemed meaningful enough to justify the effort. Learning is impossible without paying attention, and rarely is attention paid to anything seen as unimportant. When there is a "relevance gap" between the curriculum and what students need to know and be able to do beyond the classroom, apathy and failure likely result.

Accordingly, instructional tasks must be seen not as needless "why bother" demands to be resisted but rather as essential opportunities to be embraced. Once students are convinced they are doing meaningful work, they are far more likely to comply with teacher demands not because they fear negative consequences but because they are intrinsically motivated to do so.

Perhaps the easiest way for teachers to inspire intrinsic motivation in learners is to obey the "WIFM" rule of instructional choice. That is, if students become convinced that what is assigned will benefit their lives, "What's In It for Me?" will be obvious. And despite the relative lack of such meaningful tasks students are forced to complete every day, compelling and relevant assignments should not be difficult to create. All teachers need to do is identify tasks likely to promote and predict student success in school and in life (Moses 1992).

However, if the identification of indispensable learning experiences is still difficult, teachers should ask themselves what is essential *for their own children* to know and be able to do after graduation. Strange how quickly meaningful instructional choice becomes clear when one's own child becomes part of the conversation.

Students trust their teachers. If pupils are occupied with meaningless busywork, that trust is clearly violated. For by preparing youngsters for a world that doesn't exist, educators are living a lie that even the most naive students can detect. "Throwaway activities," projects and assessments having little or no value outside of the classroom, undermine motivation because students unable to connect such tasks to real-world usefulness see them as unimportant. As a result, "extended periods of time with too little stimulation, meaning relevance, or application . . . engender little learning of lasting value" (Greenleaf 2003, 17). In contrast, when "academic trust" has developed over time, students are less likely to challenge tasks they do not immediately see as valuable because they have confidence they will eventually understand their importance (Marzano and Pickering 1997).

TEXTBOOK ABUSE

One of the least relevant and most commonly accepted routines in classrooms is the use of textbooks to the exclusion of common sense. Indeed, "teachers in the United States exhibit an overreliance on textbooks for decisions about content and pacing" (Marzano 2003, 107; Stevenson and Sigler 1992). Whether this overreliance is due to well-intentioned fears about "leaving something important out," a lack of personal confidence in curricular decisions, an unwillingness to edit already constructed "paint-by-number" content designs, or simply a reprise of their own schooling is unknown.

However, whatever the reason for blind-faith, almost-obsessive textbook use, to suggest that compulsive use of textbooks is essential to ensure student learning is absurd. Do students use textbooks to learn to play video games, recall baseball statistics, recite song lyrics, or anything else they regularly and skillfully do without their "benefit"?

Textbooks *do* have an important place in classrooms. Indeed, especially in sequenced-dependent subjects such as mathematics where today's lesson is absolutely linked to yesterday's understanding, a case can be made for closely following the textbook's lockstep design. However, even then, texts should be teacher-edited reference tools *supporting* instruction and not irrevocably attached to students' hips as "academic bibles." Failing to recognize this, if instructors were trying to bore their students they could do little better than to require them to mindlessly learn minutia or to complete endless drills or exercises simply because a textbook author felt it important to include in a general scholarly work.

But there is another reason why overreliance on textbooks is a bad idea. When teachers use textbooks to almost exclusively define what is taught in classrooms, they are virtually guaranteed to foster not only student disengagement but student failure as well. The reason for this should be obvious to anyone familiar with learning theory, and that reason is that as for many things, more indeed becomes less.

That American textbooks are overstuffed with "enrichment" material is of little doubt. In cross-cultural comparisons, they "are unrivaled in size and in material covered" (Dempster 1993, 434; Chambliss and Calfee 1989). In and of itself this is not necessarily a bad thing. It only becomes counterproductive when teachers using textbooks as all-encompassing authorities of what should be taught fail to recognize that some students don't need to follow their every page, others are overwhelmed by doing so, and learners on either side of the performance spectrum will often disengage when unable to connect material to their own lives.

Additionally, blind-faith addiction to textbook use without winnowing material based on importance and student needs obscures more essential material in a blizzard of less relevant facts, vocabulary, concepts, exercises, and trivialities. Within textbooks or during lectures, unnecessary embellishments, referred to as elaborations, can undermine learning because they "often divert attention away from the crucial point of a lesson," and such interference with students' focus "can be detrimental" (Dempster 1993, 434; Bransford, Stein et al. 1982). Unnecessary elaborations are like background noise. When there is too much of such clamor, it is nearly impossible for students to "hear" what is most important.

It is one thing to recreationally learn relatively unimportant information for a quiz show appearance. It is quite another for teachers to ignore limits on time and intellectual focus to force-feed students material having little or no value in the grander scheme of things. Doing so is a prescription for student misbehavior, lethargy, and failure. As has often been said, are we preparing students to be stars on *Jeopardy* or to be stars in their own lives?

As with other curricular decisions, the most effective teachers select material from textbooks using the filters of state requirements, real-world importance, and value for kids. Ignoring the instructional compass these filters provide and the "importance" imperative in motivational theory, teachers are asking for trouble. The result of this motivation-sapping disconnect with reality is boredom, disengagement, and discipline problems.

Although these difficulties are widespread and seemingly intractable, their solution, well understood by master teachers, is surprisingly simple. To the greatest extent possible, instructors must refine curricular choice through the lens of what is imperative for students to know and be able to do. The essential question at the forefront of every curricular decision should always be "Do students really *need* to know this?" It is not important enough simply to be busy. It is only important enough to be busy concerning what really matters.

By creating learning opportunities congruent with challenges outside of the classroom, the importance of "what matters" activities should be self-evident. Even if youngsters don't immediately grasp the real-world value of these "authentic" tasks, they should be enlightened as to how their learning is related to their lives outside of the classroom. Simply because this connection *should* be obvious doesn't make it so.

Only the most academically driven students learn what seems irrelevant to their lives. Thus, by explaining to students why products and performances such as mathematics projects, research papers, science investigations, oral presentations, musical compositions, and artistic exhibits, although more difficult than traditional pen-and-paper tests, will benefit them long after graduation, the case for WIFM will be made. But even if relevancy of instruction is not in and of itself enough of a reason to teach "authentically," there is another reason to do so having nothing to do with student meaningfulness or real-world application.

In a study of more than 1,500 elementary, middle, and high schools in the United States, researchers at the University of Wisconsin-Madison found that students engaging in high-level understanding and application of information to the world beyond the classroom, that is, "authentic instruction," outscored their peers on *traditional* assessments (Danielson 2002).

PERFORMANCE ASSESSMENT

The intersection of instructional activities that are doable, important, and fun is the assignment of student tasks simulating real-world challenges. "Used successfully as the predominant form of assessment in much of the world" (Baron 1990, 128), performance assessment enables students to apply their learning in creating products and/or performances as evidence that they have acquired whatever skills have been taught. Far different than the thinking typically required of all but a small minority of U.S. pupils, "high school students in most European countries complete extended essay examinations, often coupled with oral examinations, in a range of subjects requiring serious critical thought" (Darling-Hammond 1993, 23).

The value of student exposure to such thoughtful assessment is considerable. In constructing knowledge by seeking solutions to open-ended and relevant problems rather than more passively encountering it, students are more likely to see the value of what is taught and be actively engaged. Well understood by master teachers, an authentic curriculum "accepts the premise that interesting instruction and well-constructed learning tasks will evoke questions from students, tap natural curiosity, and spark personal energy for future inquiry" (Presseisen 1992, 9).

Mirroring America's instant gratification culture, U.S. educators are almost alone in the world in using and abusing fill-in-the-blank, true-false, and multiple-choice assessments. Whereas the reality outside of American schools increasingly values problem-solving creativity, time stands still in many U.S. classrooms valuing the rigidity of single-right-answer examinations.

But in failing to understand that such a black-and-white instructional dichotomy hardly prepares the next generation for the complex challenges they will ultimately face, American students continue to be graded on memorizing large amounts of discrete bits of "inert" knowledge, much of which they will unlikely ever use. It is not that cultural or discipline-specific literacy ensured by a secure foundation of essential knowledge is without value. But in too often focusing on endless facts of questionable importance, students are woefully unprepared to answer the more open-ended questions of importance yet to come.

Because authentic performance tasks replicate challenges people face in the real world, they are in and of themselves likely to be viewed as "important," and "when students feel they are doing important work, they are more likely to buy in than not" (Wasserstein 1995, 41). Moreover, because performance targets are typically accompanied by rubrics to rate students' work and models exhibiting the rubrics in tangible form, there is little or no student guesswork as to teacher expectations. And, because students, as in the real world, are given the opportunity to modify and improve their work, performance assessments are eminently "doable." Finally, because performance tasks enable students to create original work and to solve problems having no single right answer, they inspire learner interest, thought, and "fun" far more than a seemingly endless diet of monotonal lectures and mindless worksheets.

Beyond the motivating value of performance assessment, students learn best experientially. If you want to learn to swim, you have to jump into water. If you want to learn to do crossword puzzles, you have to spend long hours staring at the Sunday paper with a dictionary at the ready thinking about 34 down and 19 across. If you want to learn to use a computer, you have to sit in front of a keyboard "fooling around," muttering barely audible oaths while complaining about technology making life "easier" and eventually finding your way. And if students want or at least need to learn to write research papers, speak persuasively, work cooperatively, or sit for a job interview, the link between doing and learning is equally undeniable. Centuries ago a Chinese proverb made the case for performance assessment far more succinctly: "I hear and I forget; I see and I remember; I do and I understand."

If the ubiquitous "Learning Pyramid" claims that the average retention rate for reading is 10 percent, for hearing is 20 percent, and for doing is 75 percent are even close to being accurate, the question needs to be asked why instruction continues to be conducted primarily in a relatively passive manner. Is it a lack of instructor awareness of performance assessment's value? Is it teacher insistence on replicating their own inauthentic learning experiences when they were students? Is it simply an unwillingness to accept the labor-intensive act of creating meaningful and compelling real-world learning activities for their students? Or is it the relative difficulty in reliably grading authentic tasks compared to fill-in-the-blank tests?

However, if this last objection is indeed the primary justification for the relative lack of performance tasks in American schools, such opposition speaks volumes about the instructional focus of many U.S. educators. For in not realizing that the closer an assignment is to reality *the more difficult it will be to grade*, teacher insistence on multiple-choice and fill-in-the-blank assessments is indisputably also an insistence on preparing students for a world that outside their classroom rarely exists. Evaluating the quality of performance assessment tasks *is* relatively "messy." But then again, so is life.

Yet whatever the reason for the passive instructional approach so commonly found in U.S. schools, American teachers should be among the last to doubt that participatory learning is an extremely powerful method to acquire competence in real-world skills. Above all, in becoming instructionally effective only after countless hours teaching students, educators should realize this. Equally so, educators should also realize that unless pupils are offered more opportunities to learn by doing, schools, as Ted Sizer once said, will continue to be "places where students come to watch teachers work" (Caulfield and Jennings 2002, 35).

While the variety of performance tasks is limited only by a teacher's imagination, some of the more commonly assigned instructionally authentic products and performances include:

1. Persuasive essay/speech
2. Newspaper editorial
3. Job interview
4. Résumé/cover letter
5. Product advertisement
6. Movie or book review
7. Scientific experiment
8. Children's book
9. Oral history
10. Invention
11. Research paper
12. Movie poster
13. Poem
14. Musical composition
15. Photographic or artistic exhibit
16. Play or television script
17. Short story
18. Travel brochure
19. Music video
20. Letter to the editor

DIFFERENTIATING INSTRUCTION

While requiring students to create authentic products and performances is an essential element in motivating students, it also is an effective method of differentiating instruction. In assigning real-world tasks to students, it matters not where students academically start the term, it only matters where they end up. Supporting each student's personal journey in moving along a learning continuum ever closer to a criterion-referenced standard of performance excellence is all that matters. Thus, in making steady progress toward that goal, students seeking improvement over past results compete more against themselves than against each other.

Assigning the creation of authentic products and performances is just one relatively simple strategy to differentiate instruction and thus satisfy the doability *and* importance requirements for student motivation. Accordingly, in maximizing the capacity of every learner, it is essential for teachers to move gradually in that direction by tailoring instruction to the needs of their pupils. However for many students, if such progress occurs at all, it will be far too little and arrive too late. For despite research, morality, and common sense to the contrary, too many teachers will continue to confine instruction to the middle of their classes. This, of course, results in apathy-guaranteeing redundancy for some students and frustrating failure for others.

Great coaches or great teachers never achieve greatness for themselves or for their teams by expecting their charges to perform in ways they are incapable of performing. A one-size-fits-all force-feeding of round pegs into square holes is no more successful on gridirons or diamonds than it is in classrooms. Just as great coaches put their athletes in optimal positions to win, great teachers put their students in equally optimal positions to learn. However, doing so requires at least some efforts to differentiate instruction.

In addition to the assignment of real-world learning opportunities, master teachers meet the diverse learning needs of their students by tapping into their passions. This is readily achieved by giving them as much choice as possible in selecting topics for essays, research papers, and for oral presentations. Allowing students to select to answer particular questions on exams out of a larger list of possibilities achieves much the same end. And as previously mentioned, manipulating verb stems during student questioning is also a simple yet effective way to differentiate the learning process.

Finally, it requires almost no effort for teachers to accumulate texts and other supplementary instructional materials at a variety of ability levels. In addition to the "standard" classroom books available to every student, there is no reason not to order a few advanced copies for more able learners doing independent study and meaningful extra-credit assignments and a handful of simpler materials for struggling students. And though differentiating instruction supporting student doability and importance is no cure-all, when combined with the third element in the motivational triad of "fun," all but the most indifferent of students should self-servingly be intrinsically motivated to learn.

TASK ENJOYMENT

Arguably not as essential to student motivation as doability and importance, adding the element of fun to one's instructional practice may, however, be the crucial difference in motivating hitherto "unreachable" youngsters. Inasmuch as many students find school boring, and that it is difficult if not impossible for uninspired students to do high-quality work, anything a teacher can do to make meaningful learning more enjoyable is worth doing. In continuing the brain-based instructional theme of linking mood and cognition, highly effective teachers recognize that while "fun is the genetic reward for learning" (Rhodes 2003, 38; Glasser 1998), the reverse is equally so. Not only does pleasure result from learning; it inspires it. Thus, when tasks are fun, students are more motivated to learn, and the more they are motivated and successful in learning, the more pleasure they will experience.

Accordingly, allowing students personal choice for products and performances, adding instructional variety within each class, mentioning interesting "inside information" related to the lesson, asking open-ended questions, infusing humor in the classroom, adapting tasks to students' interests, and providing students opportunities to participate with their peers are all relatively easy ways to motivate students by making learning more enjoyable.

Because the human brain craves social interaction, well-designed group activities may elicit the most classroom fun of all. But promoting learning by increasing student motivation is only part of their instructional benefit. Working together stimulates student emotional responses which when linked to what is being learned makes the new material more memorable and rememberable. The more intense the emotional state, the more likely it will be remembered. To that end, activities such as cooperative learning evoking emotions such as excitement, pleasure, or urgency are effective instructional strategies (LeDoux 1996).

COOPERATIVE LEARNING

In a world where it is difficult to gain universal agreement that the Earth is round or that the Holocaust was real, it is nearly impossible to find research or educational experts questioning the value of cooperative instruction. Accordingly, there is little doubt that "organizing students in cooperative learning groups has a powerful effect on learning" (Marzano, Pickering, and Pollock 2001, 87). To that end, research studies have consistently shown that students teaching each other in cooperative groups or teams increases both motivation and achievement (Aronson, Zimmerman, and Carlos 1998) and "increases retention by as much as 400 percent" (Glenn 2002, 30).

Neither claimed as an educational panacea nor that every group activity is equally valuable, widespread agreement exists that cooperatively learning benefits students both immediately and in the future. Man is a social animal with both competitive and cooperative elements to his nature. As such, it is pedagogically counterproductive to isolate students and fail to harness these inherent energies in the service of educational and associational betterment. For teachers, the choice is thus not whether to incorporate what is "one of the most thoroughly researched of all instructional methods" (Slavin 1989–1990, 52), but how.

Teachers insisting that cooperative learning "doesn't work" or that it is nothing more than "glorified group work" have neither taken the time nor made the effort to research the strategy. Simply put, if cooperative learning is to be successful it must include the following three components:

1. *Individual Accountability.* Activities should be structured so that students must demonstrate learning independent of their group. Without requiring team members to perform on their own, there is a great likelihood that some students will inevitably piggyback off the work of their classmates and will neither make an effort nor exhibit competence in the task the activity is designed to promote. The most obvious way to structure individual accountability is to require each member of the team to be responsible for a unique product, presentation, or test that will be graded separately from any group assessment.

2. *Positive Interdependence.* If cooperative learning is to work, the success of the group must be strongly linked to the success of all of its members. Similar to the "all for one and one for all" dynamic in team sports, the group gains the greatest benefit when all members succeed. In this way, the learning of every group member is important to all group members. And just as in team athletics, the desire not to let teammates down is a strong motivation spurring individual achievement. However, when a team can succeed even if some of its members do poorly or do little by "riding the coattails" of teammates, positive interdependence is compromised.

   Positive interdependence is often fostered through the manipulation of grading designs. Computing the grades of individually taken assessments to arrive at a group average or requiring each member of the team to at least reach a benchmark score when linked to team rewards are two common approaches promoting positive interdependence.

3. *Team Rewards.* Although commonly done, group grades factored into individual student averages are *never* justified. It is ethically wrong for any student participating in a cooperative exercise to be penalized for another student's poor performance. Conventional wisdom notwithstanding, it is not the job of any student under the threat of a poor grade to directly "inspire" other students to do quality work. Indeed, if teachers wanted to undermine the value of cooperative learning and to create student and parent discord over the approach, there are few better ways to do so than to lower one student's grade for another's lack of effort, ability, or results. Further, how does lowering one student's grade for another's unsatisfactory outcomes reinforce the concept that students should accept responsibility for their own actions?

   Accordingly, team rewards should be limited to extra credit or privileges such as "free homework" passes. The assessment impact of a cooperative learning activity should only be to benefit students if the group succeeds or grade neutral if it doesn't. Failing to heed this advice will surely diminish the impact of this instructional strategy, which is considerable.

One only has to be a participant in or witness a team-oriented athletic event to understand the power available when humans interact in an environment both cooperative and competitive. Because team sports create a social and motivational milieu expecting and assisting maximum effort, enhanced achievement fueled by cooperative exhilaration is often the result. And what is true on athletic fields is no less so in classrooms.

The research is clear that under certain well-documented conditions, cooperative learning not only promotes scholarly achievement but prosocial behavior as well. This symbiotic marriage of intellectual and moral growth occurs not through any specific value-laden academic content but through the cooperative instructional process itself. Common sense, anecdotal observation, and numerous studies support the existence of this positive relationship.

Through attachment to a group, children learn to value others and to feel identification with and loyalty toward something larger than themselves. Whatever the superficial differences among group members, students report a greater willingness to like others as well as a greater likelihood to be liked by others. If the goal of public education is indeed to prepare students to participate in and contribute to a diverse democratic society after graduation, and if virtually everything one does in the real world involves working with other people (Gladwell 2009), what better way to realize that goal then to regularly give youngsters experience in group cooperation and decision making?

Additionally, because many if not most workplace difficulties result not from a lack of basic skills, technical competence, or low IQ scores but from poor work attitudes, poor interpersonal skills, and from inappropriate behaviors, the ability to get along with others is the linchpin in one's employability, productivity, and career success. As importantly, because such an ability is also directly related to building positive relationships and to maintaining emotional health, the entire quality of adult life is dependent upon social skills that children are not born with. Like "reading, writing, and arithmetic," acceptable behavior on athletic fields, the school bus, the cafeteria, or in the classroom must be taught.

Realizing this, can any teacher seriously insist they have no time to *at least monthly* offer a well-designed cooperative learning activity? And if nothing else, perhaps recognizing that such an offering is a win-win instructional strategy will convince them to. For in creating enjoyable activities for their students, teachers are doing the same for themselves. After all, if the classroom is a more pleasant place for students, can't the same be said for their teachers?

INTRINSIC VERSUS EXTRINSIC MOTIVATION

Once the factors of doability, importance, and fun are in place, intrinsic motivation is likely to follow. However, improving academic performance through extrinsic reinforcers such as prizes, privileges, or even good grades for many students, while influencing short-term behavior, the research is "overwhelmingly convincing that [they] do not have a positive long-term effect" (Wilson and Corpus 2001, 57; Johnson 1999; McCullers, Fabes, and Moran 1987). In fact, because in several studies students exhibited decreased motivation after attaining rewards, there is some evidence that other than instructor recognition, extrinsic motivators may produce negative effects (Wilson and Corpus 2001; Carter 1996; Simons, Dewitte, and Lens 2000).

Foremost among these negative effects is the undermining of students' interest in learning by focusing attention on the reward and by implying that the task is not inherently worthwhile (Kohn 1993). For many if not most students, personal interest and not interest in external factors is the more potent gateway to learning.

It's not that extrinsic motivators are powerless to spur student effort. Indeed, some learners, especially academically high performers, respond to little other than good grades. However, for many indifferent and struggling students that is often not the case. For them, the "coin of the realm" convincing them to buy what the teacher is selling is often instructor praise and even more often the "what's in it for me" belief that what is offered is compelling and will benefit them.

What seems clear is that regardless of how motivation is measured, teacher reinforcements such as positive feedback and recognition for a job well done are far more effective in positively altering student attitudes and behaviors than many other common forms of extrinsic motivation (Marzano, Pickering, and Pollock 2001; Cameron and Pierce 1994). And when combined with the intrinsically powerful factors of doability, importance, and fun, most students most of the time will likely be motivated to invest effort in achieving academically positive outcomes.

Just as a meaningful instructional program engagingly delivered diminishes discipline problems, the same can be said for diminishing problems of student apathy. And if offering a curriculum that is important, doable, and at least somewhat enjoyable almost certainly reduces student misbehavior and increases achievement, it is difficult to understand any educationally sound reluctance to do so.

Practice Thirteen

Partnering with Parents

A school system without parents at its foundation is just like a bucket with a hole in it. —Jesse Jackson

In addition to being expert in instructional delivery, highly effective teachers are equally expert in gauging the social and academic development of students and in conveying such insight to parents. Observing large numbers of students over long periods of time, master teachers embody the best practices of partnering with parents in speaking authoritatively as to the progress of their children individually and relative to grade-level norms.

Parents need to know if their child is showing social and academic growth from the beginning of the term and whether that growth places them at, above, or below what is typical for a child of that age. Because few parents have unbiased knowledge of how their son or daughter compares to grade-equivalent children, they often have distorted expectations of their child's relative level of ability. This may well lead to unreasonable demands for a struggling youngster or a laissez-faire approach to a child who could be performing far more proficiently.

The most effective teachers well understand that in order for parents to understand what reasonable behavioral and academic expectations for their child are, they first must know what is typical for a youngster in the same age cohort. Without this context, parents may well view an average child as gifted or a capable youngster as needing additional services. Only an observant and highly effective instructor can convey that reference to parents both orally and through examples of their child's work, reflecting progress in comparison to grade-level rubrics and exemplars.

Moreover, because teachers necessarily define fairness as equality of attention and standards, they may well come into conflict with parents viewing "fairness" through the egocentric lens of special considerations for their child (Lawrence-Lightfoot 2004). These differing perspectives may lead to an atmosphere of distrust and misunderstanding, shattering the parent-teacher alliance essential for the best interests of the child. Realizing this, and that parents bring their hopes, their fears, and their own histories about school, both good and bad, in meeting their child's teachers, conferences should convey not only essential information but also should transpire in a sensitive, confidential, and respectful manner.

PARENT CONFERENCE ESSENTIALS

A conference with a master teacher includes far more than a cursory review of an already completed and shared report card or even an understandable explanation of standardized test scores. It also includes a discussion of a child's strengths and weaknesses with respect to the master teacher's Practice One "real-world" curricular vision. That is, how is the child performing in the academic and social skills necessary for success beyond the classroom? At the least, those skills include reading, writing, speaking, listening, participating, cooperating, and interacting with peers and adults.

Since goals drive behaviors, master teachers provide parents personalized learning objectives for their child. These academic targets include specific suggestions as to what parents should do in support of those *expectations* as active participants in their child's education. To that end, elite educators use the pronoun *we* early and often to describe this school-home partnership. Whereas educators do not have the right to ask parents to be the sole teachers of their children, they do have the right and responsibility to ask them to be partners in the learning process.

To that end, the instructor mantra to parents should be "We can't educate your children alone, and you can't either." That said, "With parent contributions to the educational program, whether through knowledge, skills, or in-person support and participation, parent and teacher responsibilities blur and the student feels a cocoon of support" (Caulfield and Jennings 2002, 16).

Once a conference is held, master teachers, mindful that plans made or suggestions offered are often forgotten, make a record of the meeting. Focusing on conclusions reached, a copy of this summary is sent to parents as an official documentation of the conference, as an accountability tool to measure changes in their child's behavior, and as a way for parents and the teacher to recall what was consented to should a disagreement later occur (Stevens and Tollafield 2003).

PARENT CONFERENCES: OTHER CONSIDERATIONS

In any effective association, the cornerstones must be trust and communication. To that end, should parents have any concerns regarding instruction, curriculum, or their child's progress, they should be encouraged to contact the teacher by phone or email *before* contacting the administration. Doing so enables the educator most knowledgeable about and directly involved with the concern to discuss the issue with the parent.

In welcoming and reinforcing such contact, highly effective instructors *indirectly* mention to disgruntled parents the potential harm of bad-mouthing teachers or the school in the presence of their children. Obviously, the best way to make this point is by expressing the academic value of a united home-school front, whatever differences initially appear to be. Parents need to know that *even if school or teacher criticism is justified,* a wedge driven between the home and school will undermine their child's sense of responsibility without which a reduction in effort is almost sure to follow. In virtually all cases, and unless the parents have unimpeachable evidence suggesting otherwise, the home and school *must* stand together.

In meeting with parents, highly effective teachers stay professional at all times. As obvious as this sounds, when an aggressive and misinformed parent goes on the attack it is easy for a conference to escalate into conflict. As a result, follow-up discussions with the administration or the community will often be far more about the instructor's lack of professionalism and control than about the parent's misguided and boorish behavior. That said, allowing a meeting with parents to degenerate into a heated exchange will move the focus of the conference from where it should be, the child, to a defensive and counterproductive attempt to protect adult egos.

Even if based on unfair criticism, should a parent conference move in the direction of a heated exchange, master teachers stay in control, never add "fuel to the fire," and always encourage parents to share their concerns. Once doing so, parents should have no doubt that those concerns have been heard and understood. And if necessary, highly effective teachers have no problem saying to unhappy parents that "I regret that you feel as you do" or that "I am sorry for this situation."

Such statements will almost certainly calm an irate mother or father while not necessarily admitting to or agreeing with personal culpability. And ironically, both responses are undoubtedly true. For in wasting valuable time in baseless accusations, and in moving discussion away from the child, is it a falsehood for an educator to regret that a parent "feels as they do" or is "sorry" that an unpleasant and time-consuming "situation" has occurred?

If during a parent conference or a school open house a question is raised "out of left field," the most effective teachers will praise the parent for their good or interesting point but will avoid a quick answer that may later be regretted. There is nothing wrong with adopting a thoughtful stance in telling the parent that more time will be needed to consider their question and a response will be forthcoming. Moreover, if a parent makes a comment that is disagreed with during an open house, a master teacher will skillfully sidestep a heated debate by stating the reasons for disagreement and offer an invitation for additional discussion at another time.

To further strengthen the home-school connection, initial meetings with parents should include a positive anecdote about their child. Describing a positive quality or talent to parents sends a powerful message that the teacher is concerned for the child as both a student and as a person. If possible and appropriate, communications with parents should always begin on a positive note.

Such an expression of care cannot help but put parents of even unsuccessful students at ease. Parents feeling at ease are far more likely to listen and trust the person stimulating that nonconfrontational frame of mind. After all, what parent doesn't want to hear something positive about their child if it is genuinely expressed? And if "out of the blue" a teacher calls a parent with good news, as a follow-up to a conference, or sends a positive note home, all the better. Doing so often preempts or diminishes later problems should they occur.

OFFERING PARENTING ADVICE

Finally, should parents express an interest or openness as to what they can do at home to help their child, master teachers are more than competent at providing research-based suggestions. And because "cooperative efforts by parents and educators to modify . . . academic conditions in the home have strong, beneficial effects on learning" (Walberg 1984, 25), elite educators are more than willing to do so.

However, because any teacher seemingly judging someone's parenting should do so only at their peril, advice concerning the "curriculum of the home" should be offered only in the most supportive manner and only if parents are receptive to such guidance. *When offering any advisement, master teachers avoid condescending and overly directive "You should . . ." suggestions.* Rather, by "offhandedly" prefacing *any* recommendations with "I'm sure you know that . . ." or "Effective parents are *of course* mindful of . . ." finesse, a coequal parent-teacher partnership is promoted and reflexive defensiveness becomes an equally reflexive willingness to accept such counsel.

If indeed parents are open to advice, recommendations might include setting aside a regular time for homework, doing the same for bedtime, emphasizing the importance of reading by modeling it every day, ensuring good attendance, and holding high behavioral and academic expectations. Additionally, parents should also discuss school and everyday events with their child and should monitor and jointly evaluate television viewing. And even more importantly, parents should prepare their children for productive and successful lives in part by accepting responsibility for their actions and by encouraging the practice of deferring immediate gratification to accomplish long-term goals (Walberg 1984).

Once master teachers help parents understand realistic achievement levels for their child, it is then up to the parents to expect their child to consistently reach those levels. Indeed, the academic aspirations communicated by parents to their children or even the students' perceptions of those aspirations are strongly linked to enhanced achievement (Marzano 2003). And in reinforcing those expectations, elite educators, with the support of parents, may offer what is arguably the most important guidance of all.

As experts in childhood behavior, effective teachers recognize that the consequences of an action determine the future probability of that action. That is, conduct that is rewarded tends to be repeated, while conduct that is punished or ignored is at least in the short-term less likely to reoccur. This seemingly obvious "law of effect" when combined with a keen awareness of a child's abilities is a potent tool for parents and for teachers in affecting a youngster's career path and future success.

Virtually everything a parent does influences how a child ultimately experiences the world. Thus in a sense, the child is a "tabula rasa" or blank slate that parental actions write on. And even more importantly is the realization that the impact of those actions both good and bad are unlikely ever to be completely undone. This is so because in whatever way a child initially views himself and others, desire for predictability leads to ignoring, distorting, or rationalizing events challenging those perceptions.

As a result, however parents "label" their children regarding their worth and the worth of others continues as a self-perpetuating "window on the world" logic ultimately dictating how the child thinks, feels, acts, and relates. In large measure, children will become whatever their labels tell them they are. To that end, when appropriate, parents should characterize their children with positive attributions or descriptors such as "You are smart" or "You are a good person" much as highly effective teachers do if legitimately earned later in life.

Additionally, in an increasingly diverse world it is just as important to label young children as "tolerant" as it is for parents to aggressively model that behavior. As youngsters imitate the behaviors of their parents and others in their social network, beliefs and attitudes including prejudice are passed from one generation to another as "mind viruses" (Dyer 2009) spreading to uninfected, impressionable, and youthful hosts. Thus, for purely moral reasons, the modeled acceptance of people who may seem different than oneself is an effective inoculation against the spread of discriminatory behavior. But there are other more self-serving reasons to view differences among people in the best possible light.

Not only is the internalization of anger, fear, and hatred associated with bias emotionally and physically unhealthy, but since the principle of reciprocity dictates people often attract in others not what they want but what they are (Dyer 2009), harboring such toxic behaviors invites correspondingly negative behavior in others including friends, colleagues, and family members. Because people respond similarly to their own treatment, low opinions directed outwardly are as postageless mail often returned to sender. Thus mindful of this "you get what you give" behavioral dynamic, effective parents know better than to accept, justify, or model intolerance with "my child is too young for it to matter" rationalizations.

In contrast, praising and nurturing a child's positive conduct or talents encourages those actions and proficiencies to more fully express themselves. As a behavioral trampoline, such recognition fuels effort and elevates such inclinations far beyond their level if otherwise ignored or unnoticed. Yet such "crystallizing experiences" providing the confidence necessary for adult achievements are too often overlooked. Worse still, such positive learning opportunities may be squandered by "paralyzing experiences" in which childhood gifts are hastily judged, ignored, or actively discouraged through criticism or even punishment. Doing so will virtually guarantee those endowments will "wither on the vine" as never fully expressed what-could-have-beens.

If as Edison suggested, many of life's failures are people "who did not realize how close they were to success when they gave up," effective parents and instructors by supporting and thereby amplifying gifts already existent in children are stacking the deck that those youngsters will not increase that number.

Master teachers also realize that even if parents do not overtly derail their child's self-actualization journey with negative behaviors, they may unknowingly *imply* messages leading to that same result. To that end, academic and behavioral problems for students may have as much to do with "read between the lines" parental messages as what they directly say and do. Parents as well as teachers need to know that what they "merely" insinuate, verbally and otherwise, is often as powerful as what is stated word-for-word. And if what is consistently suggested is growth inhibiting, a child's "lights," having become extinguished, may never again be lit.

A mother or father continually ignoring a child's accomplishments may well be sending the unspoken message "Don't succeed." Parents regularly rejecting a child's suggestions with "Who do you think you are?" annoyance may covertly be telling a child "Don't think." A youngster raised in a household where discipline is erratic or overly punitive may internalize such actions as "Don't trust." Effective parents not only avoid such potential-stifling behaviors but also *actively seek* opportunities reinforcing their children to succeed, think, and trust. To that end, parents should be encouraged to recognize their child's successes, to patiently listen to their child's thoughts, and to practice fair and consistent discipline. *And such behaviors essential for parents are no less crucial for teachers.*

Elite instructors recognize that highly effective students internalize a positive vision of their future supported by a strong sense of responsibility. These characteristics are essential to success. For without personal responsibility, effort is undermined in blaming others for failures. Moreover, without a positive vision driving behaviors, negative temptations can easily lead to negative actions. And as their child's most powerful teachers, parents need to assist their children in embracing these essential character traits.

It is almost never too early for effective parents to help children shape a mental and emotional picture for how life will positively unfold. Because everything is created in reality only after being created in one's mind (Covey 1989), planting the seed within a child that a specific ability could lead to a successful career or satisfying avocation encourages such outcomes. After all, isn't the end result of education to help children make sense of their lives as productive members of society? And if that is indeed so, "the greatest gift . . . a teacher can give a student, and a parent can give to their child is the opportunity to imagine great things" (Krzyzewski 2006, 94).

Collaboratively envisioning life as an author for a son skilled in writing, as an artist for a child talented in painting, or as a musician for a daughter attached to the family piano unquestionably furthers such ends. This is even more so when a child not only seems "gifted" in a certain pursuit but undeniably enjoys that pursuit as well. For as obvious as it sounds, if children don't love what they are doing, they "are unlikely to work hard enough to get very good at it" (Levitt and Dubner 2011, 61).

The same is true even when a child's talent is a more generalized ability for learning. When this proficiency is combined with a love of knowledge *and* parental support in foreseeing a successful academic future, gaining admission to a fine college, university, or technical school may well become a self-fulfilling ambition. At home, as in school, such positive goals drive positive behaviors, they reinforce one's sense of control, and they also help to safeguard children, especially teenage children, against goal-destroying temptations of short-term and often counterproductive adolescent pleasures.

Children are continually "brainwashed" into reflexively accepting parental views of the world and themselves. By positively doing so, parents can dramatically affect their child's future for the better. And there is no good reason for waiting to do so. For youngsters "taught" by parents that they are intellectually inadequate may as a self-fulfilling prophecy fall behind early in their schooling. Unquestionably, students slow to start often learn more slowly than students starting ahead who progress at a faster pace. Known as the Matthew effect, the academically rich get richer while the poor get poorer. Accordingly, parents need to know that what they do during the elementary school years and beyond has an enormous impact on their child's future success. To that end, a strong home-school partnership should neither be ignored nor understated.

Practice Fourteen

Internalizing Kaizen

He who stops being better stops being good. —Oliver Cromwell

Paradoxically, the penultimate practice of master teachers is not to directly focus on students, but on themselves. That is, in realizing that forward movement is impossible without saying yes to change, the best teachers are not only insatiable for high-level learner results but also for their own learning. Seeking an ever-closer approximation of ideal instruction, elite instructors embody the Japanese strategy of making small improvements day-after-day leading to short-term incremental change and over time to ever-greater excellence. In contrast to the unwillingness of lesser colleagues to grow, the DNA of master teachers directs otherwise. This continuous drive for self-improvement to not only exhibit "swing for the fences" excellence on a daily basis but to continually *move those fences further back* is expressed in the practice of kaizen.

Clichéd but true, elite educators well realize the more they learn, the more they confront their own ignorance. Consequently, a willingness to continually challenge past practices, a fearlessness to try new approaches, and an unyielding drive to face change-induced anxiety are all signature attributes of kaizen: the Practice Fourteen race without end of continuous improvement.

All people have blind spots in their behavior in rarely seeing themselves as they are viewed by the rest of the world. Undeniably so, this is as true for teachers as it is for anyone else. As such, feedback on instructional practice is an invaluable if somewhat threatening tool for self-improvement. Typically, observations are conducted by department chairs, by administrators, or by peer coaches. However, in a never-ending drive for betterment, master teachers fearlessly seek additional evaluations from a group knowing more about the daily quality of their instruction than anyone else. And that group is their students.

STUDENT EVALUATIONS

The truest measure of instructional quality is not a teacher's performance during an isolated and announced administrative observation. As for a blind date or the first days of a new job, few would argue that even uninspired and uninspiring educators on their best "the boss is looking" behavior summon a level of preparation and effort rarely if ever seen for their most important audience of all. In contrast, exposed to a teacher's daily efforts, older students as consumers of a teacher's instruction are in a unique position to more accurately identify an instructor's strengths and weaknesses. Yet even when pupil evaluations have no bearing on job standing, will only be seen by the teacher being evaluated, are for improvement purposes only, and are routinely conducted on behalf of many other consumers in the workplace, apprehensive instructors rationalize opposition to student appraisals.

At the least, those opposing student evaluations of teachers insist that students are not qualified to judge instructional quality, that teachers will dumb down their curriculums to ensure positive responses, and that disgruntled students will skew results by unfairly judging their instructors. However while commonly voiced, such arguments are far more rationalizations than reality.

Obviously, by regularly observing their teachers, students especially in high school are more than capable of judging the merit of their instructors. After all, who better would know what goes on in a classroom than those there every day? Moreover, if eighteen-year-olds can vote, can drive, and can fight for their country, isn't it absurd to claim that students fifteen years of age and older can't even judge the quality of schooling they've experienced since the age of five?

The view that student evaluations will lead to rampant grade inflation is equally ludicrous. Certainly, some instructors may lower their standards to positively impact student survey responses in a tacit exchange for good grades. However, to suggest that a majority of students will not recognize or anonymously report this "something for nothing" game is to undersell their honesty, their awareness, and their concern for a quality education. Feeling no obligation to make things easier for next year's students and recognizing that the class they were forced to endure was unfairly administered or a waste of time, there is little doubt that most students would eagerly voice that truthful sentiment.

Further, the position that student assessments of teachers will become little more than a forum for unhappy pupils to unjustly vent their frustrations is equally without merit. While true that students with an axe to grind are less-than-credible evaluators, a few negative comments for an otherwise effective teacher are hardly enough to offset an overall positive appraisal. Even if the questionnaires voluntarily or otherwise are shared with the central office, administrators are well aware that a few students will at times try to get even for a poor grade by sabotaging the evaluations. It is only when comments trend negatively similar over several consecutive terms is there serious cause for concern. And because it is impossible to change what isn't acknowledged, there is much to be gained by a teacher at least hearing such criticism.

In rationalizing discipline problems, parent complaints, and poor test results, it is not surprising that weak educators would oppose confronting student narratives of their own ineffectiveness. Doing so is a classic case of denial. Believing they are far more skilled than they really are and that classroom problems are always someone else's fault, such mediocre teachers also refuse a reality check from other sources. And nowhere is this refusal seen more clearly than during staff development activities.

STAFF DEVELOPMENT

Whereas master educators attend in-service presentations hoping *for even one idea* that with reflection might lead to improved pedagogy, weak instructors view staff development much as disruptive students view substitute teachers. With a negative and arrogant "You can't teach me anything" mind-set, inert and "retired-on-the-job" educators attend conferences doing crossword puzzles, reading newspapers, or grading papers, all the while complaining about the poor quality of a presentation they have neither heard nor valued from its opening minutes.

Incredibly so, this delusion-of-grandeur thinking even occurs if the presenter is a well-respected national figure, with a boatload of books written, conferences keynoted, and awards won. For some educators, such a résumé doesn't matter. For some educators, the so-called expert has no more instructionally to offer than a worthy-of-sympathy and uneducated indigent living in a cardboard box over a steam grate in the dead of winter.

If even the most self-assured and smug instructor would undeniably agree that there is always more to learn about the subject they teach, why then should it be any less so for the act of teaching itself? Why in the larger world do successful businesses, sports teams, politicians, and people in all professions willingly embrace an "adapt or die" mind-set, when mediocre instructors *won't even consider* accepting the conviction to "adapt and *improve*"? Why is staff development reflexively viewed as a not-so-thinly veiled criticism of teacher skill, effort, or effectiveness rather than as an opportunity to grow in a job that *by any standard* is exceptionally demanding and complex? And why then is in-service training defensively rejected by some instructors when if viewed positively would likely make such extremely challenging work more doable, more rewarding, and more fun?

Yet unwilling or unable to answer these questions, status quo instructors, even when feigning interest during staff development presentations, return to their classrooms, close their doors, and conduct business as usual.

While counterproductive, this reflexively negative reaction from mediocre teachers is however at least perversely understandable. For in order to protect the constancy of their instructional world, there is little choice but to criticize staff development. This is so because if viewed positively, there might be self-imposed pressure to question their instructional approaches and to improve their already "perfect" skills.

In hearing "out-of-touch" and "empty-suited" administrative pleas for continual improvement, status quo instructors deflect such requests as read-between-the-lines criticisms and as thoughtless directives demanding teachers to work harder rather than the primary intention of staff development presentations to work smarter. And even when an administrator's generalized comments imploring instructional growth *are* specifically aimed at underperforming teachers, they will likely go unheeded by "not me" educators insisting such remarks *must be* directed elsewhere.

Thus, rationalizing their inadequacies, mired in the inertia of excuse and mediocrity, deflecting threats to the way things have "always" been done, and antagonistic to anyone even suggesting change, these "protective" instructors return to their classrooms, and in referring to students they continue to state the no-growth party line of "It's my job to teach and their job to learn." Sadly, such myopic educators never once question how it is that this same requirement they so glibly demand from their pupils shouldn't be equally demanded from themselves. Understanding the hypocrisy of this "do as I say not as I do" mind-set, master teachers embody Practice Fourteen of also being among the best learners.

While all of the practices of master teachers are extremely important, three habits of mind are preeminent among equals. At the least, if all educators accepted full responsibility for the results of their instruction, if pedagogical decisions were based solely on the greatest benefit to students rather than on mediocre teachers avoiding difficulty for themselves, and if in practicing kaizen, instructors fearlessly considered new approaches with an open mind, schools would be transformed.

"HERE THERE BE DRAGONS"

Centuries ago, mapmakers inscribed "Here There Be Dragons" at the edge of the known world. An obstacle to many, this line of demarcation was an opportunity for a few. It was those courageous outliers facing both real and imagined dangers that made a difference and whose names we know today. In each of us resides a personal brave new world few dare to explore. Yet the best educators, in fearlessly crossing self-imposed "here there be dragons" perimeters, realize that it is virtually impossible to significantly move forward without enduring risk.

Indeed, realizing that since opportunity is inseparable from danger, the Chinese use the same ideograph for both words (Lipton 1976). Yet what the ancient Chinese knew, that risk and reward almost always come together, is foreign to the culture in many twenty-first century American schools. Sadly, those working in a career devoted to helping students progress are often reluctant to do so themselves. But as Madeline Hunter said, "If you want to be a true professional and continue to grow . . . go to the cutting edge of your competence." As their own worst critics, as perfectionistic almost to a fault, and as insatiable for their own learning and continuous improvement, master teachers are not only drawn to that cutting edge of their competence; they frequently remain there.

Yet in the only profession dedicated to making the world a better place for future generations, ineffective teachers refuse to even question their practice. They remain in a past where continuing to do what they have always done, they continue to get the results they have always gotten. Viewing change as only synonymous with risk rather than also with opportunity, many remain in a status-quo existence where students pass classes as much for attendance as for achievement and diplomas are routinely awarded as counterfeit evidence of real-world readiness.

While there can be honest debate about the essential practices of the most effective teachers, there can be little doubt that our schools are far less than they could be, that even on their worst day hero teachers are the best hope for many kids to improve their lives, and that it *is* possible to educate all children well.

Things change. The Titanic was "unsinkable," communism would "bury" capitalism, and less than a year before World War II, it was "peace in our time." Until relatively recently, home computers were a novelty, "made in Japan" was considered junk, faculty lounges were clouded in cigarette smoke, and the election of a black president was "an impossibility." Underperforming schools and underachieving students can also change.

However in word and deed, "It-can't-be-done" defeatism continues unabated from those too unknowing, too unwilling, or too well defended to admit their etched-in-granite predictions are built on sand. Yet "throw-in-the-towel" prophecies can become tomorrow's "laugh-out-loud" soothsaying failures if talented and fearless educators make it so. For now as in the past, the surest way to forecast the future is to make it.

The nation defeating fascism, putting a man on the moon, winning the Cold War, and that has won more Nobel Prizes than its four closest competitors *combined* can *at least equal* the educational system of Japan, of Germany, of Finland, or of any other nation. Because this is so, the only question that really matters is then not whether schooling can be improved but whether educators have the courage and the determination to accept no less. Until that happens, students will forfeit potential, our nation will remain at risk, and countless children will continue to be left behind waiting for Superman.

Beginnings

Come to the edge.
We might fall.
Come to the edge.
It's too high!
COME TO THE EDGE!
And they came,
And he pushed,
And they flew.
—Christopher Logue, "Come to the Edge"

Although it would have been more obvious to conclude this book with a statement of "Endings," such a label would have been a misnomer. For if the purpose of education is not in and of itself for students to do well in school but to do well in life, then these past pages were anything but an ending. For with the skillful implementation of dedicated teachers, these strategies were offered as first steps to foster a more positive future for the pupils whose lives they touch. To that end, "Beginnings" was an entirely appropriate way to conclude this volume of "those who can" pedagogical practices. But there is still another reason why "Beginnings" is a more-than-suitable title for this final chapter. And ironically, it involves one last strategy reserved for teachers of older children.

In teaching high school students and beyond, master instructors convey a Practice Fifteen sense of urgency inspiring those in their charge to positively envision, plan, and create their futures with fearless assertiveness. This final practice of challenging students to courageously pursue their dreams is surprisingly also a beginning. For whatever one's qualities, without courage as the starting point to do what is imagined, those traits may never begin to surface (Krzyzewski 2006). Or as Winston Churchill observed, courage is the "first of human qualities because it is the quality which guarantees all others."

Admittedly, for teenagers who yet see life as everlasting, instilling such existential boldness is easier said than done. Indeed, "How long will I be pushing up daisies?" is a rarely asked question spurring "be-all-you-can-be" choices when days seem forever. However, even for those in the spring of life, weeks and months can quickly hemorrhage away and accumulate into "where-did-the-years-go" regrets. And as a slight error in hitting a cue ball results in an ever-larger miscalculation as it travels the length of a pool table, the same is so for errors of commission or omission in one's immediate affairs. However, the good news is that the earlier course corrections are made, the smaller the effort to do so and the greater their cumulative effect.

In looking back on life, is it possible that fulfillment can result from other than striving to maximize one's capabilities? It is possible that contentment may not found by forging a successful career, making a creative or altruistic contribution to the world, or becoming self-sufficient? And is it possible for students to some day look back at the landscape of life and never ask whether the world has been better for their existence? Of course it's possible.

Perhaps Robert Louis Stevenson was wrong that becoming all we are capable of being "is the only end of life." Perhaps in considering that "the aim of life is self-development," Oscar Wilde was equally mistaken. And perhaps "be all you can be" is nothing more than an idealized and unreachable Madison Avenue slogan based on the existential psychobabble of a long-dead psychologist. For if so, and a meaningful life can be found elsewhere than a kaizen-inspired journey toward self-actualization, there is nothing wrong with that. However, for many high school students, betting that eventual regret will not follow from at least trying to realize one's potential is a dangerous and not easily reversible wager.

In reviewing their lives, people typically reach their final years questioning whether existence has been generally meaningful, productive, and successful. If believing that to be so, a person is better prepared to live their remaining years with a sense of accomplishment and relative peace. However, if looking back and seeing a personal history filled with lost opportunities, unrealized talents, and wasted years, many people believing it is too late to change are filled with self-condemnation and despair.

As a result, it is almost never too early for students to realize that failing to look ahead, seeking excuse rather than possibility, imposing arbitrary limits on potential, and engaging the game of life timidly not to lose rather than to win will likely result in unsatisfying outcomes. While existence passes by with all the subtlety of an onrushing locomotive, each day, each moment is yet another opportunity to begin anew the journey toward a more productive, enriching, and true-to-oneself future.

In counseling students to create a positively confident vision of their adult lives, master teachers encourage children who might otherwise lead unhappy and unproductive existences to continually reinvent themselves more positively. And even though change can be threatening, in the words of Eleanor Roosevelt, "You must do the thing that you think you cannot do."

The most effective students, and for that matter the most effective teachers, accept ultimate responsibility for the quality of their lives and have formulated an optimistic vision of the eventual path they will take. For young or old, these two character traits are essential cornerstones for a fulfilling and effective existence. For without personal responsibility, daily choice and its consequences are surrendered to forces seemingly beyond one's control. Accordingly, without a positive vision as a compass and counterweight for this lack of control, long-term and "doing the thing that you think you cannot do" goals are too often sacrificed for temporary and often destructive pleasures of the moment.

Elite educators are brutally honest with their older students. Clichéd, cynical, but only somewhat simplistic, their message to them is that many people don't really care if you're unhappy, and still others are *happy* that you're unhappy. And if that is not exactly an uncomfortable truth, what is undeniable is that in most instances few people are sincerely concerned with another's problems, miseries, or excuses.

With precious few exceptions, "Are you getting it done?" are often the only five words that matter. The truth is that if students don't "get it done" by rescuing themselves from an unsatisfying and unsatisfied life, no one will do it for them. Teachers *do* affect eternity. And by inspiring youngsters to positively shape their destinies by instilling such a "seize the day" mind-set, this most important learning of all leaves little doubt that in imploring students to author a more fulfilling life, the very best teachers are "getting it done" by ironically doing the same for themselves.

Reviewing the Essential Practices of Master Teachers

Repetition is the only form of permanence that nature can achieve. —George
Santayana

1. As the purpose of school is to prepare students for life, to the greatest extent possible curriculum should reflect that vision.
2. Curriculum choice is made through a series of "filters." The first is state and local requirements, the second is what students need to know and be able to do to be successful in the "real world," and the third is whatever is irrefutably "good for kids." Any concept, fact, activity, or assignment that cannot pass through these filters is mercilessly eliminated from the instructional program of master teachers.
3. Master teachers willingly relinquish a measure of instructional autonomy in supporting a whole-school curriculum. This agreed-upon program focuses the efforts of the entire faculty, administration, and community toward instruction on the same core essential skills, how those skills will be taught, and how they will be assessed.
4. Whatever their personal beliefs, once a schoolwide curriculum is agreed upon, master teachers support it to the best of their abilities.
5. At some levels, teaching is a performance. How instructors "sell" their lessons is as important as what they are trying to sell. Among other strategies, master teacher performances include:

   - Knowing one's "lines"
   - Enthusiasm and humor
   - Fostering effective note taking
   - Positively relating to students
   - Continuous movement
   - Promoting a positive classroom climate
   - Safeguarding instructional time
   - Dressing professionally

6. Holding students accountable for their actions, master teachers avoid disempowering them through academic and behavioral ena-

bling. In demanding and expecting high standards, elite educators refuse to:

- Grant inflated credit for substandard work
- Accept "forgotten" assignments without penalty
- Ignore disrespectful or disruptive behaviors
- Grade students on unchallenging assessments
- Allow chronic lateness without consequence
- Continually extend assignment deadlines
- Grant meaningless "extra credit" opportunities
- Overlook student inattention without comment

7. Taking full responsibility for instruction when students don't learn, master teachers don't look for scapegoats. They look in the mirror.

8. Realizing that thoughts largely control emotions and actions, master teachers regularly monitor "self-talk" resulting from thinking distortions. These irrational thought patterns evoking unpleasant emotions and negative classroom actions include:

- Awfulizing
- All-or-nothing thinking
- Overgeneralization
- Personalization
- Delusions of grandeur
- Selective perception

9. Identification as a master teacher has as much to do with engaging certain habits of mind and actions as it does with not engaging in others. In closely monitoring their personal and professional lives, elite educators rarely, if ever, exhibit the following academically counterproductive behaviors:

- Reaction formation
- Projection
- Rationalization
- Pointing fingers
- Jumping to conclusions
- "Rescuing" incompetents
- Ignoring details
- Reflexively conforming to group pressure
- Offering inadequate student feedback
- Collecting psychological "trading stamps"
- Contributing to problems, not solutions
- Seeing colleague recognition as a zero-sum game
- Justifying inadequacy

10. Understanding that effective instruction begins with a smoothly run classroom free from student misbehavior distractions, master teachers use the following disciplinary strategies:

    - "Withitness"
    - Remaining calm
    - Avoiding intimidation
    - Employing consistency and structure
    - Reframing
    - Monitoring irrational beliefs
    - Praising students
    - Using positive student descriptors
    - Creating an engaging and meaningful curriculum

11. Master teachers recognize that skillful questioning can greatly enhance student attention and learning. By changing the verb stem of their questions according to Bloom's *Taxonomy of Educational Objectives*, highly effective instructors trigger student thinking and set the level of cognition. Additionally, they use skillful questioning and pause several seconds before calling for student answers. Such "wait time" increases both the length and depth of student responses.

12. Because pupils tend to mirror the characteristics of their teachers, highly effective instructors model positive behaviors for their students. This "hidden curriculum" is a support for schoolwide character education efforts and is an even more essential foundation for children not receiving such instruction at home. At the least, master teachers model the following behaviors consistently exhibited by successful people in any field:

    - Punctuality
    - Self-control
    - Responsibility
    - Respect
    - Goal setting
    - Effort
    - Critical thinking

13. Realizing that the only variable leading to success or failure that can be fully controlled is how hard one works, elite instructors empower students to succeed by promoting the understanding that effort is the key to success. Yet many students in failing to grasp this connection between exertion and achievement continue to struggle. In believing that success is largely determined by luck or innate ability, factors beyond their control, there is little likelihood these underperforming youngsters will ever control their learning or their lives. Because of this, "effort belief," the concept

that without unyielding exertion there is little chance for success, is *explicitly* taught by master teachers. Students are continually reminded of the close connection between effort and achievement in instructional choices and in "teachable moments."

14. Perhaps unable to recite "chapter and verse" of motivational theory, master teachers naturally inspire student motivation through their instructional choices. With the backdrop of a supportive classroom environment as a motivational precondition, highly effective educators intuitively focus on the essential motivational elements of task doability and importance. Any assignment lacking *either* element will likely fail to motivate all but the most academically driven students. And only by adding the third motivational component of fun are the less-able and least-interested students likely to be regularly inspired to learn.

Task doability is promoted by distributed practice, rubrics, "cognitive maps," models of exemplary work, instructional "recipes," and connecting new learning to what students already know. Task importance is promoted by assigning work having real-world importance and in regularly sharing the academic rationale for those assignments with learners. Students obey the WIFM rule. The more they are convinced that assigned tasks are personally important, the harder they are likely to work.

At the least, moderately challenging real-world tasks include: research projects, persuasive essays, public speaking, creative writing, musical compositions, scientific experiments, mathematics investigations, and photographic and artistic exhibitions. Student fun can be fostered by giving learners a choice in project topics, cooperative learning activities, instructional variety, classroom humor, and asking students higher-level open-ended questions.

15. Master teachers embody the best practices of partnering with parents in speaking authoritatively as to the progress of students both individually and relative to grade norms. Any communication between parents and teachers conducted in a sensitive, confidential, and respectful manner should, whenever possible, begin on a positive note. And at the least, parents should be informed:

- how their child is performing in the academic and social skills necessary for success in school and in life beyond the classroom. The key focus of any parent-teacher conference should be progress. For if children are not making progress, by definition they are falling behind (Enoch 1995).
- how well their child is participating in and contributing toward group work. A student only successful when working alone may later have difficulties in real-world situations when working with others is necessary (Enoch 1995).

- how to support at home their child's personalized academic and social goals discussed and agreed to at parent-teacher conferences.
- how to *directly* contact their child's classroom teacher(s) in the event of a problem or question.

16. Master teachers focus nearly as much attention on their own learning as they do on the learning of their students. Rarely satisfied with their own performance, they are insatiable in striving for even greater improvement. Consequently, elite educators embody the Japanese philosophy of kaizen: relentlessly making small changes day-after-day leading to incremental growth and an ever-closer approximation of excellence. Accordingly, master teachers attend staff development presentations with an open mind *hoping for even one idea* resulting in improved pedagogy. Master teachers never say, "I am doing all I can do." *Nobody* is doing all they can do.

17. Arguably, the greatest gift master teachers can impart is to counsel older students to create a positively confident vision of their adult lives and a carpe diem sense of personal effort, responsibility, and urgency in transforming that vision into a reality.

And finally, the following is a review of not-so-random thoughts to consider:

- Of all the variables that can be controlled once a child enters school, more can be done to improve education by improving instructor skill than by any other single factor.
- With few if any exceptions, the quality of a school, a district, or a nation cannot surpass the quality of its teachers.
- Because classrooms are laboratories of human behavior, extensive research has irrefutably identified what instructional approaches have a degree of probability to positively affect student learning. High-quality instruction is not essentially mysterious, and as such, what the very best educators do to gain the very best student results is *not* some unknowable secret.
- Refusing to apply research-based educational methods has nothing to do with a lack of money or an innate lack of teacher ability and everything to do with a lack of instructional awareness, an insistence on "teaching is an art, not a science" rigid dichotomy, and/or an unwillingness by many to change what clearly isn't working.
- The purpose of K–12 education is not in and of itself for students to do well in school but for them to do well in life. To that end, it is impossible to justify wasting precious class time forcing students to mindlessly learn insignificant facts, to thoughtlessly complete word searches, or to robotically read and memorize largely irrelevant

material in a textbook when such activities clearly have little or nothing to do with real-world challenges.

- The easiest way to look at curriculum choice is as a series of filters. The first such filter is the state-mandated curriculum, the second is reality, and the third is whether the activity, information, or assignment is significantly and undeniably "good for kids." *Whatever concept, fact, assignment, or activity that cannot pass through these screens should not be taught.*

- Typically, schools lack a clearly articulated, locally conceived vision unifying all stakeholders into promoting agreed upon learning goals furthering student achievement. Realizing this, master teachers understand that unless they fearlessly stand for a preferred future that is that vision, their individual excellence will be diluted in a school where teachers routinely labor at cross purposes with each other.

- In schools where the only academic constant is inconsistency, the rationale for a focused schoolwide array of student products, performances, and assessments is clear. Important, complex, and durable learning can only be accomplished by repetitive instruction generating meaningful student products evaluated by uniform criteria from elementary through high school. Such vertical and horizontal curricular alignment is essential.

- In fact, if educators were trying to design an ineffective instructional approach, they could hardly do a better job than the disjointed curriculum common in most schools. Given this reality, the question shouldn't be why kids are underperforming, but why wouldn't they be?

- As unintended victims of disorganized and relatively unsubstantial curriculums, children become the collateral damage of faculty and administrative inaction to implement a more thoughtful, coherent, and essential program of learning experiences.

- The most effective educators well understand that only by relinquishing a measure of autonomy for the focused power of a schoolwide curriculum anchored on state mandates, reality, and the "good for kids" filter will essential learning for all students be more than an idealized fantasy found in mythical schools and in ivory-tower textbooks.

- Teaching is at least in part a performance art. As a result, how instructors "sell" lessons is as important as what they are trying to sell. With effective delivery lying at the heart of quality instruction, underperforming teachers offer uninspired and uninspiring lessons with "It's my job to teach, not to entertain" rationalizations. But they are wrong. Their job is to do both.

- There is little doubt that the energy level of a class is a reflection of the energy level of the instructor. As enthusiasm is contagious, so too is ennui. With few exceptions, students will substitute monotonal lectures for sleeping pills and will "caffeinate" off the energy from inspiring presentations.

- Discipline problems are directly proportional to an instructor's distance from students. A teacher planted behind a desk or mistaken for a statue in front of the room is not only asking for students to "tune out" but is asking for control problems as well.
- Classroom climate can easily be improved through teaching "performances" such as *projecting a concern and liking for all students* even when fatigued, irritated, otherwise preoccupied, and even if there is little personal affinity for a child.
- Student anxiety, fear of humiliation, and embarrassment sabotage learning. Whatever a teacher's academic degrees, years of experience, or even their instructional vision, without an emotionally positive and engaging environment, learning will be compromised.
- Recognizing that minutes are an extremely precious and absolutely finite instructional resource, master teachers begin instruction promptly, eliminate unassigned time, avoid unnecessary digressions, and constructively engage students until they leave the classroom.
- Anything a teacher does showing a concern for pupils as individuals aside from academics positively affects instruction. Indeed, for some students a teacher taking interest in their lives is essential to learning. This is so because such interest offers unspoken evidence that students are liked and that they are valued.
- Enabling students to "tune out" without comment or consequence, giving easy assessments requiring little effort, accepting "forgotten" assignments without penalty, and granting inflated credit for sloppy work all have a cumulatively harmful effect on academic performance. By not holding students accountable to high academic and behavioral standards, enabling educators are not empowering students "to be all they can be" but instead to do as little as possible and be whatever they can get away with.
- Students need to understand that even though without effort there is virtually no chance for success, in and of itself, exertion does not guarantee achievement. For older students, basing a grade even partially on effort thus diverts student focus from what really matters: the quality of their work. And in the real world, quality is all that matters.
- Mystery may be effective in Hitchcock movies, in romance, and in the works of Agatha Christie, but it *never* is effective in student assessment. Flying blind leads to only one outcome, and that is as true for students as it is for anyone else. Realizing this, master teachers design rubrics to guide student efforts on performance tasks.

- Well understood by highly effective teachers, rubrics, "recipes" for achieving quality work, and models exhibiting a tangible product of what "good" looks like create a win-win situation for instructors. For in providing ultimate clarity of what quality looks like and the steps necessary to achieve it, they foster student accountability by establishing unmistakable and understandable learning standards and an efficient process for reaching them. And when students are more successful, so are their teachers.
- Looking first at themselves rather than at their pupils, master teachers improve student results by focusing on what they can *always* control, their own actions. Whereas the weakest teachers claim excuses for virtually everything, the strongest educators claim excuses for virtually nothing.
- Instructor sense of personal mastery or efficacy has clearly been correlated with enhanced student learning. That is, teachers perceiving themselves as able to dramatically impact pupil achievement realize far better student results than those perceiving themselves as unable to do so.
- The "If students fail, I fail" mantra of elite educators is simple yet undeniably powerful. It is a self-fulfilling prophecy. Teachers who believe they can make a difference *do* make a difference. Instructor beliefs in their own effectiveness lead to positive beliefs about student potential, which lead to enhanced student achievement.
- Students perceived as less able are often viewed as less worthy of sincere praise, are less likely to be called on, and when they are called on are given less time to respond. Criticized more and demonstrably valued less, struggling students intuitively sense a teacher's lack of interest and belief in them. And they often respond in ways validating those perceptions.
- In the real world, what matters is not the inputs of what people do but their ultimate results. And ineffective teachers focusing primarily on their efforts while ignoring their outcomes, in not accepting such excuses from anyone else, would be among the first to agree.
- Teachers do what they do because of their perspectives on instruction, on children, on their roles as educators, and on themselves. To that end, an instructor's emotional health has a direct and significant impact on student learning. Unquestionably, the healthier a teacher is the greater their likelihood of connecting with students. And the stronger that connection the more learning will likely occur. As successful people do in any profession, highly effective teachers monitor their self-talk in order to establish and maintain healthy thought patterns.
- Dysfunctional and largely out-of-awareness thought patterns are not alone in undermining quality instruction. Unexamined actions protecting self-esteem by shielding teachers from unpleasant real-

ities also hinder optimal pedagogy. To that end, identification as a master teacher has as much to do with engaging in certain habits of mind *and* actions as it does with not engaging in others.

- While the strongest instructors assert discipline through curricular choice, instructional delivery, high standards, clearly articulated rules and procedures, and by demonstrating personal interest in their students, the best teachers also preemptively prevent potential problems from escalating into actual ones. This "eyes in the back of the head" keen awareness of, and immediate response to, *potentially* disruptive behavior is referred to as "withitness."

- "With it" instructors continually walk around the classroom exercising proximity control. Such teachers regularly scan the entire room, making eye contact with as many students as possible, and are acutely aware of any behavior that might become disruptive. "With it" teachers recognize early markers of student stress and preemptively deescalate potential problems before they become actual ones.

- Whatever other strategies a master teacher uses to assert classroom control, it never includes internalizing problems with a student on a personal level. Once an educator loses emotional objectivity, views a discipline issue as a personal affront, and becomes angry or hurt they are on their way to amplifying an unpleasant situation into something far worse.

- Realizing the counterproductive results associated with aversive or overly punitive conditioning, master teachers project calm, confidence, and to the greatest extent possible, nonjudgmental demeanors. Misbehaving students are given a choice to comply with the teacher's request or to accept the consequences. The options for behavior are clearly and unemotionally explained, and penalties for misdeeds, unless there are highly unusual mitigating circumstances, are always implemented.

- The best educators emotionally increase the distance from problem students through the process of "reframing." Rather than seeing problems with students as personal attacks, elite educators address disciplinary issues in an unemotional, businesslike, and matter-of-fact manner without becoming emotionally distraught and without personalizing the actions of difficult youngsters. Thoughtful teachers "reframe" disciplinary incidents by seeking explanations for student behavior that change the entire meaning and feeling tone of those events.

- In separating pupil conduct from pupil worth by reframing, destructive power struggles are avoided, the teacher models the essential skill of self-control, and the classroom's learning environment is safeguarded.

- Another discipline strategy used by master teachers is the use of positive descriptors in labeling students. By defining who and what a child is, attributions such as "You are smart" or "You are a good person" *when they are legitimately earned* act as self-fulfilling prophecies in making certain behaviors likely and others far less so. For in justifying those positive descriptors, students are intrinsically motivated to do the right thing not through fear but because they have come to believe that is who they are. When positive attributions are supported by *authentically earned* praise, it is a potent combination furthering strong discipline and a productive learning environment.

- Arguably, the most effective classroom management strategy is to preempt student problems through a meaningful curriculum engagingly delivered. Though not a guaranteed panacea, the overwhelming majority of students, if intrinsically motivated to pay attention because they enjoy class and feel it benefits them, are far less likely to be frustrated, aggressive, or disruptive.

- Master teachers well understand that questions posed to students are foremost among stimuli triggering thinking and in setting their level of cognition. That is, questioning levels mirror student thinking expected in the classroom. And because the characteristics of pupil responses are strongly related to the level of teacher questions, higher-level questions stimulate higher-level responses and lower-level questions predictably stimulate correspondingly less-complex replies. Master teachers routinely inspire in-depth thinking through discussion questions requiring students to consider their views in broader contexts, to clarify and evaluate their positions, to solve problems, and to make predictions.

- By categorizing questions into Bloom's *Taxonomy of Educational Objectives*, the seemingly daunting task of composing more thoughtful questions proves quite manageable by focusing on the verb stem that describes the question for the student.

- Despite the undeniable fact that parents should provide instruction in good character, the sad reality is that what should be and what is are often two very different things. In the absence of positive role models and character instruction in many homes, if teachers are to honor the Practice One vision of preparing students for success in life, it is essential to fill that vacuum by "modeling what matters."

- Without creating a positive moral and behavioral classroom climate through their daily actions, teacher admonitions to behave properly will ring hollow and fall on deaf ears as garden-variety examples of "do as I say, not as I do" doublespeak.

- The only variable leading to success or failure one can fully control is *effort*. Along with perseverance, it is regarded by educational researchers as a key attribute necessary for developing self-controlled, self-regulated learners. Accordingly, children need to learn that "all in" effort can largely compensate for a perceived lack of innate ability or "luck" and that with few exceptions success can only be gained through unyielding exertion.

- The message linking perseverance with success has neither been taught nor reinforced in many homes and schools. In realizing that many students have missed the connection between effort and outcome, the most effective instructors, by consistently modeling and promoting "effort belief," enable students to internalize the mindset that effort pays off even if they initially don't accept that connection.

- The indispensable precondition for student motivation is a supportive learning environment. In poorly managed classrooms where the only routine is chaos, where discipline is lacking, where bullying is ignored, and where students feel anxious, uninspired, or invisible, few children will be motivated to learn, whatever the quality of the curriculum.

- In order to persuade anyone to learn, or for that matter to do virtually anything else, the task must be *both* doable and important. If *either* factor is absent, little effort will be expended at best and no effort will be made at worst, *no matter how much of the other variable is present*. The reason for this is simple. If tasks are doable but perceived as unimportant, few people will spend much energy on such "trivial" pursuits. If assignments are important but not seen as doable, most people will give up rather than struggle with seemingly "impossible" undertakings.

- Arguably not as essential to student motivation as doability and importance, adding the element of fun to one's instructional practice may, however, be the crucial difference in motivating hitherto "unreachable" youngsters. Inasmuch as many students find school boring, and it is difficult if not impossible for uninspired students to do high-quality work, anything a teacher can do to make meaningful learning more enjoyable is worth doing.

- Parents need to know if their child is showing social and academic growth from the beginning of the term and whether that growth places them at, above, or below what is typical for a child of that age. Only an observant and highly effective instructor can convey that reference to parents.

- Master teachers provide parents personalized goals for their child. These objectives include specific suggestions as to what parents should do in support of those expectations as *active* participants in their child's education. Additionally, should parents express an interest or openness as to what they can do at home to help their child, master teachers are more than competent at providing suggestions.

- In realizing that forward movement is impossible without saying yes to change, the best teachers are not only insatiable for high-level-learner results but also for their own learning. Seeking an ever-closer approximation of ideal instruction, elite instructors embody the strategy of making small improvements day-after-day, leading to short-term incremental change and over time to ever-greater excellence. This continuous drive for self-improvement is expressed in the Japanese practice of kaizen. To that end, the best teachers are perhaps not so ironically also among the best learners.
- In teaching high school students and beyond, master instructors convey a sense of urgency for students to positively envision, plan, and create their futures with fearless but reflective assertiveness. As heroes of their own story, students are challenged to boldly follow their thoughtfully conceived dreams. For whatever talents a student possesses, without the courage to pursue what is imagined, the full potential of those abilities will neither be cultivated nor realized.

Appendix

The appendix contains five documents that may be useful as explanatory guides for a few of the schoolwide and classroom strategies well understood and often used by master teachers. As they are only *general frameworks*, feel free to adapt or borrow them as you see fit.

Figure A.1 is an example of a generalized vision directing all activities within a school. Posted in all classrooms, it is an omnipresent reminder what the end result of schooling should be. If an activity does not *clearly and significantly* support the vision, it should be discontinued.

Table A.1 is a high school research paper rubric providing students with the grading criteria informing their efforts. Ideally, a similar but an obviously less-detailed rubric should guide the research efforts of younger students. As mentioned in the book, master teachers support unified schoolwide curriculums based on horizontal and vertical assessment consistency.

Table A.2 is a research paper evaluation form given to high school students after assessing their work. Please note that this form is clearly aligned as a companion document with the far-more-detailed research paper rubric.

Table A.3 is an oral presentation rubric providing students with the grading criteria informing their efforts. As with the research paper rubric, a similar but less-detailed version of this document should guide the efforts of younger students in preparing their speeches.

Table A.4 is an oral presentation evaluation form given to high school students after assessing their work. As with the research paper evaluation form given to students, this companion document is clearly aligned to work with its far-more-detailed oral presentation rubric.

FITNESS FOR LIFE OUTCOMES

Students Will Be Lifelong Learners

Students Will Be Creative and Effective Problem Solvers

Students Will Be Informed and Active Citizens of the Local, National, and World Communities

Students Will Be Effective Communicators

Students Will Be Positive, Productive, Cooperative, and Compassionate

Students Will Appreciate and Care for Their Health and Wellness

Students Will Be Prepared for Diverse Responsibilities and Challenges

Students Will Explore and Appreciate the Arts

Students Will Be Ethical and Accept Responsibility for Their Actions

Students Will Respect Contributions of All Members of Society

Students Will Understand and Respect Cultural Differences

—Tri-Valley Central Schools, Grahamsville, New York

Figure A.1

Table A.1. Research Rubric

	Distinguished	Proficient	Competent	Unsatisfactory
CONTENT (this section is weighted twice in the paper's evaluation)	The paper clearly accomplishes the assignment's purpose throughout, using a variety of appropriate writing techniques. The target audience is clearly identifiable and maintained throughout the paper. The content matches the audience.	The paper accomplishes the assignment's purpose, skillfully using more than one appropriate writing technique. The content matches the audience.	The paper accomplishes the assignment's purpose.	The paper lacks a clear purpose.
Evidence support	The paper is supported by a large variety of logical, appropriate, accurate, and always relevant evidence that may include facts, details, examples, statistics, quotations, and reasons to create a compelling, relevant, clearly focused, and original thesis.	The paper is supported by several types of accurate evidence that may include facts, details, examples, statistics, quotations, and reasons to effectively support the author's thesis. The content never strays from the paper's primary focus.	The paper includes some evidence that only occasionally is inappropriate, inaccurate, or strays from the paper's primary focus. The use of the above still allows for satisfactory accomplishment of the author's thesis.	The paper contains irrelevant and/or inaccurate evidence throughout or lacks support of any kind.
Originality	The paper's primary topic or its slant on a commonly researched topic is original.	The paper's primary topic or its slant is highly unusual and rarely researched by high school students.	The paper's primary topic or its slant is relatively common for high school students.	The paper's primary topic or its slant shows a complete lack of originality.
Use of sources	The paper draws on a variety of source types,	The paper draws on a variety of source types,	The paper draws on at least two different	Only 70 to 90 percent of the minimum number of

	Distinguished	Proficient	Competent	Unsatisfactory
	including most recent research for current topics. It exceeds the minimum number of required sources by at least 50 percent, using each source meaningfully (several citations are attributed to most sources). Cited material is appropriately placed within the text and effectively supports the thesis. Throughout the paper, sources are skillfully woven together in support of each paragraph, which, in turn, support the thesis.	including some recent research for current topics. It exceeds the minimum number of required sources by at least 25 percent, using each source meaningfully (several citations are attributed to most sources). Cited material is appropriately placed within the text and effectively supports the thesis. There is clear evidence that sources are skillfully woven together in support of many paragraphs, which, in turn, support the thesis.	source types. It meets the minimum number of required sources, using each source meaningfully (several citations are attributed to most sources). Cited material is almost always appropriately placed within the text and supports the thesis. There are some instances in which sources are woven together in support of some paragraphs, which, in turn, support the thesis. Several paragraphs are mainly composed of paraphrasings or direct quotations from a single reference source.	required sources is used. (Note: any source listed in Works Cited, but not quoted or paraphrased in the text, will not be counted as a source to meet the minimum number of required sources.) The cited material is neither placed appropriately within the text nor serves to support the thesis. There is little or no evidence that sources have been woven together to support the thesis. Most paragraphs are mainly paraphrasings or direct quotations from a single reference source.
Reference citations	The paper has no evidence of quoting or paraphrasing without proper citation.	The paper has no evidence of quoting or paraphrasing without proper citation.	The paper has no evidence of quoting or paraphrasing without proper citation.	Some information in the text may border on unintentional plagiarism.

STYLE

	Distinguished	Proficient	Competent	Unsatisfactory
Repetition and conciseness	The paper, including the title, is compelling, intriguing, memorable, and clear throughout.	The paper, including the title, is memorable and clear throughout. The text always reads	The paper has some memorable passages, a title that matches the content of the paper,	The paper does not capture the reader's interest, and a lack of clarity is evident. The

	Distinguished	Proficient	Competent	Unsatisfactory
	The text always reads smoothly. Repetition of ideas and/or words may be used as a rhetorical device to create the desired effect but never unnecessarily or to interfere with readability. No evidence of wordiness occurs. The sentence structure of the paper is often varied, effectively blending different sentence types and lengths. Paragraph length and design is often varied.	smoothly. Repetition may be attempted to create the desired effect but never unnecessarily or to interfere with readability. Wordiness is only rarely evident. The sentence structure of the paper is varied and uses different sentence types and lengths. Paragraph length and design is varied.	and the intent and meaning are generally clear throughout. Occasional repetition and wordiness rarely interfere with readability and meaning. The sentence structure of the paper relies almost entirely on short, simple, declarative sentences. The paper shows only occasional evidence of paragraph variety in length or design.	title is missing or does not match the content of the paper in any way. Repetition and wordiness frequently interfere with readability and meaning. The paper is composed of numerous fragments and/or run-ons. Any complete sentences are short, simple, declarative sentences. Paragraph length and design is repetitive.
Vivid imaginative language	Vivid and imaginative language is used throughout the paper to effectively enhance the author's meaning and purpose. Active voice and strong verbs are used to create energy, rhythm, and power of expression.	Vivid and imaginative language is used to enhance the author's meaning and purpose. Active voice and strong verbs are used.	A limited, but clearly evident, attempt has been made to use imaginative and/or vivid language. Passive voice and weak verbs are regularly used when active voice and strong verbs would be preferable.	Imaginative or vivid language is rare. The paper relies almost entirely on passive voice and weak verbs.
Introduction and conclusion	The paper's introduction is original, compelling, and clearly foreshadows the major theme of the paper. Its conclusion is	The paper's introduction is compelling and clearly foreshadows the major theme of the research. Its conclusion is	The paper's introduction attracts the reader's interest and foreshadows the major theme of the research.	The paper's introduction is poorly written, does not attract the reader's interest, and/or does not clearly foreshadow the

	Distinguished	Proficient	Competent	Unsatisfactory
	original and summative, is powerfully crafted, and clearly ends with the paper's strongest and most memorable points.	summative and very well crafted.	Its conclusion is summative and competently written.	direction or theme of the research. Its conclusion is not summative and/or is poorly written.

MECHANICS

	Distinguished	Proficient	Competent	Unsatisfactory
Grammar, spelling, agreement, verb tense, and usage	The paper is flawless on grammar, spelling, agreement, verb tense, and usage. Rare and minor errors in punctuation may be noted.	Rare, minor errors in grammar, spelling, punctuation, agreement, verb tense, and usage are noted, which do not interfere with the paper's readability or meaning.	Some errors in grammar, spelling, punctuation, agreement, verb tense, and usage are noted, which occasionally interfere with readability or meaning.	Numerous errors in grammar, spelling, punctuation, agreement, verb tense, and usage are noted, which result in an incoherent or unintelligible paper.
MLA format	The paper always meets standard MLA manuscript form for margins, pagination, indentations, etc. The paper *meaningfully* exceeds the assignment's minimum length requirement by 20 percent. The appearance of the manuscript is exceptionally neat and clean (no handwritten insertions, cross outs, typos, erasures, etc.). The paper follows MLA form in Works Cited and	The paper always meets standard MLA manuscript form for margins, pagination, indentations, etc. The paper *meaningfully* exceeds the assignment's minimum length requirement by 10 percent. The appearance of the manuscript is neat and clean, as are any handwritten corrections. Typos are rare. The paper follows MLA form in Works Cited and reference citations with a	The paper meets almost all MLA manuscript form requirements for margins, pagination, indentation, etc. The paper meets but does not significantly exceed teacher requirements for length. The appearance of the manuscript is generally neat but may have several typos and/or handwritten corrections. However, these issues do not interfere with the paper's readability or meaning. The paper follows MLA	Often, reference to and use of MLA manuscript form is not apparent or is unidentifiable. The paper does not meet the minimum length requirement set by the teacher. The appearance of the manuscript may be untidy and may contain numerous typos and/or handwritten corrections that significantly interfere with its readability and meaning. The paper indicates little or no apparent attention

	Distinguished	Proficient	Competent	Unsatisfactory
	reference citations without any errors.	few insignificant errors.	form with several errors in Works Cited and/or reference citations.	to correct MLA form and/or omits reference citations bordering on plagiarism.
ORGANIZATION				
Transitions and sequencing	The choice of organizational pattern matches the purpose of the paper. The introduction, body, and conclusion are clearly delineated by appropriate and creative transitions within and between paragraphs. An excellent sense of unity and logical sequencing of information within the introduction, body, and conclusion are noted.	The choice of organizational pattern matches the purpose of the paper. The introduction, body, and the conclusion are usually marked by appropriate and occasionally creative transitions within and between paragraphs. The connections and sequencing of information within the introduction, body, and conclusion are logical.	The choice of organizational pattern matches the purpose of the paper. The introduction, body, and the conclusion are separate sections of the paper but may not always be marked by appropriate transitions. The connections and sequencing of information within the introduction, body, and conclusion are generally logical.	The choice of organizational pattern does not match the purpose of the paper. The introduction, body, and conclusion are not apparent as separate sections of the paper and appropriate transitions are often or completely lacking. The information within sections of the paper is often illogically sequenced.
Paragraph coherency	All paragraphs begin with an effective transition and contain a topic sentence effectively placed for the paragraph's purpose. All supporting sentences for each paragraph align perfectly with the topic sentence.	All paragraphs begin with an effective transition and contain a topic sentence. Nearly all supporting sentences align with the topic sentence.	Most paragraphs begin with a transition. All paragraphs contain a topic sentence. Some paragraphs may have a supporting sentence that does not align with the topic sentence.	Paragraphs lack transitions, topic sentences, and/or supporting sentences that align with the topic sentence.

Source: Tri-Valley Central School, Grahamsville, New York

Table A.2. Research Paper Evaluation Form

	Distinguished	Proficient	Competent	Unsatisfactory
CONTENT (this section is weighted twice)				
Evidence support, variety, and timeliness	4	3	2	1
Use of sources	4	3	2	1
Thesis clarity, focus, and originality	4	3	2	1
STYLE				
Title (optional for extra credit)	4	3	X	X
Readability and clarity	4	3	2	1
Conciseness	4	3	2	1
Word/idea repetition avoidance	4	3	2	1
Vivid and imaginative language (optional for extra credit)	4	3	X	X
Sentence and paragraph variety	4	3	2	1
Introduction	4	2	2	1
Conclusion	4	3	2	1
MECHANICS				
Grammatical error avoidance	4	3	2	1
Length appropriateness and standard page format	4	3	2	1[a]

	Distinguished	Proficient	Competent	Unsatisfactory
Typographical errors, proofreading, neatness	4	3	2	1
MLA citation format	4	3	2	1[b]
ORGANIZATION				
Logical sequencing	4	3	2	1
Transitions	4	3	2	1
Paragraph coherency	4	3	2	1

Total Points

Total Points Divided by 19 Descriptors

Final Numerical Grade

Rating Scale

3.50–4.00 =	2.75–3.49 =	2.00–2.74 =	1.75–1.99 =	1.50–1.74 =
90%–100%	80%–89%	70%–79%	60%–69%	50%–59%

See Comments on the Back of This Sheet.

[a] Twenty percent or more short of minimum length = 0; papers more than 30 percent short of minimum length will be penalized five points for each additional 5 percent short of the minimum length requirement.

[b] Paper did not include a Works Cited page and/or in-text reference citations, 0 points.

Table A.3. Oral Presentation Rubric

	Distinguished	Proficient	Competent	Unsatisfactory
CONTENT (this section is weighted twice)				
Support	The speech clearly accomplishes and maintains the assignment's purpose throughout. The speech is supported by a variety of logical, appropriate, and accurate evidence which may include facts, details, examples, statistics, quotations, and reasons to create a compelling, relevant, convincing, and original thesis.	The speech accomplishes the assignment's purpose with rare, minor digressions. The content fulfills the presentation's purpose. The speech is supported by several types of accurate evidence which may include facts, details, examples, statistics, quotations, and reasons strongly supporting the author's thesis. The talk's primary topic or its slant on a common topic is highly unusual for a high school student.	The speech accomplishes the assignment's purpose. Some minor digressions are noted, yet do not detract from the talk's purpose. The speech includes evidence which only occasionally is inappropriate or inaccurate. However, this still allows for the accomplishment of the author's thesis. The talk's primary topic or its slant shows limited originality.	The speech does not accomplish the assignment's intended purpose. The speech contains irrelevant and/or inaccurate evidence throughout or lacks support of any kind. The presentation shows a complete lack of originality in primary topic or slant on a more commonly authored subject.
ORGANIZATION				
Idea Coherency	Choice of the organizational pattern matches the purpose of the speech. The introduction, body and conclusion are clearly marked by appropriate transitions. An excellent sense of unity and	Choice of the organizational pattern matches the purpose of the speech. The introduction, body, and conclusion are almost always marked by appropriate transitions. Connections and	Choice of the organizational pattern matches the purpose of the speech. The introduction, body, and conclusion are separate sections of the speech, and are usually marked by appropriate	Choice of the organizational pattern does not match the purpose of the speech. The introduction, body, and conclusion are not apparent as separate sections of the speech. The information within

	Distinguished	*Proficient*	*Competent*	*Unsatisfactory*
	logical sequencing of information within the introduction, body, and conclusion are noted.	sequencing of information within the presentation's introduction, body, and conclusion are logical.	transitions. The connections and sequencing within the assignment's introduction, body, and conclusion are generally logical.	sections of the speech is illogically sequenced, i.e., chronological, cause/effect.
Introduction and conclusion	All ideas begin with an effective transition and contain a clear statement of the main point to be developed. All supporting information aligns perfectly with each main idea. Where appropriate, explanations for evidence are provided. The talk's introduction is original and compelling and clearly foreshadows the major theme of the presentation. The speech's conclusion is original and summative, is powerfully crafted, and clearly ends with the talks strongest and most memorable points.	All ideas begin with an effective transition and contain a clear statement of the main point to be developed. Nearly all supporting information aligns with each main idea. Where appropriate, explanations for evidence are provided. The talk's introduction is compelling and clearly foreshadows the presentation's major theme of the presentation. The speech's conclusion is summative and is very well crafted.	Nearly all ideas begin with a transition and contain a statement of the main idea to be developed. In rare instances, some information does not align with some main ideas. Where appropriate, explanations for evidence are sometimes provided. The talk's introduction attracts the audience's interest and foreshadows the major theme of the presentation. The speech's conclusion is summative and is competently composed.	The transitions between new ideas are not evident. New ideas are introduced but have no supporting information. Explanations of information, when necessary, are missing. The talk's introduction is poorly crafted, does not attract the audience's interest, and/or does not foreshadow the direction or theme of the presentation. The speech's conclusion is not summative and/or is poorly composed.
DELIVERY				
Sentence variety	The speech is compelling, intriguing	The speech is memorable. The text	The speech has some memorable passages.	The speech does not capture the audience's

	Distinguished	Proficient	Competent	Unsatisfactory
	and memorable. The speech flows smoothly using creative transitions between and within ideas. The sentence structure of the speech is varied, effectively blending different sentence types.	flows smoothly, facilitated by transitions within and between ideas. The sentence structure of the speech is varied and uses different sentence types.	The text makes some use of transitions. The sentence structure of the speech relies almost entirely on short, simple, declarative sentences.	attention. Within the text, transitions are lacking. Any complete sentences within the speech are short, simple, declarative sentences.
Vivid, imaginative language	Vivid and imaginative language (e.g. similes, metaphors) is used throughout the speech to effectively enhance the speaker's meaning and purpose. Active voice and strong verbs are used to create energy, rhythm, and power of expression.	Vivid and imaginative language is used at times within the speech to enhance the speaker's meaning and purpose. Active voice and strong verbs are used.	A limited, but clearly evident, attempt has been made to use imaginative and/or vivid language within the speech. The passive voice and weak verbs are used regularly when active voice and strong verbs would be preferable.	No imaginative or vivid language is apparent within the speech. The talk relies almost entirely on passive voice and weak verbs.
A/V aids	The presentation is highly innovative and creative, using A/V aids, if appropriate, to enhance the talk's effectiveness.	The presentation's creativity is apparent using A/V aids, if appropriate, to enhance the talk's effectiveness.	The presentation's approach is occasionally creative, using A/V aids, if appropriate.	The presentation is completely or almost totally read with little or no meaningful inflection. A/V aids, if used, do not contribute or may interfere with the meaning of the speech.
Confidence, eye contact, volume, pacing, mannerisms	The speaker exhibits strong confidence, energy, and stage presence. Eye contact is	The speaker exhibits confidence and stage presence. The speaker only occasionally reads	The speaker shows signs of a rehearsed familiarity with the content. The presenter	Numerous distractions from content and facts are observed. The speaker shows few

	Distinguished	Proficient	Competent	Unsatisfactory
	spread evenly throughout the audience. Notes are used only for quick reference. Volume and pacing are consistently altered to add interest and emphasis. Facial expressions and body movements appropriately match the content of the speech. No nervous mannerisms are noted.	from notes and maintains good eye contact throughout the audience. Volume and pacing are altered to add meaning and emphasis. Facial expressions and body movements match the content of the speech. At most, one or two nervous mannerisms may be noted, yet they do not detract from the overall effectiveness of the talk.	reads from notes but still establishes eye contact during a clear majority of the talk. Facial expressions and body movements do not detract from the content of the speech.	signs of preparation or rehearsal. Facial expressions and body movements detract from the content of the speech.
Question responses	If audience questions are posed, the responses are clear, thorough, and spoken in a powerful, confident manner.	If audience questions are posed, the responses are clear, thorough, and at times, spoken in a powerful, confident manner.	If audience questions posed, most are answered in a clear manner.	If audience questions are posed, most are not answered in a clear or satisfactory manner.
Fluency	The speaker exhibits exemplary command of the language with no sentence fragments, run-ons, slang, improper usages, or incorrect subject-verb agreement. Articulation is excellent with no mumbling, stammering, or slurring of words. The	The speaker exhibits proficient command of the English language. Few, if any, sentence fragments, run-ons, slang, improper usages, or incorrect subject-verb agreement are noted. Articulation is very good with very few instances of mumbling.	The speaker exhibits acceptable use of standard English, yet the talk may contain some colloquial expressions, sentence fragments, run-ons slang, improper usages, or incorrect subject-verb agreement. Articulation is acceptable and fosters	The speaker relies heavily on informal and colloquial English. Numerous sentence fragments, run-ons, slang, improper usages, or instances of incorrect subject-verb agreement occur. Articulation is poor. Numerous examples of

	Distinguished	Proficient	Competent	Unsatisfactory
	presentation is polished with no unintended pauses, "uhms," "ahs," "you knows," etc.	stammering, or slurring of words. The talk is a mostly polished presentation with only one or two unintended pauses, "uhms," "ahs," or "you knows," occurring. Such lapses of correct articulation never disrupt or detract from the quality or flow of the speech.	an understanding of the content. Occasional instances of mumbling, stammering, or slurring of words may be observed. "Uhms," "ahs," "you knows," occur, but do not interfere with the content of the talk.	mumbling, stammering, or slurring of words are noted. The presentation is filled with "uhms," "ahs," and "you knows," that detract from and interfere with the content of the speech.
Length	All teacher requirements for format, assignment criteria, deadlines, and process are met. By adding additional and *meaningfully* important material to the talk, its duration exceeds the minimum length requirement by twenty percent.	All teacher requirements for format, assignment criteria, deadlines, and process are met. By adding additional and *meaningfully* important material to the talk, its duration exceeds the minimum length requirement by ten percent.	Almost all teacher requirements for format, assignment criteria, deadlines, and process are met. The presentation's length meets but does not significantly exceed the assignment's minimum length requirement.	The requirements for format, assignment criteria, deadlines, length, and process are not satisfactorily completed.

Source: Tri-Valley Central School, Grahamsville, New York

Table A.4. Oral Presentation Evaluation Form

	Distinguished	Proficient	Competent	Unsatisfactory
CONTENT (this section is weighted twice)				
Content supports main idea (thesis)	4	3	2	1
Thesis clarity	4	3	2	1
Thesis originality	4	3	2	1
ORGANIZATION				
Introduction	4	3	2	1
Body supports and clarifies thesis	4	3	2	1
Transitions and sequencing/flow	4	3	2	1
Summary and conclusion	4	3	2	1
DELIVERY				
Sentence structure variety	4	3	2	1
Articulation	4	3	2	1
Volume range and pacing	4	3	2	1
Mannerisms	4	3	2	1
Disfluency avoidance	4	3	2	1
Energy, confidence, and presence	4	3	2	1
Eye contact	4	3	2	1

	Distinguished	Proficient	Competent	Unsatisfactory
Vivid and imaginative language (optional for extra credit)	4	3	X	X
Language command	4	3	2	1
Length	4	3	2	1

Total Points

Total Points Divided by 19 Descriptors

Final Numerical Grade

Rating Scale

3.50–4.00 = 90%–100%	2.75–3.49 = 80%–89%	2.00–2.74 = 70%–79%	1.75–1.99 = 60%–69%
			1.50–1.74 = 50%–59%

See Comments on the Back of This Sheet.

References

Abrams, B. J., and A. Segal. (March-April 1998). "How to Prevent Aggressive Behavior." *Teaching Exceptional Children* 30, no. 4: 10–20. HighBeam (1P3-33469268).

Aiken, E. G., G. S. Thomas, and W. A. Shennum. (1975). "Memory for a Lecture: Effects of Notes, Lecture Rate and Informational Density." *Journal of Educational Psychology* 67: 439–444.

Alderman, M. K. (September 1990). "Motivation for At-Risk Students." *Educational Leadership* 48: 27–30.

Alexander, P. A. (1984). "Training Analogical Reasoning Skills in the Gifted." *Roeper Review* 6: 191–193.

Alexander, P. A., J. M. Kulikowich, and S. K. Schulze. (1994). "How Subject-Matter Knowledge Affects Recall and Interest." *American Educational Research Journal* 31, no. 2: 313–337.

Apter, B., C. Arnold, and J. Stinson. (2010). "A Mass Observation Study of Student and Teacher Behavior in British Primary Classrooms." *Educational Psychology in Practice* 26, no. 2: 151–171.

Armario, C. (December 7, 2010). "'Wake-Up Call': U.S. Students Trail Global Leaders." Associated Press. http://www.msnbc.msn.com/id/40544897/ns/us_news-life/t/wake-up-call-us-students-trail-.

Aronson, J., J. Zimmerman, and L. Carlos. (April 20, 1998). "Improving Student Achievement by Extending School: Is it Just a Matter of Time?" Paper presented at the PACE Media/Education Writers Seminar. http://www.wested.org/online_pubs/po-98-02.pdf.

Ashton, P. T., and R. B. Webb. (1986). *Making a Difference: Teachers' Sense of Efficacy and Student Achievement*. New York: Longman.

Barker, G. P. (February 1996). "Don't Work Too Hard!" *The Education Digest*: 17–20.

Baron, J. B. (1990). "Performance Assessment: Blurring the Edges among Assessment, Curriculum, and Instruction." In *Assessment in the Service of Instruction*, edited by A. Champagne, B. Lovitts, and B. Calinger, 127–148. Washington, DC: American Association for the Advancement of Science.

Beaty-O'Ferrall, M. E., A. Green, and F. Hanna. (March 2010). "Classroom Management Strategies for Difficult Students: Promoting Change through Relationships." *Middle School Journal* 41, no. 4: 4–11. HighBeam (1P3-2010801461).

Begley, S. (November 7, 2003). "Expectations May Alter Outcomes Far More Than We Realize." *Wall Street Journal*. HighBeam (1P2-1505927).

Benard, B. (November 1993). "Fostering Resiliency in Kids." *Educational Leadership* 51: 44–48.

Bennett, W. J. (1986). *What Works: Research about Teaching and Learning*. Washington, DC: U.S. Department of Education.

Berne, E. (1964). *Games People Play: The Psychology of Human Relationships*. New York: Random House.

Beyer, B. (1992). "Teaching Thinking: An Integrated Approach." In *Teaching for Thinking*, edited by James W. Keefe and Herbert J. Walberg, 93–109. Reston, VA: National Association of Secondary School Principals.

Beyer, B. (2000). "What Research Suggests about Teaching Thinking Skills." In *Developing Minds: A Resource Book for Teaching Thinking*, edited by A. Costa, 275–286. Alexandria, VA: Association for Supervision and Curriculum Development.

Bishop, J. (Fall 1995). "The Power of External Standards." *American Educator*.

Block, P. (1987). *The Empowered Manager: Positive Political Skills at Work.* San Francisco: Jossey-Bass.

Bloom, B. (1956). *Taxonomy of Educational Objectives Book 1: Cognitive Domain.* New York: David McKay.

Bond, N. (Fall 2007). "12 Questioning Strategies That Minimize Classroom Management Problems." *Kappa Delta Pi Record* 44, no. 1: 18–21. HighBeam (1P3-1343459471).

Borich, G. D. (1992). *Effective Teaching Methods,* second edition. Upper Saddle River, NJ: Merrill/Prentice Hall.

Bradley, A. (April 1997). "Hardly Working." *Teacher Magazine* 8, no. 7: 20–21.

Bransford, J. D., B. S. Stein et al. (1982). "Differences in Approaches to Learning: An Overview." *Journal of Experimental Psychology: General* 3: 390–398.

Bransford, J. D., and N. J. Vye. (1989). "A Perspective on Cognitive Research and Its Implications for Instruction." In *Toward the Thinking Curriculum: Current Cognitive Research,* edited by L. B. Resnick and L. Klopfer, 173–205. Alexandria, VA: Association for Supervision and Curriculum Development.

Bright, N. (October 2011). "Five Habits of Highly Effective Teachers." *The School Administrator* 9, no. 68: 33–35.

Brophy, J. (October 1987). "Synthesis of Research on Strategies for Motivating Students to Learn." *Educational Leadership* 45, no. 2: 40–48.

Brophy, J. (2006). "History of Research on Classroom Management." In *Handbook of Classroom Management: Research, Practice, and Contemporary Issues,* edited by C. M. Evertson and C. S. Weinstein, 17–43. Mahwah, NJ: Erlbaum.

Caine, R. N. (November 2000). "Building the Bridge from Research to Classroom." *Educational Leadership* 58, no 3: 59–61.

Caine, R. N., and G. Caine. (1994). *Making Connections: Teaching and the Human Brain,* revised edition. Menlo Park, CA: Addison-Wesley.

Caine, R. N., and G. Caine. (1997). *Education on the Edge of Possibility.* Alexandria, VA: Association for Supervision and Curriculum Development.

Cameron, J., and W. D. Pierce. (1994). "Reinforcement, Reward, and Intrinsic Motivation: A Meta-Analysis." *Review of Educational Research* 64, no. 3: 363–423.

Cardellichio, T., and W. Field. (March 1997). "Seven Strategies That Encourage Neural Branching." *Educational Leadership* 54, no. 6: 33–36.

Carter, B. (1996). "Hold the Applause! Do Accelerated Reader™ and Electronic Bookshelf™ Send the Right Message?" *School Library Journal* 42, no. 10: 22–26.

Caulfield, J., and W. Jennings. (2002). *Inciting Learning: A Guide to Brain-Compatible Instruction.* Reston, VA: National Association of Secondary School Principals.

Caulfield, J., S. Kidd, and T. Kocher. (November 2000). "Brain-Based Instruction in Action." *Educational Leadership* 58, no. 3: 62–65.

Chacon, C. T. (2005). "Teachers' Perceived Efficacy among English as a Foreign Language in Middle Schools in Venezuela." *Teaching and Teacher Education: An International Journal of Research and Studies* 21, no. 3: 257–272.

Chambliss, M. J., and R. C. Calfee. (1989). "Designing Science Textbooks to Enhance Student Understanding." *Educational Psychologist* 24, no. 3: 307–322.

Cheung, E. (March 2004). "Goal Setting as Motivational Tool in Students' Self-Regulated Learning." *Educational Research Quarterly.* HighBeam (680269061).

Clement, M. C. (October 2010). "Preparing Teachers for Classroom Management: The Teacher Educator's Role." *Delta Kappa Gamma Bulletin* 77, no. 1. HighBeam (1P3-2260439171).

Clifford, M. M. (September 1990). "Students Need Challenge, Not Easy Success." *Educational Leadership*: 22–26.

Collette, A. T., and E. L. Chiappetta. (1989). *Science Instruction in the Middle and Secondary Schools,* second edition. Columbus: Merrill.

Coppedge, F. L. (September 1993). "Excellence in Education—Meeting the Challenge with Effective Practices." *NASSP Bulletin* 77, no. 554: 34–40.

Cotton, K. (May 1988). "Classroom Questioning." North West Regional Educational Laboratory.

Coulson, A. J. (2011). "The Impact of Federal Involvement in America's Classrooms." Testimony presented to the Committee on Education and the Workforce, U.S. House of Representatives, Washington, DC, February 10.

Covey, S. R. (1989). *The 7 Habits of Highly Effective People*. New York: Simon & Schuster.

Covington, M. V. (1992). *Making the Grade: A Self-Worth Perspective on Motivation and School Reform*. New York: Cambridge University Press.

Crowe, M., and P. Stanford. (July 2010). "Questioning for Quality." *Delta Kappa Gamma Bulletin* 76, no. 4. HighBeam (1P3-2072982971).

Csikzentmihalyi, M., and J. Nakamura. (1989). "The Dynamics of Intrinsic Motivation: A Study of Adolescents." In *Research on Motivation in Education*, edited by C. Ames and R. Ames. New York: Academic Press.

Cuban, L. (December 2008). "The Perennial Reform: Fixing School Time." *Phi Delta Kappan* 90, no. 4: 240–250.

Curran, K., and K. Reivich. (May 2011). "Goal Setting and Hope." *National Association of School Psychologists. Communique* 39, no. 7. HighBeam (1P3-2352132571).

Dale, E. (1984). *The Educator's Quotebook*. Bloomington, IN: Phi Delta Kappa.

Danielson, C. (2002). *Enhancing Student Achievement: A Framework for School Improvement*. Alexandria, VA: Association for Supervision and Curriculum Development.

Danielson, C. (December 2010/January 2011). "Evaluations That Help Teachers Learn." *The Effective Educator* 68, no. 4: 35–39.

Danner, F. W., and D. Lonky. (1981). "A Cognitive-Developmental Approach to the Effects of Rewards on Intrinsic Motivation." *Child Development* 52, no. 3: 1043–1052.

Darling-Hammond, L. (November 1993). "Setting Standards for Students: The Case for Authentic Assessment." *NASSP Bulletin* 77, no. 556: 18–26.

Dempster, F. N. (February 1993). "Exposing Our Students to Less Should Help Them Learn More." *Phi Delta Kappan*: 433–437.

Dunkel, P., and S. Davy. (1989). "The Heuristic of Lecture Note Taking: Perceptions of American and International Students Regarding the Value and Practice of Note Taking." *English for Specific Purposes* 8: 33–50.

Dweck, C. (1986). "Motivational Processes Affecting Learning." *American Psychologist* 41, no. 10: 1040–1048.

Dyer, W. (1991). *Your Erroneous Zones*. New York: HarperCollins Publishers.

Dyer, W. (2009). *Excuses Begone! How to Change Lifelong, Self-Defeating Thinking Habits*. Carlsbad, CA: Hay House, Inc.

Enoch, S. W. (March 22, 1995). "Taking Charge of the Parent-Teacher Conference." *Education Week*: 46, 48.

Epstein, M. (July/August 1995). "Opening Up to Happiness." *Psychology Today*: 42–46.

Ericsson, K. A., R. Krampe, and C. Tesch-Romer. (1993). "The Role of Deliberate Practice in the Acquisition of Expert Performance." *Psychological Review* 100, no. 3: 363–406.

Ernst, K. (1972). *Games Students Play (and What to Do about Them)*. Milbrae, CA: Celestial Arts.

Feather, N., ed. (1982). *Expectations and Actions*. Hillsdale, NJ: Erlbaum.

Feldman, R. S., and T. Prohaska. (August 1979). "The Student as Pygmalion: Effect of Student Expectation on the Teacher." *Journal of Educational Psychology* 71, no. 4: 485–493.

Fisher, H. L. (April 2003). "Motivational Strategies in the Elementary School Setting." *Kappa Delta Phi Record* 39, no. 3. HighBeam (1P3-321146091).

Fullan, M. G. (March 1993). "Why Teachers Must Become Change Agents." *Educational Leadership* 50, no. 6: 12–17.

Fullan, M. G. (1994). "Coordinating Top-Down and Bottom-Up Strategies for Educational Reform." In *The Governance of Curriculum*, edited by Richard F. Elmore and Susan Fuhrman, 186–202. Alexandria, VA: Association for Supervision and Curriculum Development.

Gable, R. A., P. H. Hester, M. L. Rock, and K. G. Hughes. (2009). "Back to Basics: Rules, Praise, Ignoring, and Reprimands Revisited." *Intervention in School and Clinic* 44, no. 4: 195–205.

Garavalia, L. S., and M. E. Gredler. (December 2002). "An Exploratory Study of Academic Goal Setting, Achievement Calibration and Self-Regulated Learning." *Journal of Instructional Psychology* 29, no. 4: 221–230. HighBeam (1G1-95148384).

Gazin, A. (1990). "What Do You Expect? A Teachers High—or Low—Expectations Can Wield a Profound Influence on Students. Here's How to Set the Bar High for Every Child." *Instructor*. HighBeam (1G1-121150474).

Gazzaniga, M. S. (1998). *The Mind's Past*. Berkeley, CA: University of California Press.

Ghaith, G., and H. Yaghi. (1997). "Relationships among Experience, Teacher Efficacy, and Attitudes toward the Implementation of Instructional Innovation." *Teaching and Teacher Education* 13, no. 4: 451–458.

Gladwell, M. (2008). *Outliers: The Story of Success*. New York: Little, Brown and Company.

Gladwell, M. (2009). *What the Dog Saw: And Other Adventures*. New York: Little, Brown and Company.

Glasser, W. (1969). *Schools without Failure*. New York: Harper & Row.

Glasser, W. (February 1990). "The Quality School." *Phi Delta Kappan* 71, no. 6: 425–435.

Glasser, W. (May 1992). "The Quality School Curriculum." *Phi Delta Kappan* 73, no. 9: 690–694.

Glasser, W. (1998). *Choice Theory: A New Psychology of Personal Freedom*. New York: Harper Collins.

Glenn, R. E. (March 2002). "Using Brain Research in Your Classroom." *Education Digest* 67, no. 7: 27–30.

Goleman, D. (1995). *Emotional Intelligence: Why It Can Matter More Than IQ*. New York: Bantam Books.

Greenleaf, R. K. (May 2003). "Motion and Emotion." *Principal Leadership*: 14–19.

Gusky, T. R. (1988). "Teacher Efficacy, Self-Concept, and Attitudes toward the Implementation of Instructional Innovation." *Teaching and Teacher Education: An International Journal of Research and Studies* 4, no. 1: 63–69.

Hansen, J. M., and J. Childs. (September 1998). "Creating a School Where People Like to Be." *Educational Leadership* 56, no. 1: 14–17.

Hattie, J. A. C. (2009). *Visible Learning: A Synthesis of Over 800 Meta-Analyses Relating to Achievement*. New York: Routledge Press.

Haycock, K. (1998). "Good Teaching Matters . . . a Lot." *Thinking K–16* 3, no. 2: 1–14.

Henderson, J., N. Winitzky, and D. Kauchak. (Winter 1996). "Effective Teaching in Advanced Placement Classes." *Journal of Classroom Interaction*: 29–35.

"Hidden Costs of Tenure." (2005). *Small Newspaper Group*. http://thehiddencostsoftenure.com/.

Hirsch, E. D., Jr. (Fall 1996). "Reality's Revenge: Research and Ideology." *American Educator* 20, no. 3: 4–6, 31–46.

Hirsch, E. D., Jr. (October 2001). "Seeking Breadth *and* Depth in the Curriculum." *Educational Leadership*: 22–25.

Honea, J. M. (December 1982). "Wait-Time as an Instructional Variable: An Influence on Teacher and Student." *Clearing House* 56, no. 4: 167–170.

Howard, J. (1990). *Getting Smart: The Social Construction of Intelligence*. Lexington, MA: The Efficacy Institute.

Hull, J. (December 2011). "Time in School: How Does the U.S. Compare?" Center for Public Education. http://www.centerforpubliceducation.org/Main-Menu/Organizing-a-school/Time-in-school-How-does-the-US-compare.

Hunter, M. (1969). *Teach More—Faster!* El Segundo, CA: TIP Publications.

Hunter, M. (1982). *Mastery Teaching*. El Segundo, CA: TIP Publications.

Johnson, D. (1999). "Creating Fat Kids Who Don't Like to Read." *Book Report* 18, no. 2: 96.

Jones, R. (December 1998). "Researchers' Ways to Raise Student Achievement." *Education Digest* 64, no. 4: 19–26.

Kagan, S. (May 1995). "Group Grades Miss the Mark." *Educational Leadership* 52, no. 8: 68–71.

Keiper, R. W., and H. M. Evans. (September/October 1994). "'Act Well Your Part': Teachers and the Performing Arts." *The Clearing House* 68, no. 1: 22–24.

Kiewra, K. A. (1985). "Investigating Note Taking and Review: A Depth of Processing Alternative." *Educational Psychologist* 20: 20–32.

Kiewra, K. A. (March 2002). "How Classroom Teachers Can Help Students Learn and Teach Them How to Learn." *Theory into Practice* 41, no. 2. HighBeam (1G1-90190494).

Kohn, A. (1993). *Punished by Rewards: The Trouble with Gold Stars, Incentive Plans, A's, Praise, and Other Bribes.* Boston: Houghton Mifflin.

Kounin, J. S. (1970). *Discipline and Group Management in Classrooms.* New York: Holt, Rinehart & Winston.

Krzyzewski, M. (2006). *Beyond Basketball.* New York: Business Plus.

Kunda, Z. (1990). "The Case for Motivated Reasoning." *Psychological Bulletin* 108, no. 3: 480–498.

Landfried, S. E. (November 1989). "'Enabling' Undermines Responsibility in Students." *Educational Leadership*: 79–85.

Larson, J. R., Jr. (1984). "The Performance Feedback Process: A Preliminary Model." *Organizational Behavior and Human Performance* 33: 42–76.

Lawrence-Lightfoot, S. (August 2004). "Building Bridges from School to Home: Meeting the Challenges of the Positive, Productive Parent-Teacher Relationship." *Scholastic Instructor.* HighBeam (1G1-121150475).

LeDoux, J. (1996). *The Emotional Brain: The Mysterious Underpinnings of Emotional Life.* New York: Simon & Schuster.

Lee, J. (2010). "Students Can Benefit from Goal-Setting." *The Daily Bruin*, October 15. http://www.dailybruin.com/article/2010/10/students_can_benefit_from_goalsetting.

Lee, V. E., and J. B. Smith. (February 1996). "Collective Responsibility for Learning and Its Effect on Gains in Achievement for Early Secondary School Students." *American Journal of Education* 104, no. 2: 103–140.

Levitt, S. D., and Dubner, S. J. (2011). *SuperFreakonomics.* Harper Perennial: New York.

Lewis, C. C., E. Schaps, and M. S. Watson. (September 1996). "The Caring Classroom's Academic Edge." *Educational Leadership* 54, no. 1: 16–21.

Lipton, J. (December 6, 1976). "Here Be Dragons." *Newsweek*, 17.

Locke, E. A., and G. P. Latham. (2002). "Building a Practically Useful Theory of Goal Setting and Task Motivation: A 35-Year Odyssey." *American Psychologist* 57, no. 9: 705–717.

Lubinski, D., and L. G. Humphreys. (1997). "Incorporating General Intelligence into Epidemiology and the Social Sciences." *Intelligence* 24, no. 1: 159–202.

Lumpkin, A. (July 2007). "Caring Teachers: The Key to Student Learning." *Kappa Delta Pi Record* 43, no. 4: 158–160. HighBeam (1P3-1319845401).

Madden, L. E. (March 1997). "Motivating Students to Learn Better through Their Own Goal-Setting." *Education* 117, no. 3. HighBeam (1G1-19471169).

Mankin, K. R., K. M. Boone, S. Flores, and M. R. Willyard. (December 2004). "What Agriculture Students Say Motivates Them to Learn." *NACTA Journal* 48, no. 4. HighBeam (1P3-768193311).

Manlove, D. C., and P. G. Elliot. (1979). "Absent Teachers . . . Another Handicap for Students?" *The Practitioner* 5, no. 4: 13.

Manzo, M. V. (May/June 1998). "Teaching for Creative Outcomes: Why We Don't, How We All Can." *Clearing House* 71, no. 5: 287–290.

Marzano, R. J. (Summer 1993). "How Classroom Teachers Approach the Teaching of Thinking." *Theory into Practice* 32, no. 3: 154–160.

Marzano, R. J. (2003). *What Works in Schools: Translating Research into Action.* Alexandria, VA: Association for Supervision and Curriculum Development.

Marzano, R. J., and J. S. Marzano. (2003). "The Key to Classroom Management." *Educational Leadership* 61, no. 1: 6–13.

Marzano, R. J., J. S. Marzano, and D. J. Pickering. (2003). *Classroom Management That Works: Research-Based Strategies for Every Teacher.* Alexandra, VA: Association for Supervision and Curriculum Development.

Marzano, R. J., D. J. Pickering et al. (1997). *Dimensions of Learning, Teacher's Manual,* second edition. Alexandria, VA: Association for Supervision and Curriculum Development.

Marzano, R. J., D. J. Pickering, and R. S. Brandt. (February 1990). "Integrating Instructional Programs through Dimensions of Learning." *Educational Leadership:* 17–24.

Marzano, R. J., D. J. Pickering, and J. E. Pollack. (2001). *Classroom Instruction That Works: Research-Based Strategies for Increasing Student Achievement.* Alexandria, VA: Association for Supervision and Curriculum Development.

McCombs, B. L., and J. S. Whisler. (1997). *The Learner-Centered Classroom and School: Strategies for Increasing Student Motivation and Achievement.* San Francisco: Jossey-Bass.

McCullers, J., R. Fabes, and J. Moran III. (1987). "Does Intrinsic Motivation Theory Explain the Adverse Effects of Rewards on Immediate Task Performance?" *Journal of Personality and Social Psychology* 52, no. 5: 1027–1033.

McGlynn, A. P. (November 1999). "Perk Up Lectures and Involve Students." *The Education Digest* 65, no. 3: 50–52.

McGrory, K. (2009). "Research: Report: Costly Plan Failed to Improve Schools." Living Wisdom School. http://livingwisdomschool.org/research-report-costly-plan-failed-to-improve-schools/.

McKenna, T. (May 2002). "The Power of Expectations. (The Personnel Touch). (Brief Article)." *National Petroleum News.* HighBeam (1G1-87427699).

Moses, M. (December 1992). "What's Worth Assessing?" *School Administrator* 49, no. 11: 18–19.

Nation's Report Card. (2011). http://nationsreportcard.gov/.

Nation's Report Card: Reading 2011. National Center for Education Statistics, November 2011. http://nces.ed.gov/nationsreportcard/pubs/main2011/2012457.asp.

Neck, C. P., and A. W. H. Barnard. (March 1996). "Managing Your Mind: What Are You Telling Yourself?" *Educational Leadership* 53, no. 6: 24–27.

OECD. (2001). *Education at a Glance 2011: Highlights.* OECD Publishing. http://dx.doi.org /10.1787/eag-highlights-2011-en.

Olsen, M. N. (1971). "Identifying Quality in School Classrooms: Some Problems and Some Answers." Special Report to the Metropolitan School Study Council (New York).

O'Neil, J. (September 1996). "On Emotional Intelligence: A Conversation with Daniel Goleman." *Educational Leadership* 54, no. 1: 6–11.

O'Neill, J. (July 2004). "Teachers Learn to Set Goals with Students." *Journal of Staff Development* 25, no. 3: 32–37. HighBeam (1P3-650849871).

Ornstein, A. C. (June/July 1996). "Motivation and Learning: A Psychological Perspective." *High School Magazine:* 40–42.

Parkay, F. W., and B. H. Stanford. (2004). *Becoming a Teacher,* sixth edition. Boston: Allyn and Bacon.

Patrick, B. C., J. Hisley, and T. Kempler. (2000). "'What's Everybody So Excited About?': The Effects of Teacher Enthusiasm on Student Intrinsic Motivation and Vitality." *Journal of Experimental Education* 68, no. 3: 217–236.

Pennell, M. L. (March 2000). "Improving Student Participation in History Lectures: Suggestions for Successful Questioning." *Teaching History: A Journal of Methods* 25, no. 1. HighBeam (1G1-636 52491).

Phelps, R. P. (2008). "The Role and Importance of Standardized Testing in the World of Teaching and Training." Paper presented at the 15th Congress of the World Association for Educational Research, Cadi Ayyad University, Marrakesh, Morocco, June 3.

Presseisen, B. K. (1992). "Thinking Skills in the Curriculum." *In Teaching for Thinking*, edited by James W. Keefe and Herbert J. Walberg, 1–13. Reston, VA: National Association of Secondary School Principals.

Pritchett, P., and R. Pound. (1990). *The Employee Handbook for Organizational Change.* Dallas: Pritchett & Associates, Inc.

Reeder, S. (2005). "Cost to Fire a Tenured Teacher? More Than $219,000." *The Hidden Costs of Tenure.* http://thehiddencostsoftenure.com/stories/?prcss=display&id=295712.

Renzaglia, A., M. Hutchins, and S. Lee. (1997). "The Impact of Teacher Education on the Beliefs, Attitudes, and Dispositions of Preservice Special Educators." *Teacher Education and Special Education* 20, no. 4: 360–377.

Resnick, L. B., and L. E. Klopfer. (1989). "Toward the Thinking Curriculum: An Overview." In *Toward the Thinking Curriculum: Current Cognitive Research*, edited by L. B. Resnick and L. E. Klopfer, 1–18. Alexandria, VA: Association for Supervision and Curriculum Development.

Rhodes, M. (May 2003). "Brain-Based, Heart-Felt." *Principal Leadership*: 38–40.

Ribas, W. B. (September 1998). "Tips for Reaching Parents." *Educational Leadership* 56, no. 1: 83–85.

Riley, P. (1994). *The Winner Within: A Life Plan for Team Players.* New York: Berkley Publishing Group.

Rimm, S. B. (April 1997). "An Underachievement Epidemic." *Educational Leadership* 54, no. 7: 18–22.

Ripley, A. (November 26, 2008). "Can She Save Our Schools?" *Time*, 36–44.

Ripley, A. (December 2010). "Your Child Left Behind." *The Atlantic.* http://www.theatlantic.com/magazine/archive/2010/12/your-child-left-behind/8310.

Rockoff, J. (May 2010). "Taking Attendance with Teachers." Columbia Business School Ideas at Work. http://www4.gsb.columbia.edu/ideasatwork/feature/7213498/Taking+Attendance+with+Teachers.

Rosenthal, R., and L. F. Jacobson. (April 1968). "Teacher Expectations for the Disadvantaged." *Scientific American* 218, no. 4: 19–23.

Rowe, M. B. (1974). "Reflections on Wait-Time: Some Methodological Questions." *Journal of Research in Science Teaching* 11, no. 3: 263–279.

Rowe, M. B. (1986). "Wait Times: Slowing Down May Be a Way of Speeding Up!" *Journal of Teacher Education* 37, no. 1: 43–50.

Sabatino, D. A. (1987). "Preventive Discipline as a Practice in Special Education." *Teaching Exceptional Children* 19, no. 4: 8–11.

Schmitz, B., and E. A. Skinner. (1993). "Perceived Control, Effort, and Academic Performance: Interindividual, Intraindividual, and Multivariate Time-Series Analysis." *Journal of Personality and Social Psychology* 64, no. 6: 1010–1028.

Scott, T. M., P. J. Alter, and R. G. Hirn. (November 2011). "An Examination of Typical Classroom Context and Instruction for Students with and without Behavioral Problems." *Education & Treatment of Children* 34, no. 4: 619–641. Highbeam (1G1-271811395).

Sedlak, M., C. Wheeler, D. Pullin, and P. Cusick. (1986). *Selling Students Short: Classroom Bargains and Academic Reform in the American High School.* New York: Teachers College Press.

Seligman, M. E. P. (1975). *Helplessness: On Depression, Development, and Death.* San Francisco: Freeman.

Shores, R. E., S. L. Jack, P. L. Gunter, D. N. Ellis, T. J. DeBriere, and J. Wehby. (January 1993). "Classroom Interactions of Children with Behavior Disorders." *Journal of Emotional and Behavioral Disorders* 1, no. 1: 27–39.

Simons, J., S. Dewitte, and W. Lens. (2000). "Wanting to Have vs. Wanting to Be: The Effect of Perceived Instrumentality on Goal Orientation." *British Journal of Psychology* 91, no. 3: 335–351.

Slavin, R. E. (December 1989/January 1990). "Research on Cooperative Learning: Consensus and Controversy." *Educational Leadership* 47, no. 4: 52–54.

Snyder, C. R., D. B. Feldman, H. S. Shorey, and K. L. Rand. (2002). "Hopeful Choices: A School Counselor's Guide to Hope Theory." *Professional School Counseling* 5, no. 5: 298–308.

Sorrentino, J. (2010). "Waiting for Superman: What It Means for You and Your Child." Education.com. www.education.com/print/waiting-superman-means-parents.

Sousa, D. A. (May 1992). "Helping Students Remember What You Teach." *Middle School Journal* 23, no. 5: 21–23.

Stevens, B. A., and A. Tollafield. (March 1, 2003). "Classroom Practice: Creating Comfortable and Productive Parent/Teacher Conferences." *Phi Delta Kappan* 84, no 7. HighBeam (1G1-98572482).

Stevenson, H. W. (1990). *Making the Grade in Mathematics: Elementary School Mathematics in the United States, Taiwan, and Japan.* Reston, VA: National Council of Teachers of Mathematics.

Stevenson, H. W., and J. W. Sigler. (1992). *The Learning Gap: Why Our Schools Are Failing and What We Can Learn from Japanese and Chinese Education.* New York: Simon & Schuster.

Stigler, J. W., and J. Hiebert. (Winter 1998). "Teaching Is a Cultural Activity." *American Educator*: 4–11.

Strong, M., J. Gargani, and O. Hacifazlioglu. (September 2011). "Do We Know a Successful Teacher When We See One? Experiments in the Identification of Effective Teachers." *Journal of Teacher Education.* HighBeam (1G1-266629716).

Stuart, C., and D. Thurlow. (March 2000). "Making It Their Own: Preservice Teachers' Experiences, Beliefs, and Classroom Practices." *Journal of Teacher Education* 51, no. 2: 113–121. HighBeam (1G1-60575568).

"Student-Teacher Ratios in Public Schools." (2010). *National Center for Education Statistics.* http://nces.ed.gov/programs/coe/indicator_qpt.asp.

"Study Backs Up Strategies for Achieving Goals." *Dominican University of California.* http://www.dominican.edu/dominicannews/study-backs-up-strategies-for-achieving-goals.

Sutherland, K. S., J. H. Wehby, and P. J. Yoder. (2002). "Examination of the Relationship between Teacher Praise and Opportunities for Students with EBD to Respond to Academic Requests." *Journal of Emotional and Behavioral Disorders* 10, no. 1: 5–13.

Sylwester, R. (November 2000). "Unconscious Emotions, Conscious Feelings." *Educational Leadership* 58, no. 3: 20–24.

Tauber, R. T., C. S. Mester, and S. C. Buckwald. (March 1993). "The Teacher as Actor: Entertaining to Educate." *NASSP Bulletin* 77, no. 551: 20–26.

Tienken, C. H., S. Goldberg, and D. DiRocco. (October 2009). "Questioning the Questions." *Kappa Delta Pi Record* 46, no. 1: 39–43. HighBeam (1P3-1872899091).

Titsworth, B. S., and K. A. Kiewra. (2001). "Spoken Organizational Lecture Cues and Student Note-Taking as Facilitators of Student Learning." *Contemporary Education Psychology* 29: 234–237.

Tobin, K. (Spring 1987). "The Role of Wait Time in Higher Cognitive Level Learning." *Review of Educational Research* 57, no. 1: 69–95.

Toch, T., R. M. Bennefield, and A. Bernstein. (March 24, 1996). "The Case for Tough Standards." *U.S. News & World Report*, 52–56.

Toch, T., and M. Daniel. (October 7, 1996). "Schools That Work." *U.S. News & World Report*, 59–64.

Tomlinson, C. A., and M. L. Kalbfleisch. (November 1998). "Teach Me, Teach My Brain: A Call for Differentiated Classrooms." *Educational Leadership* 56, no. 3: 52–55.

Traynor, P. L. (March 2002). "A Scientific Evaluation of Five Different Strategies Teachers Use to Maintain Order." *Education.*

Tumposky, N. (April 2003). "Motivation: What Do Teachers Need to Know?" *Kappa Delta Pi Record.* HighBeam (1P3-321146071).

Veenman, S. (1984). "Perceived Problems of Beginning Teachers." *Review of Educational Research* 54, no. 2: 143–178.

Walberg, H. J. (1984). "Improving the Productivity of America's Schools." *Educational Leadership* 41, no. 8: 19–27.

Walberg, H. J., and W. C. Fredrick. (1991). *Extending Learning Time*. Washington, DC: U.S. Department of Education, Office of Educational Research and Improvement.

Walker, H. M., G. Colvin, and E. Ramsey. (1995). *Antisocial Behavior in School: Strategies and Best Practices*. Pacific Grove, CA: Brooks/Cole Publishing Company.

Wall, A. (May/June 1993). "How Teacher Location in the Classroom Can Improve Student's Behavior." *Clearing House* 66, no. 5: 299–301.

Wang, M. C., G. D. Haertel, and H. J. Walberg. (December 1993/January 1994). "What Helps Students Learn?" *Educational Leadership* 51, no. 4: 74–79.

Wason, P. C. (1960). "On the Failure to Eliminate Hypothesis in a Conceptual Task." *Quarterly Journal of Experimental Psychology* 12, no. 3: 129–140.

Wasserstein, P. (September 1995). "What Middle Schoolers Say about Their Schoolwork." *Educational Leadership* 53, no. 1: 41–43.

Weaver, R. L., S. Wenzlaff, and H. W. Cotrell. (October 1993). "How Do Students See Master Teachers?" *The Education Digest* 59, no. 2: 12–15.

Weber, B. J., and L. M. Omotani. (September 1994). "The Power of Believing." *The Executive Educator* 16, no. 9: 35–38.

Wedel, C., and V. Jennings. (January/February 2006). "Motivated Students Begins with a Motivated Teacher." *Agricultural Education Magazine* 78, no. 4: 6–7.

Weinstein, R., C. R. Soulé, F. Collins, J. Cone, M. Mehlhorn, and K. Simontacchi. (1991). "Expectations and High School Change: Teacher-Researcher Collaboration to Prevent School Failure." *American Journal of Community Psychology* 19, no. 3: 333–363.

Westwater, A., and P. Wolfe. (November 2000). "The Brain-Compatible Curriculum." *Educational Leadership* 58, no. 3: 49–52.

Whitaker, T. (2004). *What Great Teachers Do Differently: 14 Things That Matter Most*. Larchmont, NY: Eye on Education.

White, K., R. Hohn, N. Tolleson. (October 1997). "Encouraging Elementary Students to Set Realistic Goals." *Journal of Research in Childhood Education* 12, no. 1. HighBeam (1P3-33739633).

Wiggins, G. (November 1989). "The Futility of Trying to Teach Everything of Importance." *Educational Leadership* 47, no. 3: 44–59.

Wiggins, G. (May 1992). "Creating Tests Worth Taking." *Educational Leadership*, 26–33.

Wiggins, G. (1995). "Curricular Coherence and Assessment: Making Sure That the Effect Matches the Intent." In *Toward a Coherent Curriculum*, edited by James Beane, 101–118. Alexandria, VA: Association for Supervision and Curriculum Development.

Wilburn, K. T., and B. C. Felps. (1983). "Do Pupil Grading Methods Effect Middle School Students' Achievement? A Comparison of Criterion-Referenced versus Norm-Referenced Evaluation." (ERIC Document Reproduction Service No. ED 229 451).

Wilen, W., M. I. Bosse, J. Hutchison, and R. Kindsvatter. (1999). *Dynamics of Effective Secondary Teaching*, fifth edition. Boston: Allyn & Bacon.

Williams, M. M. (November 1993). "Actions Speak Louder Than Words: What Students Think." *Educational Leadership* 51, no. 3: 22–23.

Williams, P. A, R. D. Alley, and K. T. Henson. (1999). *Managing Secondary Classrooms: Principles and Strategies for Effective Management and Instruction*. Boston: Allyn & Bacon.

Willis, S. (September 1996). "Managing Today's Classroom: Finding Alternatives to Control and Compliance." *Education Update* 38, no 6. http://www.ascd.org/publications/newsletters/education-update/sept96/vol38/num06/Managing-Today's-Classroom.aspx.

Wilson, L. M., and D. A. Corpus. (September 2001). "The Effects of Reward Systems on Academic Performance." *Middle School Journal* 33, no. 1: 56–60.

Wilson, W. W., and A. A. Clegg Jr. (1986). "Effective Questions and Questioning: A Research Review." *Theory and Research in Social Education* 14, no. 2: 153–161.

Wolfe, P. (1998). "Revisiting Effective Teaching." *Educational Leadership* (November): 61–64.

Woolfolk, A. E., and W. K. Hoy. (1990). "Prospective Teachers' Sense of Efficacy and Beliefs about Control." *Journal of Educational Psychology* 82, no. 1: 81–91.

Woods, R. C., and R. V. Montagno. (December 1997). "Determining the Negative Effect of Teacher Attendance on Student Achievement." *Education* 188, no. 2. HighBeam (1G1-20479508).

Wright, S. P., S. P. Horn, and W. L. Sanders. (1997). "Teacher and Classroom Context Effects on Student Achievement: Implications for Teacher Evaluation." *Journal of Personnel Evaluation in Education* 11, 57–67.

Wubbels, T., M. Brekelmans, J. Van Tartwijk, and W. Admiral. (1999). "Interpersonal Relationships between Teachers and Students in the Classroom." In *New Directions for Teaching Practice and Research*, edited by H. C. Waxman and H. J. Walberg. Berkeley, CA: McCutchan.

Yasseen, B. M. B. (January 2010). "The Effect of Teachers' Behavior on Students' Behavior in the Classroom." *International Forum of Teaching and Studies* 6, no 1. HighBeam (1P3-2005869541).

Yilmaz, Cevdet. (February 2011). "Teachers' Perceptions of Self-Efficacy, English Proficiency, and Instructional Strategies." *Social Behavior and Personality.* HighBeam (1G1-251277760).

Zimmerman, B. J., and M. Martinez-Pons. (1986). "Development of a Structured Interview for Assessing Student Use of Self-Regulated Learning Strategies." *American Educational Research Journal* 23, no. 4: 614–628.

Index

academic enabling, 25–26, 27, 28, 137; consequences of, 25–26, 29–30, 31; examples of, 25, 26, 138, 143; rewarding "hard work," 30

administrators, xi, 11, 26, 29, 46, 52, 55, 58–59, 60, 61, 128, 130

Allen, Woody, 20

all or nothing thinking. *See* illogical/ irrational beliefs and thinking

American Idol, 97

anticipatory set, 103

Are You Smarter Than a Fifth Grader?, 2

Aristotle, 48

authentic activities/products/tasks, 2, 9, 109, 110, 111, 112; examples of, 2, 9, 109, 112

aversive conditioning. *See* discipline

awfulizing. *See* illogical/irrational beliefs and thinking

bell curve, 39

Bloom's *Taxonomy of Educational Objectives*, 74, 79, 81, 139, 146

brain-based instruction/learning: connecting new knowledge to old, 14, 102–103, 140; "downshifting," 18, 19, 100; effects of emotions on learning, 18–19, 99, 113, 114; learning what is "important," 106

Challenger tragedy, 59

change resistance, 8, 10, 10–11

character education, 83, 139, 146

Christie, Agatha, 34, 143

Churchill, Winston, 133

classical conditioning, 19, 65

classroom climate. *See* instructional performance

classroom management. *See* discipline

cognitive maps, 103, 140

confirmation bias. *See* illogical/ irrational beliefs and thinking

cooperative learning, 2, 114, 115, 116, 140; individual accountability, 115; positive interdependence, 115; team rewards, 115

critical thinking, 1, 2, 61, 75. *See also* modeling behavior

crystallizing experiences, 124

curriculum, 1, 3, 6–7, 9; "filters," 3–4, 5, 9, 70, 109, 137; schoolwide/whole-school, xiv, 5, 6, 7, 9–10, 46, 137, 149; state-mandated, 3, 9; vision, xiv, 1, 4, 5, 6, 7, 9, 11, 149

Darwin, Charles, 104

delusions of grandeur. *See* illogical/ irrational beliefs and thinking

differentiating instruction, 73, 112–113

discipline, 17, 22, 23, 63; aversive conditioning, 66, 145; avoiding intimidation, 65–66, 139; clear and consistent rules and consequences, 63, 66, 71, 139, 145; control prompts, 67; meaningful curriculum, 71, 117, 139, 146; monitoring irrational beliefs, 68–69, 139; "parental" body language, 66; "parental" slogans, 67; positive labels/attributions/ descriptors, 69–70, 123, 139, 146; praising students, 18, 19, 21, 22, 70, 139, 146; proximity control, 18, 64, 67, 145; reframing, 67, 68, 69, 139, 145; remaining calm, 64, 64–65, 66, 67, 69, 139; "withitness," 63–64, 139, 145

distributed practice, 101–105, 140; promoting higher-level thinking, 104; promoting pattern recognition, 101–102, 104. *See also* brain-based